BURN THIS CITY

ALEKSANDR VOINOV

44
raccoons

Content words: suicidal ideation, organized crime, threats of sexual violence, dubcon, mental health (depression), minor character death (past, off-page), murder (mostly off-page), grief, bereaved spouse, drug use (voluntary and involuntary), corruption, domestic violence (off-page), bisexual rep, demisexual/graysexual rep

CONTENTS

ABOUT BURN THIS CITY

Some passions can set a city aflame.

Consigliere Jack Barsanti has worked his way up from nothing, survived a vicious Mafia war and, proving his loyalty, done time for his crime family, the Lo Cascio. He's devoted his life to defusing tensions, reining in volatile men, and keeping the peace between the three crime families in Port Francis to prevent another bloody war. All the time harboring one devastating secret that would cost him everything.

Enter Salvatore Rausa. A boss himself, Sal doesn't care about peace or the feelings of other made men. The war has cost him the wife he dearly loved, and he's bided his time to prepare for payback. But he needs intel to wipe the Lo Cascio off the map first.

Nobody in their right mind would lay a hand on a rival family's consigliere. Nobody except Sal. When he grabs and bags Jack Barsanti, he knows the clock is ticking. He needs to work quickly to make Jack spill his secrets. Except as he interrogates Jack and uncovers the weaknesses of his enemies, he gets a whole lot more than he bargained for.

BURN THIS CITY

Aleksandr Voinov

DRAMATIS PERSONAE

Lo Cascio crime family
Andrea Lo Cascio, boss, and his wife Petra Lo Cascio
Jack Barsanti, consigliere
Vic Decesare, Jack's predecessor
Mauro, soldier, and his wife Hannah

Dommarco crime family
Guy Dommarco, boss, and his wife Sarah Dommarco
Don Cassaro, consigliere

Rausa crime family
Sal Rausa, boss, and his wife Catarina "Catia" Rausa, previously Tomasi (deceased)
Enzo, capo

Other mafiosi
Gianbattista Falchi, retired consigliere
Silvio Spadaro, hitman (also appears in "Dark Soul")

Italian terms and Mafia ranks

Toccando ferro – "Touch wood"

Pentito – "repentant" – one who has cooperated with law enforcement, traitor

Boss – head of a crime family

Consigliere – advisor to a boss

Underboss/acting boss (sottocapo) – often the one in line to succeed the boss

Capo/Caporegime – a captain, runs a crew

Soldato or soldier – member of a crew, full member of a crime family

Associate – somebody who's connected to a crime family, but hasn't been "made" and is thus not a full member.

1

The newly minted husband and wife smiled at each other with a devoted warmth that could easily mellow and deepen over the next five or six decades. Only a jaded man would feel differently, and Jack Barsanti wasn't nearly jaded enough to not suffer a little at how tenderly they held the knife together as they cut the huge white cake. It wasn't every day that a beautiful heiress married a rich, good-looking man out of love.

It could have been easy to merely calculate how much the bride's family was worth and whether the value of her family's construction company exceeded the value of the real estate empire that he already controlled. In terms of synergies, this was Port Francis' marriage of the year.

Jack reached for another glass of the very drinkable prosecco and watched the crowd mingle in the ballroom around the buffet and a generously staffed bar. Both families had flown in every single relative in good standing, and perhaps some in bad. There were even a few he thought had been coerced into coming through some more or less gentle arm-twisting.

More interesting were those guests who were not related by blood to the bride and groom. First and foremost, the Lo Cascio, the bridal family's long-time business partners. Jack knew very well just how deep those arrangements went, considering he'd sealed a lot of them with a handshake in the name of the Lo Cascio, as had his predecessor before him. Some might argue whether the family would have been financially better off without that partnership and the fees that came with it. What could not be argued was that this was how things got done here, and the Lo Cascio had always upheld their end of the deal. Jack moved through the crowd, catching fragments of conversation or individual words, but lingering nowhere.

While the bride's family was tied to the Lo Cascio, the Dommarco had lent their weight to that of the groom. Jack didn't know the particulars of the relationship, but assumed it looked very similar on paper and in practice. He spotted Guy Dommarco and his wife Sarah chatting with the groom's parents—four prominent, upstanding members of the community not out of place in the local Rotary Club.

Of course, the happy couple had been forced to invite everyone who mattered in Port Francis—this was a Sleeping Beauty kind of situation: even their wealthy and powerful families didn't want to piss off one of the fairy godfathers.

Just six years ago, if both crime families had attended the same event, it would have played out very differently; people would have been checking the magazines in their submachine guns instead of texts on their phones. Jack smiled wryly into his drink and checked his own phone, balancing it somewhat awkwardly in one hand. He missed the days when those damn things hadn't been the size of paperbacks.

"Jack! So good to see you!"

Hearing the familiar voice, Jack smiled and slipped his phone into his pocket. Don Cassaro shook his hand and patted his shoulder with affection, and Jack made sure his nod was almost a little bow, because Cassaro was easily the most well-connected man in the room. After the "War", he'd kept promising he'd "retire" to the golf course, but maybe Cassaro found it hard to give up his role as the Dommarco consigliere in favor of a younger man. Cassaro knew everybody who was anybody in the city, in the state, and further afield. That well-filled Rolodex made him a force to be reckoned with on his own without having to draw on the authority of his boss.

"Mr. Cassaro." Jack reached out and plucked a glass of prosecco from a passing silver tray to offer it. "I saw you in the winter garden earlier but didn't want to disturb you."

"You can disturb an old man anytime." Cassaro accepted the glass as the humble offering it was meant to be. "How have you been doing?"

Jack laughed softly, if only for the benefit of anybody watching him talk to Cassaro. He took a few steps to the side, away from the buffet. "I've been good. Keeping busy. You know how it is."

Cassaro smiled, but whether the man genuinely liked him or merely indulged him was up for debate. His gut told him it was the former, but his mind always second-guessed that instinct. He had to question everything—it was his job to anticipate the tantrums and violent impulses of other

3

men, and move the china out of the way before they could smash it.

"I do. I'm not hearing much in the way of bad news," Cassaro said.

"Business is on track. Things are calm and peaceful, just the way I like them."

"There's that thing about swans," the old man mused. "They glide along serenely, while paddling their feathery asses off under the water."

Jack let out a full-throated laugh. "That's me. Paddling my feathery ass off." He took a mouthful of the prosecco, noting again that the stuff went down so easily he could get completed wasted from it without feeling it creep up on him. A few people had glanced over when he'd laughed, but this was a wedding reception, and he wasn't the only guest who was being a little more demonstrative, a little louder, a little brighter. "But it's all working out, *toccando ferro*."

"Walk with me." Cassaro made a show of taking him by the elbow, serving up a large helping of "kindly uncle", despite the fact that everybody in the room knew what the old guy was capable of and could even now arrange with a phone call or a nod. Those who didn't know didn't count. Jack had found that over the lifetime of a made man, power waxed and waned, but more importantly, it evolved and shifted. Cassaro had been in the life for going on five decades and had likely killed more men than Jack knew.

He walked by Cassaro's side like a favored nephew, away from the crowd attending to the happy couple, through another huge room where people danced, past buff, hard-eyed waiters, some of them with facial scarring you didn't acquire during a normal career in hospitality, and out into the carefully landscaped garden and bright early afternoon. Jack found himself drawing a deep breath of the cooler air that no longer carried that cloying mix of perfumes and food odors.

Cassaro led him toward the pond near the eastern wing of the manor. Light filtered golden and reddish through the tall trees, while flawless white and pink lilies sat stark and inviolate between the rich dark greens of their leaves.

"I keep hearing that Andrea is still a loose gun." Cassaro could have let Jack's elbow go, but he didn't, and Jack realized it was meant to fool any onlooker that this was still a chat of no consequence. Yet, with those words, Cassaro had set Jack on edge as if he'd suddenly reached for a gun. He must have jerked, because the old man's grip tightened. "Can't be easy. The boy's got a temper."

So that was the reason for the friendly chat. Somebody on the Dommarco side was worrying that Andrea might cause trouble. The longer the peace lasted, the more nervous those who remembered the War became.

"I'm not going to dispute it, Mr. Cassaro," Jack said so low his voice didn't carry. "But what's said in private doesn't have to make it out the door. We're different people in private, all of us."

A rumble in the man's chest could have been a chuckle. Very hard to read his face as they stood side by side, looking at the lilies which, in their purity, seemed incongruous rising from a muddy miniature lake. "I'm also hearing that you are doing a good job keeping your young, impetuous boss on the right track."

"Oh, I can't take credit for that."

"You could, but you don't, which makes you a good consigliere. Certainly with a boss like that."

Jack pressed his lips together, thinking for a few moments, trying to pinpoint what exactly had triggered these concerns. They had to be small enough. A friendly chat between consiglieri was a far cry from a formal sit-down. "To my mind, keeping the peace is simply best for business. There's no reason why the good times shouldn't last, and if business is good, everybody's happy."

A simplification that was nearly criminal in itself, considering how many factors went into maintaining the equilibrium in Port Francis, as well as the constant careful management of those same factors. Andrea Lo Cascio often didn't take the time to understand such details. He was too preoccupied with his family and his toys—his customized cars, his mistresses, his yachts—and impressing anybody around him who might be useful.

"An old friend of mine used to say 'peace is a damned sight harder than war'. War is easy. You stick a gun in a guy's face and—boom. Do that a few times and you got war. Peace now, that's a game you play in a hundred different ways." Cassaro tapped his lips with the first and index fingers of his free hand. "You've always struck me as a man of peace, but how equipped are you to face another war?"

Maybe those concerns were not so small after all. But such information had to be inveigled from the consigliere. If not timed correctly, outright questions made people uneasy.

"Arguably, you know more about it than I do. Mind you, I'll do what it takes. I've paid my dues; I'll do it again."

Above the pond, dragonflies flitted back and forth, here

one second, gone the next, no more than sparks of metallic green and blue.

"Jack." Cassaro changed his grip on Jack's arm and now took both of his hands in his, which reminded Jack of the way his local priest had often spoken to his parishioners. "Of course. I didn't say I doubted that."

"So what's the problem?" He searched Cassaro's dark brown eyes for any hint of suspicion and found himself similarly weighed.

"One of our associates has been gone a while. He was mixed up in all kinds of things, and some of those might have involved Lo Cascio interests. We're still piecing the situation together. Mind you, he might just have grabbed the money and run without telling anybody where he's headed."

An associate, so at least not a made man, but in Port Francis, people "vanishing" left a particular taste.

"I'll take that to Andrea, but I can already tell you that no hit has been sanctioned. I'd know about this." And if a hit had gotten past him unnoticed, he had much more urgent problems than dealing with a Dommarco-associated lowlife going on the run or dying. "Thanks for bringing this to my attention. And thanks for the caution."

Cassaro let Jack's hands go and clicked his tongue in vague acknowledgement, but he didn't pursue the topic further. Every time they met, Jack was tempted to ask him what exactly had happened during the War from his point of view. Jack had only witnessed the very beginning of it as a freshly made capo. His had been a battlefield promotion because the sheer scale and viciousness of the War between the Rausa, Lo Cascio and Dommarco crime families had taken bigger players than him off the board permanently, and they'd needed to replenish the ranks fast. But how the three-way war had started, or exactly why it had carried on as long as it had was still a mystery to Jack. Everybody's recollections differed so wildly that he'd never managed to piece it all together.

Navigating the shifting quicksands had been both scary and exhilarating, and still, Jack much preferred the peace-time. When, after six years of bitter war, Andrea's father had ordered him to broker peace between the families, Jack had at first felt he'd been promoted way beyond his competence. But there had been nobody else left. Jack's predecessor's health had already been failing, and there was so much bad blood that the Dommarco refused to even listen to the original Lo Cascio consigliere.

Jack still remembered the day when he, as acting consigliere, had finally managed to get Guy Dommarco to sit down with Andrea's father, terrified the meeting would just lead to a final flare-up. To his surprise, Guy Dommarco had been reasonable enough, and Andrea's father had made generous concessions in return for peace. And in that way, Jack's reputation had been made and his position became permanent. With every year that the peace held, people seemed to respect him more.

"Let's go back this way." Cassaro turned, this time without taking Jack's arm. The slow walk through the exten-sive park around the manor was enjoyable—the September afternoon was still warm, though not so warm that Jack felt uncomfortable in his formal suit. Across the lawn he noticed a large white tent that would serve as a much more relaxed barbecue area and bar for later in the evening, with staff already setting up.

When the path curved back toward the house, Jack spotted a man he hadn't seen in years—even rumors of him had been difficult to come by.

Salvatore Rausa sat on a white marble bench. He leaned against the backrest as if he'd been poured there, his only company four crystal tumblers, two of them empty, and two of them filled with an amber liquid. He held one against his flat stomach and stared sullenly into the distance.

Jack cast a quick glance at Cassaro, but if the old fox had led him here on purpose, he didn't show it.

Salvatore Rausa was the boss of the third crime family involved in the War. Unlike Guy Dommarco, he'd refused to come to the negotiation table, regardless of how many threats were issued, and, in the end, promised generosity. He was still a presence—his family had painted its name in red across the city and the state—but he kept such a low profile he was damn near invisible. As a rule, Jack didn't like invisible players.

Jack took a step toward the man, and another. "Mr. Rausa?"

Rausa looked up at him with a kind of piercing glower that indicated he still wasn't interested in talking. Now in his late thirties, Rausa looked confident, healthy, well-groomed, his wavy hair was tousled, and his light hazel eyes were bright and clear. If he'd retired—if he'd stopped being a player—he might not even know who Jack was. Though the fact that the Dommarco consigliere had all but walked Jack directly to him should at least signal that he wasn't a hapless wedding guest. Rausa studied Jack for a few intense moments, raked him head to toe, then emptied his whiskey glass, leaving the ice cubes to clink together. "Andrea want anything?"

"No, Mr. Rausa. I just wanted to say hello."

Rausa seemed on the verge of sneering, but didn't. "Yeah. And hello to you too, I guess. And you, Don. Now kindly fuck off, this is a wedding."

Jack lifted an eyebrow, but forced himself to smile. "Of course." He withdrew, deciding Rausa was planning to get drunk, and that was his privilege. Still strange that he didn't have anybody with him—no capo, soldier, or his own consigliere.

The Rausa had seemingly collapsed at about the same time as the War had ended. People had died and vanished, and Salvatore Rausa, up until then underboss, had become boss without any contest or opposition. Maybe he'd spent the time since on whipping his outfit back into shape or focused on repairing the tremendous damage, but, whatever the case, Jack was pretty sure Salvatore Rausa was the reason the Rausa clan had faded from view.

Jack had already turned back toward Cassaro when he heard Rausa's voice: "Jack Barsanti, isn't it?"

Jack hesitated, but turned around again for politeness' sake. "That's correct." And now he felt the full weight of that moody stare. Something was off about Rausa, something beyond lining up whiskey tumblers like shot glasses, and sitting out here while the actual party was still mostly indoors. Fact was, Jack didn't know enough about Rausa to even guess what the problem was. Though, if he could establish a connection, he might be able to finally get Rausa to the table, and remove one unknown that had, in a faraway corner of his mind, been nagging him for years.

He lowered his hands and angled his body toward the man in a show of openness. "If you want me to arrange a meeting with Andrea ..."

"Lo Cascio can get fucked," muttered Rausa.

Jack turned away with a shake of his head and caught a miniscule twitch of Cassaro's lips. As casual as this chance meeting had been, it seemed no progress could be made today.

They'd nearly circled the manor when Jack excused himself to check on Andrea. In no particular hurry, he returned to the ballroom, idly scanning the crowd for the face of his boss—or that of his boss's wife, because she'd know where her husband was.

Petra Lo Cascio stood in a small group of other wedding guests, but seemed to have caught the general gist of his questioning eyebrow raise. She nodded toward the large central staircase, so Jack climbed the stairs with another glass of prosecco he'd picked up on the way.

He found Andrea sitting in one of the rooms open for guests to regroup or make phone calls, which Andrea was ostensibly doing. He was smiling for the camera of his phone and said, "Daddy loves you too," so Jack stood back and blended into the background.

Of course, the event would go on into the night, so the nanny was looking after the kids. Andrea had his faults, but the birth of his children had turned him into a fiercely proud father—and both his son and daughter were cute kids, as far as Jack was concerned. He himself played a distant role as uncle, and was happy to agree with Andrea's strong opinion that his children were beautiful and talented. Every father thought so during those years before his children turned rebellious or contemptuous.

"Jack." Still that paternal glow on his face, Andrea waved him closer. "Had to check in on the kids. Hard not to get fond of the little fuckers," he said, as if grasping for that much more hardened part of himself. "You should get a couple. Would do you a world of good."

Jack nodded noncommittally. "I'll be sure to pick up one or two with a sixpack and a loaf of bread."

Normally, that would put an end to that particular suggestion. The birth of his son had kicked off an occasional prodding from Andrea, such as telling him that, one day, Andrea's son would play with Jack's son, and that they'd be like brothers. When Andrea had achieved the provision of a sibling a year later, he'd teased Jack that he was now "two ahead". Considering how competitive the man was, Jack had been happy to let him revel in his superior masculine fertility.

This time, though, Andrea's jaw set in that stubborn way that told Jack he was being serious. "*As I said*," his boss said slowly, firmly, as if he were talking to a dumb soldier. "It would do you good."

Keeping his face blank, Jack nodded, as he usually did when Andrea had a truly awful idea.

"Because, see, you're family, Jack. You're the guy I have to trust one hundred thousand percent with my life. With Petra. With my kids." A noticeable vibrato in his voice on the last word betrayed how much of a gap in Andrea's emotional armor his kids were—he loved his wife, but he adored and worshipped his children. That slight tremble in Andrea's voice made Jack's hair stand up on his arms and on his neck.

There was less emotion in a kill order, a lot less emotion whenever he talked about business or vast amounts of money.

"I know you do. And you know I'm loyal."

"Yeah, listen. I want to think you are. You have a good head, and I need that." Andrea pushed out a breath that was almost more a hiss. "I have to be able to trust you with my children. You're their uncle. So ..." He grimaced. "I don't want to think you're somehow not right when it comes to them, understand."

Holy. Mother. Of. God.

Jack's blood ran so cold he half turned away in case Andrea could read the shock on his features. The first thought he could string together was to wonder how long Andrea had harbored that suspicion, and how much damage it had already done. His second thought drew him right back to the darkest hours of his life. The night spent staring into an icy spring-swollen river which had been more inviting than waking up the next morning. He'd battled that black abyss, barely escaping with his life. But it had cost him. He tried to shake off the full-body memory. The thing was, he couldn't back out of this: unwittingly or not, Andrea had cut off all his escape routes.

"I know you don't have much of a private life. Petra says the same. You've been married to your job, and it's appreciated. We're lucky to have you, you hear?"

"I do." Jack drew a deep breath and faced Andrea again. "Sorry, I'm just surprised. I never wanted to ... never wanted you to think less of me."

"I don't." Andrea walked up to him and drew him into one of his fraternal hugs, but Jack's skin crawled when he felt

Andrea's body heat. Hard slaps between the shoulder blades followed. "Get some of those apps. People meet each other on those dating apps all the time. Worst case, I'll ask my aunt and she can point you at any number of girls with the right kind of pedigree." Girls from the right families, those who already knew what was going on and who didn't have to be brought in or taught not to put their pretty noses in their husband's business.

"Yeah, you're right."

"Of course I am." Andrea held him firmly by the arms and pushed back to look Jack in the eye. "We all want you happy, okay?"

Jack forced a smile. "Thanks, Andrea."

Andrea slapped him on the shoulder a couple of times. "Good man. Have you seen my wife?"

Jack forced his mind to work, tried to recover his internal composure, tried to not show how much this short exchange had unnerved him. "Downstairs."

"Don't worry, I'll find her." Andrea rushed off, giving Jack time to put his game face back on. But it took a while.

2
_____

A week after the wedding, Jack chose to take the long way around the bay. The silver-grey Porsche 718 Cayman handled like a dream even on wet leaves, and normally he'd have enjoyed taking the car out for a spin. Letting let the sound system blast every last thought from his mind for an unnecessary 45-minute detour through the forest was the closest he got to taking a vacation these days. But the album he'd been listening to had grated, so he now drove in silence, peering every now and then at the phone in its holder, half-worried he might be called back for something urgent.

Come to think of it, he'd lived the past few years like a top-rated neurosurgeon, always on call, never able to relax because things always deteriorated when he turned his back.

The darkness robbed him of the beautiful fall colors and the way the rust and yellows contrasted with the refreshing blue shades of the bay.

He thought he saw lights from some yachts further out,

though this time of the year, the richest inhabitants of the bay were beginning to decamp to their winter haunts of the Caribbean or St. Moritz. Besides the asphalt in front of him and a glimpse of a lighter darkness between the trees, his only company were the headlights following in his wake, though not close enough to blind him. Mauro had no reason to trail him that closely—if this trip had been dangerous enough to justify somebody hugging his rear tires, he would have had Mauro sit right next to him, riding shotgun.

Mauro was one of the soldiers who provided Jack's personal security whenever necessary. Seemed he was concerned enough about the risk of an ambush and the relatively remote location of Jack's house up in the hills to insist on following him and checking on the house.

Earlier this day, during their catch-up, Andrea had been very relaxed about the missing Dommarco associate, which made Jack believe that his boss really knew nothing about the matter, and also that he didn't understand its significance. Had it been otherwise, Andrea would have been angrier and more accusatory.

"Maybe he's just fucked off to Vegas for a week, how's that my problem?"

Jack drummed his thumbs against the steering wheel, both impatient to arrive at the house and not quite willing to face the consequences of the decisions he needed to make. It was almost midnight, and Jack couldn't wait to get to the house and rest. Back in town, Andrea would obviously be still awake for a few more hours. The man rarely went to bed before three in the morning and didn't rise before noon. Jack guessed that worked for some if they were still in their thirties. By now, Andrea should have adapted his lifestyle to fit his family's, after all, he was married and had two children under the age of five, but Jack could imagine how any such suggestion would be taken. Whether Petra had tried to rein him in or not, Andrea kept up his wild bachelor lifestyle and assumed that everybody did the same.

But Jack had just turned 45, and he required the assistance of very serious quantities of espresso to keep up with Andrea's schedule, even if he managed to hide it. Andrea would consider it a sign of weakness.

He shook his head and stared at the street ahead. Some turns in this part of the drive required attention, and while the darkness allowed him to spot cars coming from the other direction from miles away, he didn't want to hit a deer or other large animal. At least this last bit of the climb up into the hills felt more familiar. Forest at night was always the same, and the drive had stretched out much longer than he'd expected or even had been emotionally prepared for. He'd planned to come up with a solution on the way, but his thoughts were a jumbled mess that he couldn't untangle while focused on night driving.

The gate opened and let both the Porsche and Mauro's Beemer in. Another very short and much slower drive, and he parked the car at the side of the house. He couldn't wait to get inside—the angular shapes beyond the trees looked like a friendly fortress now.

The Beemer's tires crunched gravel as Mauro drove up close enough that Jack could have touched the car without extending his hand much. The window buzzed down. "Need a hand?"

Jack scoffed and opened the Porsche's trunk. "I'll

manage." What clothes he needed fit snugly into his overnight bag, along with his laptop.

"All right," Mauro drawled and killed the engine. "Just a quick check."

"Sure." Jack led the way, unlocked the door and deactivated the alarm. He dropped his bags on the chair next to the fireplace and busied himself with starting a fire, while he listened to Mauro moving through the house, opening cupboards and doors. Since the house was almost an open floorplan with plenty of large windows and thus reflections, he didn't even have to pay attention to know exactly where the soldier was.

Mauro returned. "Right, looks clean. Are you sure you're going to be okay?"

Jack raised his eyebrows and tilted his head. "I packed enough socks, the bar is filled up, and Gino's has delivered enough food to survive here for a couple of weeks." He looked around demonstratively. "I'll be fine."

"You know the boss would prefer me staying here."

"He also prefers blondes, and yet ..." Jack smiled at Mauro's beginning smirk. "Listen, you go home to Hannah. I'll call if I need a pick-up or anything more dramatic happens than me running out of pasta. Which is unlikely. You know Gino's."

Mauro still didn't seem convinced, so Jack shed his jacket and patted the gun holstered at his belt. "I can look after myself."

It wasn't like they were on enemy turf. This was one of the smaller villas up in the hills, and he was so rarely here he'd be astonished if anybody targeted him. He fully expected to go in a more traditional drive-by shooting, unless he returned to Memorial Bridge one night and ended things himself. But Mauro didn't need to know any of this.

Mauro held his gaze for a couple of moments, then glanced toward the kitchen. "Gino's, eh?"

"Definitely Gino's," Jack confirmed. "I'm taking a break, not starting a diet."

"Good on you. And you'll call?" Mauro looked around, as if checking whether he'd looked into all the rooms and corners, but the way his weight shifted betrayed that Jack had won the argument. Nobody was eager to pull boring guard duty when he could hang out with his crew or sleep next to his wife. This place offered solace to somebody like Jack, but the same peace and quiet held no appeal to somebody like Mauro.

"I'll call." He wasn't going to add "I promise"—they weren't that familiar with each other, and ultimately Jack was under no obligation to reassure a soldier. His aim was to get him out the door without worrying him too much. He'd struggled so hard to get the time away from the bustle of Port Francis, and constantly awaiting Andrea's pleasure, and all those late-night phone calls. He needed this to clear his head and so Mauro needed to get the hell out.

"Well, I guess." Mauro shrugged his heavy shoulders. "Nobody knows you're here."

"That too."

And that was how he liked it. Andrea knew. A faceless housekeeper knew. After all, she'd taken delivery of the restaurant food, checked there was wood for the fire, and that all bed clothes and towels were fresh. But, to her, Jack was nothing but a rich guy from the city who wanted his vacation home ready for a few days. There were dozens like him with houses like this scattered around the hills. His name had never been mentioned, and a totally legitimate company was listed as the owner. Ah, anonymity. Priceless.

He stood and subtly herded Mauro back toward the front door. "Thanks, I'll let you out."

"All right." Mauro nodded. "Have a good break."

Jack breathed a sigh of relief when Mauro left. On the security screen, he followed the soldier's progress down the natural stone path winding past manicured shrubs. Mauro was still watchfully gazing left and right until he'd reached the Beemer. On cue, Jack opened and then closed the gate for the car and then sagged against the wall in the corridor as if he'd sprinted a dozen miles without warm-up.

Restlessly, he walked through the house—it only had two floors. When he'd first bought the place three years ago, he'd briefly considered replacing the ornamental wall with its open doorway with a solid wall and door to add privacy for the downstairs master bedroom, but he'd decided against it. The house had never been meant to be shared. He wasn't going to entertain anybody here, and he'd never had any use for the guest bedroom upstairs.

After he'd locked away his gun in the safe, he hung up the few clothes he'd brought in the spacious walk-in closet. Jack kept a few shirts and suits hanging, plus some workout clothes folded neatly on shelves, mostly so it felt less like an empty design hotel suite, but with little effect. Now he added the light woolen coat he'd worn to that collection. The architect had clearly intended for a couple to have plenty of space for their clothes, and Jack's five suits, ten shirts, and three pairs of shoes drove home how poorly they filled it. Whoever had built the shelves had anticipated handbags, many more shoes, jewelry, suitcases and ties, and all the other stuff that accumulated over the years.

Jack placed his current book on the nightstand, then walked around the corner to the bathroom to drop off his toiletry bag. As much as the large shower beckoned, he ignored it for now—the thought of stepping out of steamy warmth onto cold stone with bare feet made him shudder. He switched on the underfloor heating so he could enjoy a long shower later to beat the lingering tension out of his muscles.

Upstairs, he placed his laptop on the large empty desk and plugged it in for tomorrow's hard workday, though he'd likely get distracted by what the estate agent had called "his one-million-dollar view"—well, make that two million— over the flank of the hill and out to the ocean. As stunning as it was, he preferred the view from the living room, down the hill and over the bay. The house was mostly glass with a few wood and natural stone walls, but its real value was in the fact that it was also completely private. No neighbors could peer into his windows, and likewise he didn't even catch a glimpse of other people's properties. Unlike the other side of the bay, this area hadn't been ruined with development, and further construction had been banned, adding another cool half million to the value of the house.

Of course, in deepest darkness, none of the views mattered. On a clear night, the landscape could be down-right magical, especially when a full moon poured a silver pathway across the bay and the trees cast dark blue shadows. No moon tonight, though.

He still switched off all the lights, opened the double doors of the living rooms and stepped out into the night to enjoy the quiet, deeply breathing in the clean air that held a promise of fall. The season was about to turn, teetering between the overripe sluggishness of a radiant summer and the sobering chill of autumnal decay.

To his struggling peasant ancestors, fall had meant slaughter season, hunting season, with nature tightening the purse strings so only the strongest of her children would survive. They couldn't have dreamed of the life he led now.

Ah, blessed silence. No phone calls, no people, just quiet hills, trees, sky, wind. Jack almost wished he were still a smoker to keep his hands busy and settle his nerves. Hell, in his youth he'd have added some weed to that, but these days marijuana only made him tired and hungry, and ultimately he could no longer afford the loss of control over his own thoughts. Better to stay in the here and now, settle into a kind of domestic vacation boredom that would be punctured with short bursts of intense work.

After the past week, that seemed like heaven. Only, of course, it couldn't last. He had to come to some final decisions and make a phone call he didn't want to make. But for today—and maybe even tomorrow, if he pushed it—he could still avoid it. He could still tell himself the same thing he'd told Andrea: that he needed the quiet so he could focus on reviewing the annual numbers.

He'd deal with the personal stuff after that.

3

Salvatore Rausa didn't think of himself as much of a hunter. He didn't enjoy crawling through the underbrush or getting eaten alive by mosquitos. But a few hunting trips with Enzo and occasional, but utterly brutal, paintball weekends with some of the other boys had prepared him as much as possible for this kind of stalking.

Still, did Barsanti have to make it quite so easy?

Sal was tempted to strike now. The bodyguard had left an hour ago and now Barsanti stood alone outside the house in shirt and trousers, door open behind him. What if Barsanti only planned to spend the night here—maybe with a woman?—and left in the morning? They'd miss out on the chance to do it.

That Barsanti had left his usual haunts was already lucky. Separating him from that bastard Andrea Lo Cascio had started to seem nearly impossible, and snatching Barsanti in the city would attract far too much attention.

Plus, it would warn the head of the Lo Cascio clan that something was afoot.

Sal might have ignored the Lo Cascio consigliere if the man hadn't approached him at the wedding last week. Not considerate enough to allow a man to get seriously drunk in peace, Barsanti had dared to walk straight up to him and play at goddamned politics. If not for the alcohol, Sal might have strangled him then and there; he wasn't going to meet Andrea Lo Cascio for any reason other than to finish him off with a bullet between his motherfucking eyes.

He almost hadn't recognized Barsanti; he'd been a lean, jackal-faced capo when he'd shown up on Sal's radar, what, something like fifteen years ago? Now he filled out his frame very differently, though he still looked like he could run a marathon and then climb a sheer rock face without ropes or support.

Over the years, Sal had been aware of him but hadn't paid him much mind, and certainly hadn't followed his career—the families in Port Francis only dealt with each other when absolutely necessary. Even Barsanti's optimistic attempts to get everybody talking after the War hadn't changed that fundamental truth.

But Barsanti's ill-considered approach at the reception had given Sal an idea. Enzo hadn't been impressed.

"What, boss, you're going to change the plan now?"

"Yes. If it means less blood ..."

"Big fucking 'if.'"

Yeah, well, if crawling around between trees and undergrowth meant he'd end up with even one or two fewer wounded or dead soldiers, then, fuck it, this little "hunt" would be worth it.

Considering Barsanti intended to spend the night in this designer fishbowl, he had the feeling they'd get lucky.

Next to him, Enzo shifted his weight and lowered the binoculars. "I'm starting to see your point."

Sal cast a glance at his capo. "Right?"

"He seems like a reasonable guy," Enzo said.

Sal scoffed. "And you get that from what? A nice suit and a terrible grasp on security?"

"No. Books." Enzo vaguely gestured toward the house. "They look read too."

Well, those. They weren't the kind of books rich people bought, like old-school leather-bound encyclopedias or books whose jacket colors matched the interior. There were two high bookshelves in that house and the contents were a mix of paperbacks and hardcovers that seemed well-used and organized in a system that wasn't by color or size.

Finally, Barsanti seemed to shake himself out of his reverie. Going back inside, he switched on some lamps positioned on small tables and on low shelves. That formal white shirt helped them track him by reflecting even the dimmed light.

"Let's get the cameras up."

They continued to monitor Barsanti's movements in the house as they worked their way around the perimeter, hiding cameras that looked through every window and glass pane—from the bathroom to the office upstairs to the master bedroom and the formal dining room. They couldn't achieve a hundred percent coverage, but at least they'd always have a very good guess in which room Barsanti was and where he was moving, which was everything they'd need for their purposes.

Everything connected straight out of the box, all the cameras were happy to chat with their mobile phones and their laptop.

"I fucking love plug and play," Sal muttered when they were back in his Ford F-150 truck they'd parked halfway down a logging road. Enzo grinned at him, balancing the slim laptop on his knees while swiping through the different cameras.

Technology was amazing when it was this intuitive. They could focus on learning the layout of the house and how to follow Barsanti's movements inside. No need to sit in the man's garden with binoculars all night, hoping for some revelation that might or might not come.

They watched more or less in silence, interrupted only when they broke out the thermos with coffee and unwrapped the meatball subs Enzo had conjured up in Sal's kitchen a few hours earlier.

Sitting side by side in the truck, Sal realized again how lucky he was to have a capo like Enzo. He could be both vicious and playful, but he definitely made too much of his Sicilian roots and had recently become obsessed with Ancestry.com. The site had convinced him he was descended from medieval Norman crusaders, which allegedly explained the blond hair and grey eyes running in his family.

"What're you thinking?" Enzo licked his fingers and crunched up the aluminum foil into a tight little ball.

"That I appreciate how you're up for this kind of shit."

Enzo pulled his lips back from his canines in that wolfish grin of his. "Ever tell you how I got that restraining order as a teenager?"

"Girl told you to get lost?"

"Her parents thought I was no good. I'd sit out there in my cousin's car and watch her house all week for a chance to talk to her."

"Can't blame the parents."

"Really can't," Enzo agreed good-naturedly.

After a while, Sal asked: "So, how did it end?"

"Told you. Restraining order."

"And you fell in line?" Sal raised an eyebrow. "Seriously?"

"Turns out, I'm not into women who don't know what they want." Enzo said it lightly, but the statement hung between them in a way that made Sal refocus on Barsanti wandering his house like a ghost. The man was restless; he'd sit down, reach for a book, then put it back again to choose a different one, run a hand through his hair while pulling at it, and then put that book down too.

After a while of wandering in and out of the kitchen and around the furniture in the living room, Barsanti eventually walked into the master bedroom, where he stripped out of his clothes.

"Enzo." Sal nodded toward the screen.

"Anything interesting happening?"

"Depends."

"Letting his hair down finally." Barsanti stripped to his socks, boxers and undershirt, first putting the clothes away before he put on dark running shorts, one of those compression T-shirts, and finally running shoes. "Reckon he'll run outside?"

"I imagine he'll be using the gym at this hour. There's no light along the road."

That turned out to be true. Barsanti switched on the light in the gym. He chose the treadmill, and after a light trot, sped up to a full-throttle run that had Sal mildly impressed. Gaze empty, Barsanti ran his heart out for a solid forty minutes, then gradually slowed down, face still blank but now glistening with sweat, chest pumping hard. He didn't have much patience for the cooldown; once he'd slowed to a light jog, he brought the treadmill to an abrupt stop and stepped off.

He pulled off his top, which hung, soaking wet, from his grip, and tossed it into a basket in a corner, then proceeded to do some stretches.

Enzo glanced meaningfully at Sal. "What are you thinking?"

"He's ripped, but he's still the consigliere of my enemy." Sal narrowed his eyes. "You?"

Enzo drew back slightly. "Just saying, good to know in advance that he's fit. Think he's a fighter?"

"That's why I brought you. In case he is." Sal watched Barsanti stretch his quads. The restless, driven man they'd been observing for the past few hours didn't fit the tentative, friendly dealmaker he'd so briefly encountered at the Prizzi wedding. He also didn't fit Sal's memory of the quietly focused capo Barsanti had been about fifteen years ago. Neither of those had looked as if they were being chased by demons.

Guilt? Bad news he needed to shake off? Or the tension of waiting for a major plot to fall into place?

Of course, a few hours of observation wouldn't give him the key to the man's secrets. He'd hoped to catch Barsanti in the act with the wrong woman or scheming with the wrong people, something to get a bead on why he'd isolated himself here. Men like that didn't leave the city just for an uninterrupted treadmill workout.

Barsanti finished up and left the gym, already pulling at his waistband. By the time they'd switched cameras to the bathroom, he was completely naked.

He's ripped, but he's still the consigliere of my enemy, Sal repeated to himself.

More than ripped, actually. Barsanti was on the wrong side of forty, though arguably on the right side of fifty, but no middle-aged paunch had taken hold. His chest was well-defined, the fur on his front either sparse or trimmed, and his short salt-and-pepper hair that had been so well-groomed was now raked back and plastered to his skull with sweat, making him look less *businesslike*. At the wedding, he could have been a car salesman—though for an expensive European brand—a bit too polished, too eager to please. But this now was a man who had dropped all that as he stepped into the walk-in shower and started the water, head bent forward under the spray, his whole body pumped up after that run, veins popping on his arms.

Hot steam soon obfuscated their view, though the hint of muscle, legs, shoulder, flank, ass in the condensing steam was strangely hypnotic. And, fuck, he took his time—after the way he'd punished himself on the treadmill, he clearly felt he deserved half an hour under the hot water.

Sal only lingered that long in a shower when he wasn't alone in there. "Motherfucker," he muttered.

Enzo lowered the thermos as he coughed. "What?"

"Just." Sal made a circling motion with his hand, weirdly annoyed at Barsanti's self-indulgence. "Fuck this guy. We should just walk up to his door, put a gun in his face, and bag him. We're wasting our time here."

Enzo gave him that "Now you're speaking my language" look, but hesitated. "We might get more intel if we wait until tomorrow."

There. Barsanti left the shower, dripping and glistening, crossed the bathroom as he was, and grabbed a towel from the rack. He wiped his face first, dried his hands, and then scrubbed it over his head. One swipe mostly straightened out his hair—it was too short to get untidy. As he began to dry himself with a second, larger towel, it was easy to see his skin was flushed from the hot water and the exercise.

Sal shook himself. "All right." He'd chosen Enzo as his capo because he always came through when it counted. He never evaporated when the work got ugly. Some guys, once they'd been made, basked in their newfound status and slacked in their efforts. Of course, they never made it higher up the greasy pole, unlike Enzo who threw himself into the work with a certain type of glee that Sal found appealing.

Enzo took nothing too seriously—not killing, nor dying, not his pride. He didn't love the politics of the business enough to aspire to boss or underboss, because that would remove him from the thick of the action. But he'd also always lived by that classic Cosa Nostra chestnut: never hold down a legitimate job. And with his anarchist heart and wicked smarts, he'd never have to.

Wearing nothing but a towel, Barsanti walked around the house to dim some lights and switch off others. A last drink in the kitchen—looked like a protein shake—then back into the bathroom to brush his teeth and comb through his hair. He discarded the towel and padded naked into the bedroom, where he slipped under the covers, propped up against the low headboard, and switched on a large flat TV mounted on the wall opposite. The lamp on the nightstand offered no more than a glimmer, but that and the changeable glow from the TV allowed Sal to make out the lines of his legs under the covers, his naked chest, and his sharp features, which remained impassive.

Without his smile and smooth words, Barsanti seemed oddly diminished, all eyes, processing whatever he saw on the screen without judging it, and periodically tapping around on his phone. Aside for Enzo next to him in the truck, who sipped coffee and kept an eye on the night forest around them, the consigliere was the sole focus of Sal's attention, but he didn't yield any of his secrets.

What was abundantly clear now had already been pretty clear before tonight—Jack Barsanti was a smart man, polished, thoughtful, but also disciplined and fit. More dragon than the pit viper Andrea Lo Cascio. Tonight was likely a waste of time. Still, Barsanti remained the most promising target to start with. A mere capo didn't have enough intel. The only way to solve the Lo Cascio problem was to use the same approach as any gardener when dealing with ivy—you had to scrape off and dig up every last piece and burn every leaf or it would come back with a vengeance. Andrea Lo Cascio hadn't appointed a new underboss or acting boss after taking over from his father. Sal had watched while the previous holder of that position had been chopped into pieces, dropped into a plastic barrel, and deposited into the foundation of a luxury development going up in the city roundabout that time. That meant there were two men at the top of the Lo Cascio: Andrea himself and Jack Barsanti.

On the screen, Barsanti ran a hand down his chest, then further to slide beneath the covers. He shifted his weight and pulled one knee up. Sal watched as Barsanti began toying with his cock, in no particular rush, but also with no teasing, no finesse. He jerked off in the same businesslike way he'd gone about everything so far; there was no true urgency. If anything, Sal thought, he most likely touched himself out of boredom or to help himself fall asleep. When he pushed the covers further down, Sal found himself fascinated by Barsanti's good-sized, thick cock, and his strong hand around it.

Enzo cleared his throat and reached for the door handle. "I'll have a look around. Back in a bit."

"Not going to watch the show?" Sal nodded to the screen.

Several emotions flicked across Enzo's face, surprise, suspicion, embarrassment, but he settled on pure openness, and Sal was glad for it. "First, I gotta piss; second, I want to stay clear-headed. Okay?"

There was no harshness in his voice, and he'd have stayed if Sal had asked him to. Enzo was probably worried about where this might lead otherwise, and Sal agreed with him, though neither of them was a sixteen-year-old with raging hormones. "Sure. Go piss."

Enzo opened the door, and surprisingly chilly night air rushed in to replace their companionable warmth.

Sal focused on the screen again, watched Barsanti's artless movements. As his arousal increased, Barsanti's face changed. He gritted his teeth so hard Sal could see the tension in his jaw muscles, and when he got to the edge, he closed his eyes, and pushed his head back against the wall, stretching out his throat as his motions became punishing. He remained like that for several long moments, then reached for something outside the bed, wiped over his chest with it and then cleaned his hands. Finally, he slid down deeper into the covers, switched off the TV first, and then the lamp.

Darkness. Peace.

Laptop on his knees, Sal sat alone and enjoyed the frisson of arousal tightening his balls. A strange thing to get from an enemy, and he wasn't quite sure how he felt about it, but his body didn't particularly care who Barsanti was, or what blood-drenched history had maneuvered them both to this exact time and space. As far as his body was concerned, things were very black and white. Mostly black.

He near-closed the laptop, put it down on the seat and pushed the door open. Enzo had walked a few steps down the unpaved road into the forest, and was looking up into the sky, where the cloud cover had broken open enough to reveal stars here and there. He cast a quick glance over his shoulder when Sal approached, but remained standing where he was until Sal stopped by his side.

"So?"

"He's done. Just a quick one before sleep."

Enzo glanced at him sideways. "You sound bored."

"Meh. Straight guy rubbing one out. Not exactly thrilling stuff." Sal pushed his hands into his pockets and peered into the forest, listening, but he only heard a faint rustling of leaves. No movement, no snapping twigs, though the thought alone made Sal want to turn around and get back to the fake safety of the car. He knew better than most people that no place was ever truly safe. Cars certainly weren't.

The forests around Port Francis were surprisingly deep and wild, as the occasional over-confident camper found out the hard way, and Sal was too much of a city kid to ever feel really comfortable more than a few steps away from a road. He'd gone out into the wild often enough to know that he could easily get lost, which was why he usually went with more experienced hunters. And while he might enjoy the comradery, he was also more than happy to sleep in his own bed, and have a fridge stocked with food he didn't have to stalk first.

Enzo, by contrast, was at ease living off the land. Apparently, Enzo's father had been a passionate hunter and his family had been poor enough that the only meat that landed on the table had to be dragged out of the forest. Enzo had told him that he'd shot and killed "Bambi's Mom" when he was just nine years old, and he hadn't been much older when he'd learned how to skin and butcher.

"I figure there's nothing more tonight. We should go home."

Enzo stood there, clearly thinking, then half turned to Sal. "Want me to come to your place?"

Sal's first thought was that it would save them time tomorrow when they returned early to their stake-out, but then he saw the tension around Enzo's eyes. "Nah. Come by at seven. Make sure you get some rest—long day tomorrow."

The tension softened, so Sal reached out and placed an arm around Enzo's shoulders and pulled him against his side before letting him go. "Come on. You drive."

4

J ack stopped shaving and fixed his eyes in the mirror. He held the safety razor in a death grip over the rim of the sink.

Coward.

But he knew that already, didn't he? If he were truly as courageous as some people seemed to think, he would have already enacted his Plan B and retired. Or ended it all. There was no way he could ever be truly honest with Andrea and keep his job and his life, but instead of accepting that and getting the hell out one way or the other, he hadn't. Instead, he'd smiled and nodded and tried to fit in. But now he'd reached the end of this particular rope, and found all it offered was a noose for him to put his head through.

"I'll do it. Fuck you."

He looked away and ran probing fingers over his jaw to check for any remaining stubble, then washed his face, dried it and rubbed some cooling after-shave balm into his skin.

He preferred a barber doing all that, but making the long drive back just to get swaddled in hot wet towels held no appeal. Mostly he wasn't up to dealing with anybody on the outside—he was in that state of mind where *"Buongiorno, Signor* Barsanti" was already overly familiar and just too much. And he'd put the fear of God into the whole barbershop if he had a meltdown when they asked him whether he wanted a newspaper.

He buttoned up his shirt and pushed it into his trousers, then combed his damp hair, all the time with the beginnings of a decision sitting heavy in his guts. He'd given himself a full eighteen hours to mull this through—and that was already too long. The few facts hadn't changed and there was nothing he could do to move or twist them. He'd tried approaching the whole problem laterally, out of the box, unconventionally, had briefly considered doing the exact opposite of what he had to do, had turned everything around and around in his mind, but he kept running against the same old walls.

"We all want you happy, okay?"

He knew Andrea well enough to be certain that Andrea wouldn't let this one slide. As far as Andrea was concerned, he'd started the clock, and the past had taught Jack one thing —Andrea had no patience whatsoever. He was the kind of man who escalated from a hunch to a plan to pulling the trigger in a matter of days, not weeks.

Sometimes it was all Jack could do to slow Andrea down, or break him out of his internal spirals where he whipped himself into a frenzy, and made rash decisions because he trapped himself in a web of paranoia and prejudice. It was one of the less endearing qualities of his boss, but also made Jack a vital part of the Lo Cascio. Few people approached Andrea directly, and all capos knew that their own business, as well as that of their soldiers and associates, should be brought to Jack, who did his damned best to defuse all the hand grenades, anti-personnel mines, scandals and "beef", before any of it reached Andrea. Ultimately, it was a consigliere's job, but Jack often wished Andrea would calm down enough to interrogate his own hunches before he made decisions nobody could reverse except God—and He never did.

Jack settled down for a breakfast of coffee and yogurt with some cut-up fruit he'd found in the fridge. He pulled his phone from the charger, tapped open messages, typed Beth's number, and then a message.

Hey, what's your schedule like today? I'd like to see you.

He forced himself to put the phone down and eat. He'd finished the yoghurt and was halfway through his coffee when the screen lit up.

Working today. :(How are you doing? Long time, no text.

Yeah, it's been awhile. Sorry about that. Can you meet up after work?

The next response was faster, thank God.

It'll be late, but sure. Everything okay?

Yeah, just wanted to talk face-to-face.

Breathlessly, he waited. He didn't like playing this game, but he was flat out of other options.

Oh, sure. I get off work at ten and can come right over.

Great. I'm not in the city. I'll send directions. I'll have food to make it worth your trip out here.

Gotta get back to work now, but look forward to seeing you.
Sending the directions now.

He texted her the address and detailed directions because it wasn't unheard of for people to get lost here, then deleted the whole exchange. The temptation was strong to smash the phone on the stone floor of the kitchen, but he put it carefully down on the breakfast bar. Still, it was difficult to look at it, so he stood and headed upstairs to get some work done.

Jack only broke away from the laptop to hit the indoor gym for an agonizing two hours, trying to beat the worries out of his system until his bones groaned and his muscles screamed. Half an hour in the hot Jacuzzi afterward, plus a Tylenol washed down with a protein shake represented something of a physical armistice after all that pain, but he definitely wasn't thirty anymore. He'd feel this session tomorrow.

Again, he tried to withdraw with a book to the couch, but just like yesterday, the words rushed straight past him and ended up meaning nothing while his mind continually reminded him of all the ways this was bound to go terribly wrong. With a silent curse, he put the book back where he'd found it and picked up one of the lighter novels he'd read a hundred times in prison, and which no longer required much focus or imagination.

Outside, the shadows grew longer, the shift in light betraying that the sun was on the other side of the hill; both the sky and the water in the bay darkened and deepened with the expectation of night. Jack looked up every now and then, memories of prison coming to him as he skimmed the well-worn scenes. Echoing voices, too-small, grimy rooms, and guards who still called him "Mr. Barsanti", because everybody had known exactly who he was; most had also known their families and loved ones were fair game should anybody harm as much as a hair on his head. Who needed a protector in prison if "Lo Cascio" was both promise and threat?

He finished the book and checked his phone again.

No calls, but a message: *Leaving now.*

Time to get the food ready. Briefly, he surveyed the treasures in the fridge—his order had included more food than he could eat by himself, but he always liked having options.

He took the large lasagna dish out and removed the plastic wrap. After referring to the notes the restaurant had included, he set the correct temperature for the oven, and pushed the lasagna inside. He busied his hands with putting together a small arugula and cherry tomato salad with a basic oil and vinegar dressing. Once that was done, he spent a moment contemplating the wine shelf. He'd never learned all that much about wine—he had a dealer he trusted and who bought wines directly from small vineyards in Italy that were too precious, and whose harvests were too small, to ever make it into any kind of wholesale catalogue. He placed a bottle of Chianti and two glasses on the kitchen island, then started a fire in the fireplace.

Another text: *How far is this place?*

He tapped out an answer: *No rush, just follow the directions. How do you feel about lasagna?*

Fifteen minutes later, the fire was burning nicely—flames danced between the logs and spread that cozy living heat that had nothing to with hot water gurgling through pipes or hot air being pumped. He'd always found himself hypnotized by fire and its utter lack of compromise. Open flame was never civilized. It was only banked by material that couldn't catch fire, like stone tiles and concrete, but it wasn't for lack of trying.

After a quick glance in the mirror, he ran fingers through his hair and gave himself a side eye. The offer he was going to make was good. He didn't allow himself to think further than that this time around.

The phone rang in his pocket, and he answered. "Yes?"

"Jack? I'm down at the gate."

"I'll buzz you in. Gimme a sec." He walked to the front door and peered at the security panel. There she sat, alone in her beaten-up, bright yellow Toyota, and his stomach flipped, not at seeing her, but at what he'd set out to do. He buzzed the gates open and watched her drive through, then pressed the button to shut the gates behind her.

He opened the door, arms crossed against the evening chill while he watched Beth park her car next to his, then all but jump out and hurry up the path and stairs to him. Considering they'd met when she'd been a wispy bleached blonde, that had been the image he'd had of her for a long time, even when she'd cut off all her hair and let the bleached strands grow out. It suited her liquid brown eyes much better. No more perm either, but he noted she'd started to wear makeup again after about a year without any.

"I'm sorry I'm late." Without hesitation, she hugged him, a friend's hug, neither lingering nor powerful, but surely comfortable.

"Not your fault. Sorry for making you drive all the way

here. Can I take your jacket?" She wore a biker-style black leather jacket with a few spikes and studs. On her small frame, it looked a lot more like borrowed toughness than real attitude.

"Sure!" Once inside, she handed it to him and stopped to take in the house, and that made him smile, but she also looked fidgety in her tight blue jeans and hoodie. "Can I use the bathroom?"

"Of course. Just that way and then left."

"Great, thanks!" She dashed off, leaving him to hang up her jacket near the front door. He checked on the lasagna, but while a promising aroma was emanating from the oven, the timer said the food needed at least another twenty minutes. He poured the Chianti and set out a small bowl of olives, then laid the breakfast bar as a table. He wasn't in the mood for a more formal setup in the dining room on the other side of the house. The kitchen and living area around the fireplace were much cozier.

She returned and climbed onto the stool opposite, took her wine glass and offered it to him. He lifted his glass and gently touched them together before taking a sip. "I'm liking the hair."

"Right?" She shook her ponytail at him with a grin. "And look at you."

"Look at me?"

"Ageing very gracefully, oh yes, sir."

He chuckled into his wine. "Thanks to my mom. She had the good genes in the family. I was lucky."

She paused and regarded him. "I don't think you've ever talked about your family."

"Not much to tell, to be honest. They've both retired to a

small village in the Mediterranean. We have roots in that region." He shrugged, speared an olive with a toothpick and began to scrape the flesh from the stone with his teeth, which bought him a few moments. "How have you been? It's been, what, five months since we caught up?"

"Something like that." Her light faded a little, as she grew more thoughtful. "I dropped out of culinary school." She lowered her gaze and drew her lower lip between her teeth. "It wasn't for me. I'm sorry."

"Any particular reason?"

She took a deep breath, but still didn't make eye contact. And yet again, Jack wished he could get his hands on her ex. That fucker had gotten off way too lightly. "I started work as a cook to see if I liked it, but ..." Now she pressed both lips together. "Seems I can't cope with it."

Ah yes, the well-known rudeness and shouting behind the scenes. Jack could have fixed that. If he'd had a word with Gino's owners, provided some background, sat down with them and explained Beth's special circumstances. But the truth was, he didn't want her anywhere near Gino's or any of the other Italian restaurants in town.

"It's a tough job," he murmured and reached out to place a finger under her chin.

When she raised her head, her brown eyes were brimming with tears, and that catapulted him back to the night they'd met. She'd looked like a shot deer, still alive but unable to protect herself, waiting for the killing blow.

He walked around the bar and pulled her into his arms. Now she clung to him, sniffling against his chest, and he ran a hand over her hair, but did nothing else. That night, he'd given her his coat, and noticed her wracking shudders through the heavy wool, her body almost violently clinging to life.

"I'm very proud of you," he said, conjuring up the deepest, warmest layers of his voice. "It takes a lot of strength to know what's bad for us."

"You think? You're not disappointed?" She looked up, still holding onto him.

"You said you were interested in culinary school, and it seemed like a good idea at the time. That's all we can do. Trial and error. Sometimes it doesn't work out." She'd seemed so alive when she'd presented the idea to him, a wild "one day I will" dream, an ambition that had seemed out of reach then, but she was willing to strive for, and he'd enjoyed seeing the hunger in her. It'd taken courage to even make the attempt after everything she'd been through.

"But the money ..."

"Fuck the money," Jack said softly. "Do I look like I'm hurting for it?"

Now she looked at him and wiped at her eyes, so he reached out behind her and offered her the kitchen roll. She accepted with a teary smile and a nod, ripped off a sheet and dabbed at her eyes, then blew her nose. "I didn't believe I was heading for the right house."

"Why not?" He cast a glance at the timer. Two more minutes.

"It does explain a few things." She took a few deep, fortifying breaths, and he stepped back and around to his seat. "Like, everything. I mean, I knew you were loaded. But not how loaded."

"That's the right word." Like a gun. Or with a weight.

Focus on her. He shook his head. "Do you have any other plans?"

"I think I want to work with my hands. I've looked at some courses online, and I think I'll become an electrician. I talked with a few people and they said they'd take me on as an apprentice. I've read the demand for electricians is growing faster than for other professions—eight percent per year. That sounds pretty good, right?"

"Eight percent is very impressive." A doubling in nine years.

"And I can get qualified in ten months if I focus on it." There it was, the light in her eyes.

The timer. He stood and grabbed oven gloves to take the lasagna out. "I hope you're hungry."

"I'm just off work so yeah I'm hungry."

He succeeded in cutting out a piece of lasagna tidily and it didn't collapse on her plate. He managed the trick for his own too, then put the lasagna back in the oven but switched off the heat.

She dug in the moment he'd picked up his fork again. "Oh my God, that's crack. No way I'll finish all of it, but this is *so good.*"

He smiled, enjoying her response to Gino's best almost as much as the food itself. Lasagna was the ultimate comfort food in his book, but such a hassle to make at home. Better to leave that effort to restaurant staff who could hover over the bubbling sauces for hours until they'd fully revealed their flavor. While he could have put a passable lasagna together if forced to, he didn't usually have the patience and sheer stretches of time it took to make a truly good one.

While they ate, she gave him the whole run-down—how

she planned to start her own business and market to women primarily so they wouldn't have to deal with sexist assholes not taking them seriously. All Jack could offer was that it wasn't easy to get a good electrician in town, and a reliable one with manners would stand out like a unicorn. She'd be a hot commodity. Plus, of course, nobody would shout at her while she was re-wiring their house.

"But enough about me, what about you?" she asked after polishing off a good half of her portion.

"Been keeping busy."

"You do look tired. Stressed?" Then, after a small pause: "Working too hard?"

"Oh, without a doubt." He took a mouthful from the Chianti, forcing himself to focus on the mingling tastes until the wine overpowered the beef and tomato and cheese. He held the wine above his plate and watched her face carefully, inviting the question.

"So ... what do you actually do?"

"I'm a consultant."

"Oh. Consulting on what?"

"Business. I make sure people don't kill each other." He grinned to turn the truth into a kind of joke. "And that pays pretty well."

She picked up her fork but now merely played with her food, taking small bites for the taste, but eventually, she pushed the plate away. "Can I ask why you needed to see me so urgently? I thought it must be something bad. If it is, can we just talk about it and get it over with?"

Damn. He'd done his best to keep the urgency out of the texts he'd sent. His stomach flipped again, and he needed a moment to work through the nausea that came with it.

Maybe the lasagna had been a terrible idea after all. He'd hoped it would soothe and settle him, like a childhood favorite. But nothing on earth had that power right now.

"It's bad, right?" she asked when he didn't answer.

He hated how perceptive she was to mood shifts. He had a good poker face, or he couldn't do what he did, couldn't have survived as long as he had, or been as useful to Andrea and Andrea's father. But nothing escaped somebody whose very survival had depended on anticipating the moods of a volatile, violent ex.

"It's kind of bad and it kind of isn't." He reached out and took her hand, glad she closed her fingers around his, completely trusting. That she still had capacity to trust was a damn miracle, but he accepted it as the boon it was. "I have an offer to make. Think about it before you answer. Will you do that? Just hear me out?"

She nodded silently.

"First, let me state: you can still one hundred percent do what you want to do. Become an electrician, or go back to culinary school—whatever works for you. Nobody shouts at the boss, you know, if you wanted to open your own restaurant. You'd have your own place to live, and, as you've realized, money wouldn't be an issue, at least not much of one. You'd be completely safe and secure, and I would never make any demands of you." He'd gone through that list so often in his head, it almost appeared as bullets before his eyes, but he shook his head and focused completely on her. Her breath came a little faster, a little flatter, and her eyes had widened a touch.

"I'd do my best to support you in everything you do. You

wouldn't have a single worry in the whole world. Not one, I promise."

In his mind, he'd been smoother, more diplomatic, and in his mental rehearsals, she hadn't looked anywhere near this alarmed. When the last sentence came out, it was a wretched, breathless thing. "I want you to marry me."

5

"What? No!" She ripped her hand from his and pushed away from the breakfast bar with enough force to almost topple the stool.

The sick humor of the situation hit Jack, and shock and pain mixed at seeing her recoil like that. Yes, it had been a big request, definitely more than she'd expected, but ... she'd reacted as if he'd invited her to join him in cannibalism or something, not matrimony. "I'm sorry."

"Jack, what's going on? Why?" Red spots danced on her cheeks. He couldn't tell whether she was outraged or anxious. "What's happened?"

"Nothing's happened. Please think about it. There's nothing nefarious in this, I swear." *Wow, look at you, Mr. Hotshot "Consultant", who's getting flustered now?* Noticing the tension in her body and especially her rigid legs, he forced himself to sit down again, but he pushed his plate to the side.

She didn't seem convinced by the gesture and remained where she was, alert like an animal who'd heard a gun crack but hadn't yet caught a whiff of cordite. "No, I mean, we're not that kind of close." A hint of insecurity vibrated in her voice, indicating she was starting to doubt it herself, doubt the truth. Because a man she'd trusted was behaving as if he had the right to define their relationship in new terms, and now she was struggling to re-evaluate everything. That was the part that hurt enough to push him over the edge.

"No, we're not. You're right."

Now her alertness ratcheted up.

Here he was, terrifying her by staying calm and unemotional, but through the habitual numbness and exhaustion, a chronic condition of his life, he was surprised to feel an acute pain somewhere in his chest. "It was a stupid idea. I wanted to make sure you'd be taken care of ..."

"In case ...?"

"No, not like that."

"Then what is it, Jack? Can't you tell me? Ideas like that don't come out of nowhere. You're not interested in me like that. I mean, you never were." Again, her eyes shifted, obviously going through their shared history to test individual facts and events to see if they yielded any other interpretation, or could be assembled into a totally different timeline that would turn their weird lopsided friendship—compassionate project? platonic soulmateship?—into a normal heterosexual relationship centered on attraction. As if she could find a way to believe Jack's patient, long-suffering love had finally declared itself.

"You're right, I never wanted to sleep with you." That destroyed any idea he'd briefly entertained that he could play this as if he were a red-blooded male who'd bided his time until she felt ready to consider a relationship again.

He'd weighed that betrayal the same way he did when faced with options that only a very evil man would seriously consider. Usually, he was able to find alternative solutions that worked just as well. But the people he moved around like pawns believed themselves to be players too, and they'd never look for alternatives to evil; they'd betray him in a heartbeat.

Beth, however ...

Yeah, she wasn't a player. He'd never regarded her as a pawn, either. She'd been part of a different world and their chance encounter had torn down the wall between her world and his. When both of their lives had been so close to ending.

"So why?"

"Listen ... I don't have an explanation. I need to marry. You're the only one I can trust."

Shit.

But he did, didn't he? By getting her to trust him, he'd come to trust her too. Maybe because none of his many alarm bells went off in her presence. If his mind were like a jacket pickpockets trained their apprentices with, sewn with bells all over, she'd never raised so much as a tinkle.

She stared at him, opened her mouth as if to say something, but closed it. Took a sharp breath, opened her mouth again, and he realized how his words must have sounded. That she was a tool, a stopgap. She was right—this was about him and only him. He was all but bribing her to accept a terrible violation of trust.

"Your family?"

He almost startled when she unwittingly jabbed the finger right into the wound. "Yes."

The fear in her eyes softened and she took a couple steps toward him. "I'm so sorry. Are they giving you a hard time?"

Not yet, but they will.

He raised a hand to wave the concern away. "Yes, but that's not your problem."

For a long while, they didn't speak, but she didn't bolt, and she was no longer scared or shocked. She seemed to gather her thoughts and then raised her chin in a show of defiance. "Maybe you could explain to them ... I get that your parents might want grandchildren, but maybe you can sit them down and explain to them that ..." She hesitated, clearly unwilling to go there. "I mean, you're a successful businessman. What's more important, you're a *kind* man. Maybe they'll stop pressuring you to marry and give you more time to find the right one."

"I don't think it'll work that way, but thanks."

They both lapsed into silence, and he found he was suddenly grasping for the last of his reserves. This had been the plan. Wave money, use his charms, deceive, lie and coerce if necessary. But that took energy and focus he felt himself desperately short of. He needed to think quickly, snatch victory from the jaws of defeat and convince her. But he knew deep down he couldn't inflict that on either of them. She deserved better.

She checked her phone screen. "I need to get home, but ..."

"You could stay here. It's a long drive."

"Oh no, I really need my own bed." Spoken in a bit of a rush, but maybe it was better that she left. "But thanks."

"Sure." He trailed behind her to the door. "Thank you for coming. I'm sorry this got weird."

She placed a hand on his arm. "Don't be. I bet you thought about it. It's not that I don't care about your situation. It's just … I can't. You know? I didn't … get through all that to give everything away again. My freedom. My own decisions." She bit her lower lip. "Do you understand that?"

"I do." He unlocked the door and opened it for her. "I won't mention it again."

"I can explain this better when I've slept. I'll call you, okay? Tomorrow?"

"Sounds good. Drive safely. I'll open the gates for you."

She nodded and put on a brave smile. The slightly tense *no hard feelings, okay?* smile he knew from her.

Hard to tell whether she rushed down the path or that was her normal speed, but he didn't want to think too much about it. He wasn't sure she would call tomorrow. She might have decided he was a creep after all and she wanted nothing to do with him, because he was like all other men, and she'd had a lifetime of grief from men in general.

Maybe they'll stop pressuring you to marry and give you more time to find the right one.

It took him several heartbeats to realize she hadn't specified a gender.

But she was already in the car and heading down the gravel road, so it wasn't like he could ask her whether she'd meant what he thought she'd meant. Maybe he should have come clean, state upfront what the problem was, but if he crossed that line, it would be easier to cross the others. He could ignore a few of them with a wife, slowly, gently, carefully, teaching her the unwritten laws and what issues and events she'd better ignore for everybody's safety. But with an outsider—impossible.

6

_____

"Look at that." Enzo handed over the binoculars, a sharp grin forming on his features.

Sal focused on the side of the house where Barsanti stood in the open door, gazing after the girl who'd arrived about an hour earlier and now seemed in a bigger rush to get back to her car than she'd been to meet him.

"That doesn't look like a booty call," Sal murmured. And it had started so nice with the wine and a steaming lasagna from the oven. The only thing missing in the picture had been roses or a box with some expensive black lacey nothings that they'd try out in the bedroom together.

"Yeah, I'm disappointed." Enzo chuckled. "Wouldn't have minded watching them fuck."

Sal scoffed. "What did you want to see? Him on top? Her riding him?"

"Not partial. Either way."

Sal wasn't surprised. Enzo was a kind of "anything goes" guy, probably the most open mind man Sal had ever encountered, though apparently he preferred couples over one guy relieving some stress. Figured.

Barsanti's late-night guest had now made it to the gate. The car stopped there.

Sal handed the binoculars back to Enzo, who stashed them. Both of them pushed up from their prone positions and moved sideways to the house through the copse of trees. They'd been about to strike when it had become clear that Barsanti was expecting a guest. His preparations—two wine glasses, two plates—had stayed their hands, though Sal had decided to leave the truck and do some more old-fashioned surveillance up close.

There were a few large trees at the back and to the sides of the house, but much less protection at the front. The lawn was broken only by the path to the house and had a few bushes and rocks, but none large enough to give cover to a tall guy like Enzo.

Or Sal. Those decorative boulders and carefully trimmed boxwood bushes were more traps than cover.

"Look, here he comes." Enzo nodded toward the gravel path, where Barsanti was now coming down at a half-run, pocketing his phone on the way.

Could he have left the door open? The night visitor had thrown the original plan into disarray, but this would work fine too. Lucky Enzo was handy with electronics. "You get in the house. Door might be open. If I don't make the grab and bag, get ready to do it when he comes back in."

"Yep." Enzo gave him another grin and a nod.

Slowly and carefully, Sal moved toward the gate. He didn't think Barsanti would pay too much attention to snapping twigs and rustling among the trees, considering he was at a full jog on the gravel, but it always paid to be careful.

The gate came into view, where the young woman stood, phone in hand, arms crossed in front of her chest. The headlights of her crappy little car tore her out of the darkness, and illuminated like that, she had no chance of seeing Sal in the undergrowth.

"I'm sorry," she called toward Barsanti, "The gate didn't open, so ..."

"Don't worry about it." He walked to one of the posts of the gate, pulled out his phone to light the area, almost on top of Sal, but then he stepped backward. "I guess a wire got fried. I'll get that fixed." He unlocked the gate manually and pushed the heavy wrought iron wings open with only a little visible effort, then waved her through.

"Thank you! Talk tomorrow!" She hurried to get back in her car and was through the gate five seconds later.

Sal's pulse beat in his ears. Barsanti wrestled the iron gate closed, as if a busted gate would protect him (not that a working one would have), but maybe he counted on appearances—few people had reason to check whether a closed gate was actually locked.

While his target was still completely focused, Sal emerged from between the trees and crept up behind him. The gravel gave him away, of course, so he struck that instant. He wrapped his arm around Barsanti's throat, jugular in the crook of his elbow, locked his hands behind the man's head and applied pressure on both sides of the neck—a quick and easy blood choke.

Surprised, Barsanti stiffened, then his arms began to flail. Smartly, he reached for the hand behind his head and tried to loosen the hold so his brain would get oxygen again. Sal pushed against that, tightened the triangle around Barsanti's neck.

As Sal knew well from training, unlike in the movies where a man could be choked for what looked like minutes, a blood choke worked within seconds, and the total slackening of the victim's body was the giveaway. That couldn't be faked. Somebody trained enough to go slack still felt different from the peaceful quiet and wholly undramatic slump that came when the technique was applied correctly. Barsanti's movements became weaker, less coordinated.

"Good night," Sal whispered in the man's ear, and there it was, that full-body relaxation. He kept the choke for another three seconds. He let Barsanti's body sink to the ground and pulled out the zip cuffs. The downside of a blood choke was that the man began to come around again the moment it ended, so he hurried to grab his wrists and linked them behind his back, then put a black cloth bag over Barsanti's head.

He was already stirring. Sal knew what that felt like, emerging rapidly from unconsciousness, adrenaline pumping, the body's primal terror at the loss of control as big as the mind's disorientation. He'd been on the receiving end often enough that he didn't go into full-on panic mode now, but during training he was also prepared that it could happen. Barsanti had good instincts, but he didn't strike Sal as a trained fighter.

Sal kept his knee in the middle of Barsanti's back and enough of his weight on him that he felt the vertebrae of his spine move slightly with the pressure. He pulled his gun and dug the muzzle into the soft hollow where Barsanti's skull met his neck, and waited, counting. On a very slow five, Barsanti began scrabbling against the ground.

"Don't make a sound," Sal ordered. "That's a gun, and I don't mind blowing your head off right here."

The scrabbling stopped. A few deep, labored breaths. A nod.

"Good. I'll help you get up and then we'll walk back to the house."

Another nod.

Sal took his weight off Barsanti's back and shifted to the side. He grabbed Barsanti under one arm and all but hoisted him to his feet. The man broadened his stance as if he were on an oceangoing vessel that was lurching left and right. Sal grabbed his elbow, and dug the gun into the man's spine, but lower down. "Walk."

Even though they were still on the gravel path, and Barsanti had to know there were no obstacles, he lifted his feet higher than necessary, and moved with hesitation as if he expected Sal had conjured up a wall from somewhere to steer him right into for laughs. It was enough to be annoying, but not enough to shove a blinded, bound man who was likely still getting his bearings after having lost consciousness for a few seconds.

It wasn't so much compassion as the thought that making him fall, picking him up again, and repeating that a few times would only slow them down, and while witnesses were unlikely to show up at this time of night, Sal was eager to get Barsanti back into the house and secure him there. That environment would be easier to control.

When they reached the stone path, Sal grabbed Barsanti's elbow tighter and dug the gun in under his short ribs, now walking side by side. Say whatever you wanted about Barsanti, his body took its cues from Sal's, falling into step when they changed direction, and neither of them ended up in the flower beds, which was quite a success. Barsanti almost stumbled when his foot hit the step leading into the house, but he caught himself without Sal's help.

Enzo stood near the door in the corridor, waiting for them to enter before he closed and then locked the door.

Sal noticed the blinds in the living room were drawn, affording them more privacy than Barsanti and the young woman had had. Sal pushed Barsanti toward the couch. "Fuck those designer chairs. Is there a normal one anywhere in the house?"

Enzo shrugged. "I'll have a look."

"You. Sit." Sal pushed the back of Barsanti's knees against the couch near the fireplace. A harder push served as emphasis, and Barsanti sat down carefully, again as if he expected Sal would trick him into crashing into obstacles, maybe glass shards or rusty iron spikes. Sal shook his head. A dose of healthy paranoia was part of the job. He wouldn't act any differently.

Instead of leaning back, Barsanti sat ramrod straight on the edge of the couch, shoulders drawn up as if subconsciously trying to protect his head. Truth was, though, Sal could have cut his throat then and there and Barsanti would only realize that way too late.

Sal watched the hooded, bound man in front of him, watched every rise and fall of his chest. If Barsanti was scared, he wasn't showing much of it. The only indications were that none of his breaths reached his belly, and his breathing was too shallow and faster than normal.

Enzo came back from upstairs, carrying a much more suitable chair with an actual wooden back and much longer legs than those low designer chairs. "Found one."

"Put it over there." Sal indicated a gap between the couches.

Enzo set it down with a slight clatter which made Barsanti jerk.

"You. Get up."

The man stood, and Sal grabbed him by the elbow again and moved him the two steps to the chair. "Sit."

He did. Sal guided his arms so the back of the chair ended up between tied arms and back, and then he took two zip ties and tied his legs to the chair. Interestingly, Barsanti's breath now sped up noticeably.

"Can I speak or are you going to shoot me?" Barsanti's voice was flat, but he wasn't pleading.

"You got something interesting to say, then? Let's hear it."

Hah. No immediate response, instead a further straightening of the spine. Not happy. Sal grinned to himself.

"I have money. There's a safe. You take it, cut me free, and leave. This never happened."

"How much are we talking?" Sal asked.

"About twenty-five large."

Sal met Enzo's gaze, who'd tilted his head, clearly curious how he was going to play this. "If we take the money, you'll have us hunted down and killed."

"I don't know who you are. I haven't seen your faces. That's why I said, cut me free and leave and I'll chalk this up as a lesson. No harm, no foul."

Sounding perfectly reasonable, voice regaining some resonance, probably as he warmed to the idea himself.

Already trying to cut a deal—tied up, powerless, potentially with a gun pointed at his head, still believing he was in control, or a step away from seizing it back. That was some faith in the world.

Maybe the offer was genuine too. Maybe Barsanti had already worked through the implications. If anybody heard of this, it would play out in one of two ways—he either was a made man who'd gotten jumped by some burglars and allowed them to escape and remain breathing. Or he'd turn every stone in this city, slit every mattress, toss every piece of furniture to find and kill them. And if Barsanti didn't do it, Andrea Lo Cascio surely would. Neither of them could afford not to.

"I'll think about it," Sal answered.

7

What burglar said something like that? Maybe Jack was still hazy, maybe shock and surprise had rattled him too much to think clearly, but now he forced himself to backtrack, because the alternative would be to lose it and freak out.

They'd definitely targeted him with a measure of preparation. The gate that no longer worked. Attacking the instant he was out of the house to let out Beth, and—

Beth.

He was almost positive that she'd gotten through the gate and driven off. Yes, he was. He remembered seeing the taillights moving away. They'd definitely targeted him, not her. Or rather, they'd targeted the owner of this nice expensive house in the hills. And whose fault was it? Beth had unwittingly provided the opportunity for them to strike, but it was him who'd insisted on Mauro leaving. Had Mauro been lurking around, these burglars might have realized that he wasn't as soft a target as he might appear at first glance, and chosen another house.

The shock of being grabbed from behind and around the throat. Sheer horror when he'd feared the attacker would break his neck, but also the greying of his vision, the knowledge he was passing out and yet could do nothing about it and then a strong hit of his own body's sedative signaling that, yes, he was dying and it would be okay. Some merciful mechanism in his brain gave him a strange, fucked-up calm and peace while his body went numb, and his vision faded. It would probably feel like that when he actually died, if he ended up like he expected to: bleeding out on a sidewalk somewhere.

But this brought the horror home, and in more ways than one. He shuddered hard.

Who were these men? Two at least. Their voices sounded muffled because of the hood over his head and his own pulse thundering in his ears; hard to concentrate while his thoughts raced and very nearly screamed at him. He forced himself to breathe—he couldn't move much, securely tied hand and foot to the chair as he was. That limited his options. The thin restraints with their sharp edges felt like plastic zip cuffs. He knew those could hold a big man. Twisting his wrists against them had proven they could hold him at any rate. He wasn't going to try again. All of this left him, still breathing but blinded, tied to a chair in his own house at the mercies of men he didn't know.

The man who'd spoken to him last was also the one who'd pressed a gun to his neck and physically maneuvered him inside. He remembered the warmth and strength of his body and the harsh, focused movements. There was nothing unsure or probing about him. Rehearsed. He'd done this a dozen times.

Didn't burglars usually try and avoid having to deal with people? If you were after jewelry or a laptop, why risk looking into the muzzle of a gun? The most prolific burglar Jack knew was a potbellied, nearly-bald guy, easily mistaken for a plumber, but had some of the sharpest senses Jack had ever encountered, as well as a natural gift for observing people. In that way, he'd been much like a seasoned pick-pocket—selecting a mark carefully because ideally the mark never realized what had happened. Similarly, burglars liked to be far away from the scene of the crime by the time it was discovered.

Robbers, though, were a different breed—they lacked the finesse of a pickpocket or burglar. These guys struck Jack more like robbers.

"So what's the problem? Do you want more money?" If they were robbers, a larger haul might sway them.

No immediate response, which made Jack's skin crawl. They weren't amateurs. But if they were professional crimi-nals of any stripe, they should know who he was, and give him wide berth. Nobody touched a made man.

Except.

Except if they were made men too. In that case, it was a declaration of war. He pushed that thought to the side as a worst-case scenario. If that was true, he was dead. Still, to lay hands on a consigliere was a move so breathtaking it wouldn't have been done lightly.

Or it was an inside job. Had Andrea already decided Jack

needed to be dealt with? Would Andrea cut off his own nose to spite his face? Before that wedding, Andrea hadn't made any noises about being displeased with him. Not a single threat, not even a veiled one. Granted, Andrea was impulsive, but even he wouldn't act so quickly when it came to removing Jack. Going against Jack so brazenly without any proof of things he still only suspected was dangerously short-sighted. Andrea *knew* the Lo Cascio were better off with Jack than without him.

If Andrea *was* behind it, these men would be drafted from among his own capos and soldiers. Except Jack was closer to all of them than Andrea was, and would surely have recognized their voices. All members of the Lo Cascio clan came to him first. Dealing with their grievances was his job. Andrea had nobody to replace him with—there was no overflowing talent pool in the organization and nobody who'd been sawing at Jack's chair. If he'd missed this going on in his own family, then he deserved no better, but he couldn't recall any grumblings. To the best of his knowledge, he was liked and respected. There were others whose positions were a lot less secure.

Dommarco? He hadn't caught a whiff of anything wrong between Cassaro and him. Why would Cassaro slather on the honey to have him killed a week later? They had nothing to gain from another war. Surely this wasn't about that missing associate?

But if these *were* made men, why wasn't he dead already? If they planned to torture him first, they were also taking their sweet time. Only one way to narrow the field.

"Do you know who I am?"

A snort. "Next you'll ask to speak to the manager."

Jack bit back on his first response. "If he can help clear things up, I'm all for talking to somebody else. The question is, do you know who I am and what this means? I can't work with nothing."

8

S al caught himself grinning. He could almost see
Barsanti's gears grinding behind the black hood.

"I can't work with nothing."

I don't want you to "work with" anything. But he didn't say
it out loud. Sitting on the on the armrest of one of the
couches, Enzo watched the scene unfold, but he seemed a
little confused. Sal found himself enjoying it all more than
he'd thought he would. The evening had started strong and
was only getting better. Not only had he gained control of his
enemy's queen, but if he played it right, he'd follow up his
revenge with a resounding victory.

He'd lived for this for years. Which made him the damn
king of delayed gratification.

Sal stepped closer to Barsanti, and punched him in the
stomach, hard. The attack had the full benefit of surprise—
no tension of muscles that cushioned or deflected any of the
force. Barsanti doubled over, spluttering and gasping breath-

lessly. Enzo was off his perch like a shot, but Sal raised a hand to stay him.

"Does that answer your question, Barsanti? Whether I know who you are and how much I care *who the fuck* you are?"

Shit, the rage rose like a red wave now that he'd made his move, and the force of it committed him much more than he'd expected. Partly because Barsanti had lived the past few years without even a hint of the pain that had torn up Sal's life, partly because Barsanti clearly believed he was untouchable, that nobody would ever make him and the others pay for what had happened, and that he'd dare to challenge him while tied to his own fucking chair. If anything, the fact that Barsanti was tied and blinded somehow stoked Sal's rage even more.

He might have pulled back and regained control of himself if Barsanti had been in a position to fight back, if he'd posed even the slightest—actual, physical—threat. Barsanti tucked in his chin like a boxer to protect his throat, tensed instinctively, pulled his shoulders up, and pushed his knees together, but those defenses were pitiful against the hail of punches.

When Enzo placed a hand on Sal's arm, Barsanti's chair had toppled and the man lay on his side, gasping hard and clearly suppressing sounds of distress. Coldly, distantly, Sal remembered that people didn't cry out when they didn't expect to attract help or mercy. Men without hope suffered in silence. He hissed out the breath that had got stuck somewhere between his ribs, and stepped back, then looked at Enzo.

"What?"

"Nothing." Enzo's eyes lacked all sentimentality. "Figured you still had questions for him."

Sal gritted his teeth, but Enzo was right. Wouldn't do to beat the man to shit and inflict wounds that made him useless. He flexed his hands and rolled his shoulders and straightened. "Get him up."

Enzo duly bent down and tried to right the chair with Barsanti tied to it—a hell of a lot of dead weight, and he might have eventually managed, but Sal lent him a hand. Between them, they got it done.

Barsanti didn't move. He sat there slumped under the pain as if it were a weight. His panting breaths were the only indication he was still alive and hadn't passed out either. Sal's fingers itched to continue the beating, or he was just on edge as years of tension found an outlet. That said, a lot of men would have already broken—for all their hard-ass antics, quite a few members of their specific circles were cowards and perfectly happy to sell their grandmothers if it saved them a minor inconvenience. Barsanti hadn't said a word after that first attempt to work out who had gotten the better of him.

"Do you know who I am? I can't work with nothing."

Well, now Barsanti knew this wasn't a random attack. And if they were both *men of honor*, as the misnomer went, he'd also already know how this would end.

Which was the place to pick up their conversation. Sal stepped behind Barsanti and rested his hands on the man's shoulders, felt their warmth and strength through the shirt. As he tightened his grip, he realized how stiff the muscles were—an attempt to muster whatever physical armor Barsanti had. Pointless. Steel and cordite put the lie to any man's strength. Fuck, for many all it took was a pair of pliers.

"I can do this the hard way or the easy way," Sal said. "Personally, I have no preference. Hard might be more fun, easy means I can go home sooner. You understand me, smart boy?" It tickled him to call Barsanti a boy, but he'd have to prod him a while to see how much fight was left in him. Besides, as Enzo had said, any psychological advantage would work in their favor. Hence the hood and ties. And doing this in the man's own house.

"I understand." The words were clipped, carefully controlled. Not a hint of begging. Yet. Sal felt the words in Barsanti's shoulders, as well as the breath he took to say them.

"Good." He let one hand crawl closer to the hood and cradled Barsanti's jaw, drawing a full-bodied shudder of revulsion from him, but didn't allow him to pull back or move his head away—more psychology. Training a man into helplessness was important. "Now that we're here, having this nice time together, I'll tell you what I want from you. I'm sure you're dying to know." Shifting his hands back, he dug them into the man's shoulders and kneaded the muscle. Barsanti didn't like that, and there was no give. "I'm going to take down Andrea Lo Cascio and his whole miserable outfit."

"And that includes me." Barsanti's voice was neutral, a professor adding a footnote to a paper.

"Every one of his associates, soldiers, capos, trusted friends. Lo Cascio is going down."

"You're not a Fed."

"No. Not a vigilante cop either. I'm an interested party."

69

"Dommarco?"

Sal bared his teeth, and exchanged a glance with Enzo, who was back on his perch on the couch. "You're going to help me. You know everything there is to know about his business. You'll give me everything. Names, addresses, businesses, accounts."

"Oh Christ." Barsanti shook his head and that was the first genuinely emotional response Sal had gotten out of him —a kind of despair at the enormity of it. "You're going to start a war."

"Don't worry about that part. You won't be around to see it," Sal snapped. "Your choice is—easy or hard?"

Judging from the state of the man's shoulders, it would be hard. Everything about Barsanti signaled resistance.

"Is Guy Dommarco behind this?"

"I already ignored that," Sal hissed. "You keep your mind on answering *my* questions."

Several seconds passed, but Sal kept his hands on Barsanti's shoulders, finding that the man's body was better about communicating what was going on inside of him than his voice or his words. The tension under his fingers ramped up like ropes twisting tighter.

"So?"

"You know I can't do that." Barsanti sounded calm, but breathy. "Besides, this could be some twisted test."

How old school. But then, Barsanti was part of a generation where business was done face to face, and unable to fit this whole event into his neat worldview, he questioned even the most basic choices put before him. Though what an interesting piece of intel. He truly seemed to think that either Dommarco or his own fucking boss might have him snatched and beaten to test whether he'd fold under pressure. Huh.

He had no argument against it. Dommarco might have decided it was time for another war, even though business had been good, and the Prizzi wedding had overall been a demonstration of harmony. And whether Lo Cascio was stupid enough to fuck with his own consigliere—well, Sal reserved judgment on that.

He took his hands off Barsanti and stepped around the chair. If this got him to his goal faster, making the small concession might be worth it. After all, he was playing this little game to save blood and time. He reached for the black hood.

"You sure?" Enzo asked.

"Yeah." He pulled it off.

Barsanti blinked in the comparatively bright light—that hood was a real bastard, Sal had tested it himself, and after a little while the total darkness inside got disorientating. Barsanti's hair was a little disheveled, his skin flushed, his lip split. Barsanti must have quietly sucked in the blood and swallowed it, though there was a smear on his chin. His light blue eyes blinked again, and Sal caught all the little, fleeting expressions on his face. Relief. Recognition. Fear. Surprise. Realization.

Now, though, Barsanti gathered himself and regarded him evenly. The skin on his left cheekbone was red and swollen—that looked like it would become a hell of a shiner. The hood had also allowed Sal to forget how attractive Barsanti was—especially without his smarmy salesman grin. His stomach tightened with appreciation.

"No, I didn't get this sanctioned by either Dommarco or Lo Cascio," Sal said.

Barsanti looked up to him, nothing but honesty in his eyes. "I believe you."

Hot fucking damn.

Strip the bullshit from the man, make him hurt and shake that confidence, and there was something underneath that almost shocked Sal. He'd seen that expression on Enzo's face years ago, when Enzo had dropped his defenses and completely surrendered. Up until then, Enzo had been attractive in an abstract way, but never compelling. It took a masterful hand to reduce Enzo to that point where nothing but honesty remained.

Barsanti closed his eyes briefly. "Shit." Though Sal felt there was an odd measure of relief in it. "I'm ..." He cleared his throat and then looked at Sal, making a show of honesty. "Thanks for ... taking the hood off."

Sal laughed in his face. "Fuck you. You don't get to thank me, you bastard." He grabbed Barsanti around the throat. "I'm going to fuck you up and fuck up your whole family and absolutely slaughter your boss—you don't get to say *thank you, Mr. Rausa.* You're dead. Your whole fucking family is dead already."

Barsanti recoiled and Sal let him go, pointedly. He was of a mind to punch him again, but Enzo was right. He did have questions and just draining some of the rage boiling inside him wouldn't get them even one step closer to the goal. Which was still to make Barsanti spill everything he knew so they could finalize their plans to wipe the Lo Cascio off the map forever for what they'd done to Catia.

"You didn't have to take it off, though," Barsanti said in a low murmur.

"You ...!" Sal got right back in Barsanti's face. The man regarded him unblinkingly. "Fuck you." But those two words came out without any of the venom from seconds ago. "Fascinating though that you'd think Andrea would do this to you. Why's that?"

"Maybe he wants to switch me out for a younger model," Barsanti said with half a smile. "Somebody more in line with his thinking on some things."

"Such as?"

Barsanti hesitated. "Violence is a young man's game."

"Is it?" Sal pulled back. Barsanti might be hiding behind Internet meme quips, but he hadn't even attempted to paper over the fact that he and his boss didn't always see eye to eye. Enough that maybe his biggest horror was that his boss had turned against him. Sure, a worrisome development for anybody in their circles, but the extent of that fear intrigued Sal. He himself hadn't interacted much with Andrea Lo Cascio, but the received wisdom was that Andrea wasn't boss so much for his talents as for whose son he'd been until his father had died of a stroke in his office. The Lo Cascio might have supported Andrea's claim in part out of respect for his old man. There must have been more experienced men available, but none of those seemed to have stepped up. Barsanti could have done it—he'd just been made consigliere when it happened, if his memory served.

"Back to the topic," Sal said. "Hard or easy?"

Barsanti lowered his gaze, and Sal caught himself staring. Fuck, the whole situation, from Barsanti's clean-cut attractiveness to his strong shoulders to how he sat there, tied up on the chair and considering his options, plucked at strings he'd thought he'd muted. Several of them had been cut, because he doubted that the stars would ever align again and give him somebody like Catia—a person he could trust and love enough to do that kind of play with without all the scars inside hurting like fuck.

"Don't make me ask again."

9

Rausa stood there, in his black military-style pants, black turtleneck, eyes blazing. And the other man was similarly dressed, but tall and blond. Both of them were armed—gun holsters sat snugly against their sides, and the second man carried what looked like a small utility pocket on his belt. A Leatherman or similar multi-tool. Useful for pulling out somebody's fingernails.

That it had turned out to be Sal Rausa was the worst and maybe the best of all possible worlds. Best because it didn't involve Andrea. Cassaro hadn't stabbed him in the back, either, and the peace with the Dommarco held.

But like a revenant from hell, the third boss in the city had apparently risen to kick the ants' nest and trample everything that Jack had so painstakingly built. Not at all a drunk has-been—the Sal Rausa in front of him seemed even more volatile and a whole lot more violent than Andrea. Those two would tear into each other like two fronts of wildfire. Capturing a consigliere in good standing signaled that Rausa meant what he said. There was no coming back from this. In private, Andrea might disagree with Jack, but he'd come down hard on Rausa if he caught wind of this.

It meant Rausa was racing a ticking clock. Once Andrea realized what was happening, the game was on. And if Jack pegged Rausa right, he'd follow his course like a falling star —nobody could catch him now or slow him down. Nothing but pure force and decisiveness could win the battle for Rausa. Jack didn't know what state his family was in—he was frankly surprised that Rausa thought he had the manpower to win the inevitable war, or perhaps he just didn't care. He had to know that even if he managed to take the Lo Cascio down, the Dommarco would have Rausa leftovers for breakfast right afterward.

Jack ran his tongue along his gums, then lips, but the sharp, lemon juice in a papercut feeling there told him the blood was from a cut in his lower lip. All teeth were still in place, a small mercy and marked contrast to the nasty throbbing all over his body where Sal had punched him. But this hadn't been the first or worst beating he'd received in his life. The first time, he'd considered it a great injustice that it was impossible to pass out at will. Thirty years on, Jack knew justice didn't exist. All he could do was wrestle the terror and protect himself as much as possible. Still woozy, he figured he must have hit his head against the hardwood floor when the chair toppled. His vision had blackened, and lights had sparked before his eyes. He might even have lost consciousness for a split second.

He met Rausa's eyes. "It'll have to be hard, and you know that. It's not a real choice."

"Maybe not."

Jack swallowed. "Alternatively, you come to the table, and we'll renegotiate. There's plenty of business for everybody in this city. I'm sure rather than fight a war, we can sit down and divide up the spoils. You take your rightful place; we all make money."

"My rightful place." Rausa sounded thoughtful. "I let you go, and you get to be the brilliant dealmaker who secures another few years of peace for everybody."

"Why not?" Jack shrugged, though his shoulders were beginning to feel stiff and ached from the unnatural position. "At this stage, it could be nothing but a ... a mistake. A show of force. Message received. I know you mean business. I know you're willing to go to war. But you don't have to."

"Simple as that."

"Yes." Jack didn't get the impression Rausa was seriously considering it, but he had to try. While he could still speak, still appeal to the man's ... well, maybe not humanity, but maybe any doubts he might harbor against going to war. Rausa had to know there was a fair chance he would get killed too. That kind of war was too chaotic to know who'd be left over at the end of it, however meticulous the planning. If he was mad because he'd been sidelined and pushed out of his former business, there was a way to appease him and give him some of it back. There would be stomping and table-thumping and shouting and threats, but in the end money and opportunity would win out.

As long as he managed everybody's egos carefully, they might just all live. Cassaro would see it the same way. Did Rausa have a consigliere?

Rausa nodded to himself, before catching his man's eye. "Enzo."

The blond man left the couch, cast a glance at Jack and followed his boss.

10

Enzo followed Sal outside through the glass door out to the garden. It was getting late, past three in the morning, so dawn wasn't far off, and Sal thought the sky was already a little less black and turning a dark Prussian blue.

"I know you have thoughts. Spit it out."

Enzo glanced back over his shoulder as if making sure Barsanti wasn't breaking the chair apart and scrambling for a gun.

"He's got some balls on him." Enzo suppressed a small yawn.

"Yeah." Sal fought the impulse to yawn as well and shook his head, despite himself impressed by the man still trying to broker peace. Fuck him, he'd probably try to fucking broker peace with fucking terrorists while kneeling in the desert sand in an orange jumpsuit, sabre already on his neck. That kind of man. Courageous to the point of stupidity. Rational. And he did have an argument. The sheer composure it must have taken him to make it.

Of course, it wouldn't work, because peace wasn't what this was about. Aside from requiring both Andrea Lo Cascio and Guy Dommarco—who had admittedly upheld some kind of peace deal—to be cool-headed men in Barsanti's mold, Sal himself would have to muster the will to accept that Andrea Lo Cascio was still breathing, and act as if the War and its aftermath had been nothing but an interruption of business as usual. He had failed at that so far because he didn't want to succeed.

There was no way he'd shake hands with Catia's murderer. The thought alone made his pulse beat against the insides of his skull, and just her name hurt and conjured all kinds of emotions and memories he couldn't use inside that house when he tried to get into Barsanti's head.

Barsanti's job required him to be a schemer and a risk manager, heading off dangers before they, to use business parlance, crystalized. Nowadays, consiglieres came with business or law degrees, and Sal could easily imagine Barsanti walking amongst lawyers unmolested.

"I'm definitely not thinking rationally." Sal gritted his teeth. "Fuck." They were both running on far too little sleep, no more than five hours each for the past couple of days, driven onward by rage, determination and, last but not least, spiky caffeine jitters.

"Rest, regroup, let him think about it some more?"

"Not on that note." Sal shook his head. "If we break here, we'll do it on our terms."

"Gotcha."

Sal glanced at him and was so tempted to ask the question: *What do you think Catia would have made of all this?*

"You're pretty wired," Enzo stated.

"No shit," Sal growled. The past few years of simmering anger had been a heavy weight to bear. Keeping the pressure in, slowly reorganizing, quietly removing pawns and people whose loyalty wasn't to be trusted. He'd also retired some people who clung to how things had been before—some had fucked off to Florida or Mexico, others had been foolish enough to think there were other options.

He'd forced himself to wait even when he thought he was ready. Just in case. Played dead. All but allowed the carrion eaters to peck out his eyes—that kind of dead. Tested loyalties. Retired a few more people. Made more money to fill up the war chest. Spent a lot of money to grease the palms of people who were not even on Lo Cascio's or Dommarco's radars. Made friends in high and low places and anywhere in between. Always with the gnawing feeling that he might be waiting too long, that the opportunity would pass.

At this point, Sal didn't even know anymore whether the agony of the wait would be worth the payoff. It seemed about even to his mind. Sometimes he wished he'd immediately gone in all guns blazing and slaughtered every last one of them.

Barsanti might not consider an easier death much of a reason to sell out his family. But Sal knew once the pain started and got bad enough, Barsanti would see it as quite the prize. Sal's job was to push him there, and Enzo would help. But tomorrow. They should have that much time, but more than that was a risk. A man could drop off the face of the earth for a day. Two days, maximum. Three—and Andrea Lo Cascio might start to miss his consigliere.

But to break Barsanti tomorrow, he needed to be clear-headed. Too much of one kind of pressure was crashing, while another one was rising. Adrenaline would only get him so far.

He walked back in and noted that Barsanti's eyes followed every single one of his steps.

"You're in luck," Sal said. "We're going to take a break. Give you get some time to think. The fun starts tomorrow."

"Lucky me." It was said so calmly it didn't even sound like sarcasm.

Now, how to secure him for the night? While he and Enzo could use some rest, Barsanti shouldn't get any at all. There was a minute risk he might be able to topple the chair, maybe break it, maybe reach a phone. Who knew what a smart guy could come up with in those long night hours when left to his own devices? Or what if, by some freak accident, somebody spotted him through a window?

The bathroom was a little more protected, and so was the gym, but planting the man plus chair in the Jacuzzi and tying the chair to the armatures came second to using the walk-in closet in the master bedroom. Between Enzo and him, they carried a re-hooded Barsanti into the bedroom and then into the adjacent walk-in closet, which could be locked from outside and had no windows. A quick search revealed no cell phone, weapons or anything sharp that could saw through the zip cuffs. Sal tied the back of the chair to two clothes rails with some of the rope from his bag of tools, and stepped back. The knots weren't the tidiest he'd ever made but functional, and the whole picture was pleasant to look at—almost architecturally symmetric, with all lines culminating in the sagging man on the chair.

"A bit shibari, isn't it?" Enzo said softly. The odd gleam in his eye looked a lot like envy.

"Can't have him hurt himself before *we* get a chance to hurt him." Sal closed and locked the door. He pushed a chair against it, and placed a lamp with a glass shade close to the edge of the seat. Not enough. He went to the kitchen and found a shiny metal mixing bowl, which he placed where the lamp would fall if it got shoved. Its breaking on the carpet might not be enough to wake him up, but this should do the trick.

He picked up both his and Barsanti's phone from the nightstand. Barsanti was an Apple man; Sal preferred Android. Even so, Barsanti had enabled an old-fashioned PIN with a limited number of attempts rather than touch ID or iFace or whatever the Cupertino crew had come up with. The quickest way to get into that phone was simply to get Barsanti to spit out the PIN. If that came with a spray of blood or broken teeth, then so be it.

He switched off the light in the master bedroom and took a few deep breaths. That wired, spiky feeling inside didn't budge, and part of him wanted to rip the closet door off its hinges and finish all of this tonight, but Barsanti was dangerous. Sal didn't underestimate the reserves some men could draw on when their lives depended on it. That, plus his recent sleep deprivation, and who knew what foolishness Barsanti could get him to agree to?

While Enzo examined the contents of the fridge in the kitchen, Sal headed upstairs. The office had a more intimate vibe than the downstairs floor. The lower ceiling felt more sheltering, and two shelves separated the office from another sitting area and a guest bedroom—both of which seemed unused. Sal set down his bag in the guest bedroom. When he turned back the covers, he caught a whiff of freshly washed and tumble-dried laundry.

"You could go grab a shower." Enzo came upstairs with two large glasses of orange juice.

"Later." Sal accepted the glass and emptied it, surprised how much his body needed this now though the chill from the cold juice froze up his sinuses.

Enzo moved around the bed, sat down on the edge of it, and drank more juice while reviewing the sight angles of the "room". The nearest path down was via a spiral staircase. He could just jump down to the lower floor if necessary. In Sal's estimation, whether the house was a good place for a shootout depended entirely on whether one liked cover.

Enzo turned the glass thoughtfully in his hands, while Sal got rid of his shoes and pulled the tactical turtleneck over his head. One of his capos had been raving about these being composed of specially woven fibers that cut the risk of infection if he got stabbed or shot, but on the outside it could have simply been normal survival gear. And since his capo was very persuasive, this brand had spread well beyond his own crew. Plenty of the local tech bros dressed like that, enough in any case that Sal didn't even raise eyebrows when he picked up a latte among normal people.

Enzo's gaze followed the turtleneck, and his hands stilled on the glass. "Would you prefer me to sleep downstairs?"

"Come here."

Enzo didn't hesitate to obey and set the glass down. Without his heavy boots, Sal was a little shorter than his capo, but Enzo made up for it by stooping slightly.

"What do you want, boss?" Enzo asked.

Shit. Too easy, too tempting. "You're only doing this because I'm wired like a fucking cable plant."

Enzo gave an open-handed shrug. "Maybe I'm wired like one too."

Sal looked deep into Enzo's eyes, didn't detect any lies or subterfuge. The only thing Enzo had ever hidden was how much Catia's death had hurt him. But frankly, Sal had been so trapped in his own pain there was no fucking way he could have carried Enzo's too.

Sal placed his hand flat against Enzo's groin and pushed against the outline of Enzo's semi-hard cock. His capo blinked and inhaled sharply as Sal squeezed firmly, and he rapidly hardened. "All right. Get undressed. And yeah, you'll sleep up here." He wasn't going to kick Enzo out of bed afterward.

His orders clear, Enzo seemed to calm down, became less sharp, slightly less aware, and, Sal realized, a lot more vulnerable. He could snap out of it within seconds, but his ability to sink into a responsive, passive and even soft state had surprised Sal. He knew how cold and cynical Everyday Capo Enzo appeared to others.

Enzo pulled his shirt off first and the smell of him hit Sal —some musk from today's work, some lingering scent of lime and ginger shower gel.

Enzo sat down on the bed to take off his shoes and socks, and when he straightened again, Sal placed his hand against the man's neck and pulled his face against the side of his groin, cheek against his pants, and he kept him like that—all it took was a firm touch, no force at all. He felt Enzo tremble when he opened the button of his pants, pulled down the zip, and freed his cock an inch or so from Enzo's lips. This wasn't something that Enzo did often—Sal had a solid suspicion that Enzo had only done this with him—and it was less a matter of desire on his part, and more a matter of surrender.

He felt Enzo's breath on him, and, despite Enzo's headspace, he felt a twitching in his neck too. He still had to psych himself up to take a cock into his mouth, and Sal enjoyed the struggle playing out under his fingertips.

"You know you don't have to do it," Sal teased. "Unless you really, really want to."

"Fuck," Enzo breathed.

Between them, they could build an international cable factory empire now.

"No need to sacrifice yourself, Enzo. I can deal with it myself."

"Shut up," Enzo muttered and jerked free to take Sal's cock into his mouth. Sal placed one hand on his shoulder, the other against his neck as Enzo took him as deeply as he could, which wasn't all that deep, but this wasn't about a harsh face fuck. It was about watching Enzo space out as he won or lost his internal battle, depending on viewpoint. And what the capo lacked in experience, he made up with heart. Once he was over the whole "I'm really mostly straight" thing in his head—and Sal respected that—he followed through. Shit, did he follow through.

Sal forced himself to remain still and let Enzo take things at his own speed; he wasn't tentative, either, just re-learning the geography of a man after, what? Half a year or so? Their friendship always carried this potential, especially with Enzo wanting to serve him any way Sal required. But knowing Enzo wanted the surrender more than he wanted a male lover had ensured that they hadn't ended up together.

For Enzo's sake, Sal had hoped he'd eventually move on, find somebody who could give him what he needed, and that would be that. Instead, Enzo had become his shadow, more loyal and closer than ever. It wasn't healthy, considering a mostly straight man was now sucking Sal's cock partly because he got off on doing what he was ordered to do, instead of getting off on the things he did, but Sal figured as long as he respected Enzo and made sure they were both as safe as they could be, no harm, no foul.

Enzo eventually looked up to him, eyes glazed, whole face transformed with lack of tension and nothing guarded in him. "Sorry I can't ..."

"I don't want you to suck me off." He stroked Enzo's heated cheek with the back of his fingers. "Lose your clothes. All of them." He stepped to watch Enzo get rid of his pants and underwear. Enzo was all golden flesh and long, muscular limbs, some white scars on his lower arms betrayed a passionate student of the switchblade, and fights where he'd gotten hurt. Misspent teenage years. And the scar on his solar plexus from the branding, of course—entwined lines like a tribal tattoo. Enzo had no way of forgetting Catia either.

Sal pulled down his pants and boxers and shed his socks. Enzo stood near the bed, knees touching the frame, looking good enough to eat—attentive, obedient, turned on. Sal took the gun holster from his belt and placed it on the nightstand, then turned toward Enzo to kiss him. Enzo froze at first— being kissed jolted him, and it was even rarer than a blow job between them. Sal didn't let Enzo recover his equilibrium, but pushed him down onto the bed. He remained on top, grabbed both of Enzo's hands and held them against the mattress. "I got rope left, but that's too much of a risk if anybody shows up."

Enzo nodded. "Just to … get rid of the tension. Not really playtime."

"Tell yourself that." Sal kissed him again, deeply, with tongue, roaming all of his mouth. *Playtime* had been one of Catia's words. The first time he'd thought of Enzo in a sexual way had been observing Enzo tied up in their marriage bed, covered in sweat and goosebumps because Catia had edged him for an hour. She'd turned the big fierce capo into a quivering mass of need. Then he'd sucked Enzo off, together with his wife. Afterward, Enzo had lain between them, shivering and emotional and close to tears. Catia had broken his defenses down for good.

Enzo reached for Sal's cock and stroked it, more reverently than in an attempt to make him come. "Anything, Sal, please."

"I know." Enzo had called him by his name, maybe trying to signal that the request, hell, offer, wasn't due to that sense of surrender. "And I'll have it." He kissed Enzo again and shifted between his legs. The only bit of poor planning was that he couldn't reach his overnight bag from here to get the lube. He always kept it there for short trips. "Lube first."

Enzo shifted both of them closer to the foot of the bed. He dug into Sal's bag and after a second attempt found the pouch that held the travel-sized tube. He opened it, squeezed some of the stuff into his hand and then placed his slick hands around Sal's cock. The lube was cold but rapidly warmed while Enzo stroked him with those strong killer hands. The same hands that could strangle a man or wield a switchblade as easily as a claw hammer, now prepared him. Fuck. If Enzo had been a little more bisexual, a little more into cocks, who the hell knew where they could have gone together?

"Up." Enzo shifted again and lifted his legs. Sal was so hard and slick that he managed to breach Enzo on the first attempt, and the man tensed underneath him in a purely instinctual way. That was the real test, fucking a guy who was "mostly straight"—and who always freaked out a little every time this happened. Always slightly weird to fuck a man who was willing but whose body didn't like the intrusion. Not at first. Practice might take care of that, but it was unlikely Enzo would ever get there.

Sal thrust harder, heard that sharp intake of breath and the deep, semi-pained groan. He gave Enzo a few moments to relax, felt him shake and quiver, then pushed all the way in. Enzo clawed the sheets, eyes tightly shut, his face empty in that blissful, enraptured way that told Sal he'd gone back into his surrender and intended to stay there. Sal gritted his teeth but, once Enzo relaxed around him, he let his control slip. Fucking him hard and methodically, Sal paused when he got too close and, when he couldn't hold back any longer, he pulled out and took both their cocks in hand.

"No, Sal, please ..."

"Shut up." He wasn't going to take an even bigger risk than that. Enzo did enjoy him coming inside of him, likely part of his overall submissiveness, but he couldn't have everything he wanted. He timed his strokes just so that they both came in the same moment, Enzo falling to pieces, while

Sal kissed him again, deeply, letting most of that terrible tension go.

It helped. It really did. Sal rolled off Enzo to catch his breath, enjoyed how Enzo's eyes blazed alive, his skin flushed and gleaming. He was attractive in killer and capo mode, but with that freshly fucked expression, the smell of sex rising from him, he was gorgeous. Sal leaned over to kiss him on the brow, surprised when Enzo, still so weak and vulnerable, kissed him full on the lips. This was a tender, trusting kiss, not quite a lover's kiss.

Sal smiled. "Thank you."

Enzo scoffed. "Yeah, quite the sacrifice, right?" He shook his head and twitched as though to move before relaxing back on the sheets. Instead, he rolled onto his side to face Sal. "How are you? Better?"

"I think I could sleep now."

"Same." Enzo lifted an arm and lazily pointed toward the stairs. "Grab a shower now, maybe." He was definitely forcing himself to come back from his special place, because yeah, without ropes he had no excuse for remaining emotionally fragile and helpless, and Sal didn't have the words to tell him it was okay, that nobody expected him to function 100 percent right after sex. For the moment, they were safe. And as long as they kept up momentum, stayed on the front foot, and had their punches ready, they'd both be safe.

Enzo yawned but didn't move, so Sal pulled himself together. The tiny guest en suite wasn't nearly as luxurious as the large bathroom, but it had fresh towels, a sink, toilet and shower, so he tossed a towel out for Enzo. He washed off, but didn't take a full shower in the end; he brushed his teeth and then left the en suite to Enzo. He set the alarm for six hours, checked his gun, and slipped naked under the covers.

When Enzo joined him in the dark, it struck Sal how long he hadn't slept fully naked in the same bed as another person he trusted, or even gave a shit about. Enzo was the blessed one—he could fall into that vulnerability so easily, and he knew that Sal would always be there to catch him. But Sal didn't have the strength to do the same. Maybe once he'd had his revenge. Maybe he could crack himself open and release the pain.

11

Falling asleep on a chair wasn't easy. Jack's shoulders were crying out, but all he could manage was to roll them and pull them up against the base of his skull, hold and release, hoping to relax them somewhat. His hands were cold, but not numb. Rausa hadn't tightened the ties unnecessarily or cruelly. The only sounds he could hear were the normal creaks of any house with inbuilt wood.

He had nothing to lean his head against, and even the attempt to topple the chair so he could maybe rest his head on the ground and find some sleep that way hadn't worked —they'd stabilized or fastened the chair somehow. All he could do now was wait, and think, and drift off a few minutes at a time—it was never enough. He had already been mentally and emotionally exhausted from meeting Beth and offering his sad little proposal. And then Rausa ... Rausa had felt like wrestling a tiger, or getting run over by a truck. The side of his face throbbed and the pain from the bruise had turned into a stinging one-sided headache.

Here I am, a man who can have men murdered with a nod or an indirect hint during a phone call. The damned consigliere of the Lo Cascio clan, Andrea Lo Cascio's right-hand man, tied to a chair and locked away in a closet in my own house to be tortured and executed tomorrow by a man who had, until now, been a non-entity.

He ran through that thought the same way a Buddhist repeated his mantras, and the disbelief turned to exasperation, anger, and finally into a bleak kind of humor. Rausa had promised him a hard death, and Jack knew what those looked like. He'd seen bodies riddled with bullets, had seen corpses without fingernails, corpses who'd had a cut-off dick shoved into their mouth, had seen what men looked like who'd been beaten to a pulp with baseball bats. Whatever the bodies looked like, you could never really forget they'd been human once.

Jack had found killing difficult, especially the premeditated type, and he'd been lucky that the man he'd killed to be made had been a despicable coward and traitor. He would kill if necessary, if he had no alternatives, but it didn't thrill him like it did some others. It had felt like a bone-shaking inner restlessness and nausea before, and took a long time to wear off afterward. Threats had gotten him far with the unions, and he could actually solve problems without murder. Most normal people simply fell in line when he applied pressure the correct way, such as when a construction union put him on the payroll, or he strolled into a supplier's office and strongly suggested that some things needed to be renegotiated or the project would "die". Not to mention, once he'd been promoted to consigliere, others were all too happy to do the wet work.

Most people picked up on words quickly if they were said well, in the right context. Most people were eager to "help" once they realized who they were dealing with, and that Jack could muster backup from all directions. Ironically, while the Dommarco family had been union busters, the Lo Cascio had always syphoned money from the unions, and, in turn, provided a ruthless element that the unions were ill-equipped to legally send into the field.

If that meant they put Jack or any other Lo Cascio man on the payroll as a "consultant" and paid a nice monthly "fee" whether there were issues to handle or not, so be it. Even better when both sides paid to have their conflicts managed. Played well, that game could last forever and be highly lucrative. Just like in legal business, a skilled operator could judge easily how much he could bleed a client, and how often, before the client became too restless or weak. The rules were not to get too greedy and always give the boss his cut.

Rausa. Now he was a different animal.

A man spoiling for a fight.

For a war, even.

Despite the fact that he'd seen the last one play out and the Rausa clan had suffered terribly and never recovered. And he hadn't sold out to the Feds—even if somebody in a potential task force was bending the rules, whatever Jack would eventually spill would be inadmissible in court. And weren't rats forbidden from committing further crimes? Kidnapping and torture surely counted. So far, it was little more than threats, but Jack expected Rausa to follow through on them. Fuck, at this point, Rausa wearing a wire and some Feds sauntering in and telling Jack to cooperate *or else* was his best-case scenario.

Hell, there were consiglieri who were in prison, and full members of their families who'd shopped their friends and business partners, and even written books about it. The Cosa Nostra wasn't what it had once been, and not all the myths still worked. But this was different, this was family against family, boss against boss, and all gloves were off. If Andrea got the opportunity to strike back, he'd no doubt choose the nuclear option.

Would Jack give Rausa what he wanted? He'd seen too much to believe he could resist forever. Anything else was a stupid man's bravado. And yet, his only value as a man had been in his usefulness and his ability to know when to talk and when to not talk. Keeper of secrets, and motor mouth when necessary. No, he wasn't always fond of Andrea, but he respected the man's role and his power. He respected the rules. Sometimes he thought he mostly respected *himself* because others did. They didn't see his flaws and weaknesses, and that made them easier to deal with, in secret. Men looked at him with respect, so he could pull himself back out of whatever darkness he'd lost himself in and at least be useful.

Did any of this matter in the face of death? No. He wouldn't be around to feel the humiliation. Dead bodies had no dignity left. No longer people. They were nothing but meat. They were added to the lists of those that were never talked about again, became anecdotes, often stripped of their identities, "you know who", and "you know when". Anybody who was stupid enough to ask about them painted a target on their own back; it was important to know at all times who was in good standing and who wasn't. Who'd been a loyal friend this morning and who had vanished twelve hours later.

Jack hadn't questioned those rules, and still didn't, but it was a sobering thought. If he gave Rausa what he wanted and anybody heard of it, judgment wouldn't be kind. He doubted it would be kinder even if his body showed signs of that hard death Rausa promised. All they'd know and care about was that he'd betrayed them. His death would be regarded as an insult, and the response would be in kind and worse.

Rausa had kicked off the war the moment he had kidnapped and beaten Jack. His body would be the opening shot.

That was, if there was a body to find.

The morbid part of his mind noted that, as far as last evenings went, this hadn't been the worst one he could have imagined; a good meal with a good friend. There had been days, but mostly nights, in prison when he'd contemplated all the possible ways he could end things himself. Any of those last meals would have been far worse.

Ultimately, he hadn't wanted to die in prison and let people on the outside assume it was prison that had broken him, when the truth was that he'd been born with a huge crack right down the middle of his soul. And nothing—not the "life", the "business", or the advancement from being the son of a mere associate to made man and soldier to capo and finally consigliere had healed the crack. Part of him would never be respectable, would never be part of the "family", and he'd known that from the start.

Whether he'd risen through the ranks because of luck, or

because that inner brittleness had driven him, or whether he'd simply managed to fool the men around him, were questions he'd entertained often.

Those same questions had filled his mind that one dark night. He'd been drunk enough to probe the jagged edges of his soul, and suddenly felt that gnawing inside, much like a man close to starvation whose body suddenly remembered hunger in a final, desperate bid to survive.

In the club with Andrea and a number of capos, he'd slowly worked on getting drunk, fully aware that alcohol made him quiet and withdrawn, but he'd been in a mood all day. Seeing the dancers gyrating to the beat, colored flashing lights sparking off their sweat-glowing skin, among them a couple of shirtless young men, and how they'd sized each other up from under heavy eyelids, teeth playfully bared, every dancer lost in themselves as much as lost in the glory of the others, calculating yet carefree.

Something about the view in combination with the alcohol had set off a depth charge somewhere inside him, and he couldn't hold himself together—he'd become aware that he was, right here, beginning to lose his mind, and for an exhilarating moment he hadn't known what he'd do next —whether he'd join the dancers or attack the next warm, lithe-muscled body with teeth and claws as if he were some primordial horror. The lights had hurt his eyes, the thumping bass underneath the melody and the crowd of bodies moving with the rhythm were crushing him, so he'd cracked a joke about feeling his age and all but staggered out of the club.

In hindsight, he wondered whether that had been some kind of mental breakdown, a misfiring of all his nerves, a psychotic episode, or maybe some kind of slow-burn panic attack.

In that moment, he'd realized that he couldn't trust himself to hold it together. Control was slipping through his fingers. That all the sacrifices he'd made both voluntarily and otherwise were no longer enough to keep his demons at bay.

So, like any man pursued by evil spirits, he'd gotten into his car and driven off out of the city, toward the forest. He vaguely remembered hatching a plan to go walk into the wilderness and somehow die there, though his mind skipped how exactly. He did remember both laughing and crying at the thought that they wouldn't find him until hunting season, months and months later. He would simply stop existing, and it was the relief of it that made him laugh, though he sounded more than a little mad in his own ears.

How he'd ended up on Memorial Bridge was anybody's guess. Maybe because he knew from his childhood what a desolate place it was with its flaking paint, decaying iron underneath, dark forest on both sides and the treacherous black waters of Oak River rushing below. Originally Herman Nordmeyer Memorial Bridge, only part of the name had stuck around. Everybody in Port Francis knew this was where people went to "jump". If this had been a different sort of city, Memorial Bridge would have been the place where priests conducted exorcisms for the lost souls that surely haunted the area. Jack assumed every community had places like this—both grim and not quite real, as if, through squinted eyes, the laws of physics didn't always completely apply. In his disjointed state, he'd wondered whether those who "jumped" were actually attempting to fly because they felt on the deepest level that those laws could be haggled over here.

Jack was done. He abandoned the car, left the door wide open and walked straight to the railing, feeling both a creeping horror and a sense of relief grow with every single step. Horror won, and he stopped, leaned on the rusty railing and stared into the fathomless water gurgling below. The river had been swollen from weeks of heavy rain, and an almost full moon cast silver shadows through the gaps in the heavy clouds that promised more rain. He gazed into the darkness below, regarded the churning surface the same way, he assumed, as saints the face of God.

The water had no revelation for him except oblivion, which in that moment he assumed would suffice. He sobered enough to spare a thought whether he had any unfinished business—any revenges not taken, any personal papers that could incriminate him, anything he'd have wanted to say to a loved one. Now in his early forties, he was too old to begin justifying or explaining himself to his parents—whatever unspoken things had stood between them had been condemned to eternal silence when he'd bought them an old farmhouse in a picturesque village in a part of Italy that was a lot friendlier to their creeping arthritis, and then all but bundled them off into a plane. Internet out there sucked, so no video calls. Thank God.

They still thought his "involvement with the unions" put him and them in danger. And the situation had been dicey, but nothing he hadn't been able to handle. They were lucky they liked the artisan cheeses and ham that that area produced, and the last he'd heard, their health had improved and his father had lost enough weight that his knee replacements weren't blowing out.

No unfinished personal business, then, with his parents as settled as they could possibly be. Left the car. In his own ideal scenario, he abandoned it there, door ajar, key in the ignition, and it remained there as a kind of totemic marker of what had happened. The cops would take an interest in the gun in the glove compartment but even they would quickly form a theory based on his prison record.

Still, some part of him called for complete annihilation —burn down his house and everything else he owned, and vanish as if he'd never existed. Romantic and very, very appealing, but impossible. These days, people always left transaction histories, the footprints of this age. The sound of a car engine tore him from his thoughts, and when it came closer and he smelled the exhaust, he half turned away from the river and glanced to the side.

The headlights were uneven, one decidedly dimmer than the other, the car being held together by nothing other than inertia and rust. Jack almost assumed some teenagers were looking for the best place for some illicit drinking or smoking or petting or any combination of the above, and he felt resentful that his grim reveries had been cheapened that way—even though there was no romance in it, and he knew it despite the hollow ache of self-pity and his total inability to see past the wall of despair before him. This wasn't—and would never be—a kind of heroic act. It was the last remaining option, so whether teenagers messed with it didn't matter.

Yet, when a door clapped and heels tack-tacked on the asphalt, he looked over again. The woman's steps slowed as she looked his way, and he gathered an impression of thin legs sticking out of a blue jeans skirt, and an oddly patterned white or light blue blouse. She glanced at him, then hesitatingly stepped up to the railing herself, as if in defiance. Some kind of waitress, or maybe a prostitute, to be out and about at this time of night, though prostitutes should be able to afford better cars.

He returned his attentions to the water, aware of another human being like an itch under his skin. Eventually, he pushed away, resolved to return to his car and drive a little further, maybe take the car with him into the river.

But he saw her bony shoulders shake in the chill of the night, and his mind backtracked to that first impression of her. Not an odd pattern on the blouse at all. He gritted his teeth, but at the same time, something in his heart shifted. It was none of his business, but as he regarded her there, all alone in her blood-splattered clothes, sniffing in the darkness, he couldn't help but resent her for messing with his struggle to reach a state of acceptance, at the same time aware that she might be in a much more desperate situation than he was. He walked back to his car, picked up his coat and walked over to her. He placed the coat within her reach and leaned on the railing again, in his own space, the coat now between them.

"It's cold. You'll catch your death."

She sniffed and then broke into a sobbing laugh.

Regarding her from the side, and peering past her untidy mop of bleached blonde hair, he noticed somebody had done a number on her delicate features, and the sniffing was likely from a broken nose. A shadow of smeared blood across her chin and lips made her look ghoulish, indicating she hadn't even had the time to clean up after whatever had happened. Maybe she'd resolved to let the river wash that away.

They stood together for what could easily have been an hour, the only sound the wind in the trees and a gargling of water below them. She seemed to calm down somewhat, but the occasional sniffles told him she was still there with him, not zoned out. Oddly, she seemed to be the only anchor to reality, the only other real and true thing here except oblivion, though nothingness was diametrically opposite of her and he was stuck somewhere in the middle. No, not stuck. He was moving, or rather drifting, but it was decidedly in one direction.

"Having a bad night?" she ventured, eventually.

"Depends." He gestured toward the water. "Could go very badly or ..." The other option hadn't quite taken shape in his mind yet. It was all upside down—was it actually a bad or a good thing? Surely, an end to that pain inside was good, right?

He wrestled that question but couldn't find an answer.

"I know what you mean." She gave a resigned sigh. "What for, right? What is that shit for?"

A day ago, he'd have told her *survival*. Survival was the reason to do anything. But up here on the bridge, that wasn't real anymore.

She rubbed her arms and shifted her weight from one leg to the other. Several of her fake nails had broken off. And her bruises were darkening almost while he watched. "What is any of this shit for," she muttered to herself.

"At least you can be warm." He pushed the coat over. "It's nice."

She eyed him. "And you?"

"I'm not cold."

I'm nothing. There were no feelings, no sensations, everything felt empty and dead inside and he briefly wondered how long that had been the case. How long he'd swum only on the surface of his own soul. Years. Decades. When had he entombed himself like that?

She glanced toward his car. "Nobody waiting for you?"

He shook his head but finally managed to tear his eyes away from the blackness and release a tautness inside of him. Maybe it was because she reached for the coat and put it on. She almost vanished in it, though she didn't attempt to make herself comfortable inside of it. Her hair remained inside the collar and she didn't close it, just pulled it closer around her by crossing her arms in front of her chest. After a while, she stopped shivering.

He gave her a half smile to put her at ease. "You should get that nose looked after."

She reached up and winced when she touched it. "No, I'm ..."

"... Going to stand here?"

She looked at him then fully with her wounded, liquid eyes. "No."

"Same," he said softly, carefully, sensing the same tension in her. Hell, he didn't know what he was feeling anymore, but he could pick up her pain clearly as day.

They stood like that for hours, silent witnesses of a kind of battle that was fought with determination but no hope. Long before dawn, though the deepest part of the night seemed to have passed, she agreed to get in the car with him and have her nose looked after, though he assumed the bruises and the broken nose had kept her anchored the same way she'd done for him.

He managed to get her to a motel, then took an Uber back to the bridge to pick up his car. By then, the sun was climbing into a pale and sickly sky and Jack didn't want to do anything but sleep for a couple of days, which he would have done if Beth hadn't texted him about the coat in the afternoon.

12

When Sal checked his phone, the alarm was seven minutes out, so he deleted it and rubbed his face. Six full hours of sleep, deep and dreamless no doubt thanks to Enzo, who lay next to him on his back, not quite snoring but wheezing in his sleep. Weird to wake up with another human being. With a random hook-up, he was usually out of the door after a little rest, or, if he did fall asleep, this would be the moment to vanish.

Paid professionals always left afterward—they were welcome to shower and change, that was all. He could no longer be bothered to hunt. Hunting meant getting gradually invested in the person, wondering about them, trying to please them outside the bed, and living with that questioning inside—could this be more? Could this be *something* at least?—but Sal had found it put too much strain on the stitches in his soul. Regardless of who he met, he always compared them to Catia, and they never measured up.

Sex was different. He knew how to get people off,

enjoyed pleasing them, but as he liked to tell them from the start, "anything goes, but I'm not emotionally available". That worked for those who also weren't emotionally available, or couples who sought a discreet third who wouldn't insert himself into the relationship. If anybody asked about the ring he still wore on his hand, or sometimes on a chain around his neck, he told them he was widowed, and that was usually enough to shut down that topic.

Casual hook-ups never questioned beyond that word. Widowed. It made couples he slept with glance at each other with that sudden realization that love could die, and sometimes it won him brownie points he didn't want. He wasn't one of those pathetic fuckers who expected special treatment because of how he'd suffered. His response to suffering was very different—he'd go straight to the root of it and take out those who were responsible.

Which brought him to today's work. Another simple beating wouldn't solve his Barsanti problem. The best way to proceed was to attack the consigliere from all angles at the same time, and then exploit any cracks that appeared. Made this more complex than he'd originally thought, but Sal was nothing if not adaptable.

Enzo next to him groaned and blinked. "Fuck."

"Good morning. You can have the shower up here, I'll check on our gracious host." Sal swung his legs out of bed. He picked up his pants and put them on.

"That's unnatural. How are you so awake?" Enzo muttered.

"Busy day ahead." Sal regarded him, noticed that in the early morning, the house was filled with soft golden light, and it worked miracles on Enzo's skin, hair and eyes. "We'll need to go in hard and fast, so get the doc on standby."

Military trained, the doc hadn't switched to civilian practice, but when it came to gun and knife wounds, Sal didn't know anybody better, and he was especially good at stabilizing bodies. That dishonorable discharge hadn't taken away the man's skills or his cold-bloodedness. *Thank you, Uncle Sam, much appreciated.* The doc had worked hard to reconnect to the Rausa clan, indicating heavily he wouldn't mind killing if necessary, but Sal had kept him out of the thick of it, and paid him a generous retainer to keep him there. Paradoxically, he was too valuable to get made.

Enzo yawned. "I'll call him."

"There's another thing. Work out who that girl was last night. We might have her license plate on camera, so run it; let's see who she is."

"Yeah, will do." Enzo took his phone and sat up on the side of the bed.

"Meanwhile, I'll find out how that coffee machine works." Sal grabbed his other clothes and walked down the spiral staircase. Wow, a clear, sunny early autumn morning made the hills and bay look stunning. He started to see the point of those huge panoramic windows. Maybe someday he'd buy a plot up in the hills and build less of a security nightmare.

First things first. A quick check of the master bedroom told him that his improvised booby trap hadn't gone off. Nothing had left the closet or entered it.

Great, now coffee.

The kitchen had a gleaming metal-cased mid-range Gaggia machine. Figured that a guy who liked Apple would go for the brushed metal look with only a few buttons. Sal switched the machine on to heat it up, checked on the beans and water—the Gaggia took the water straight from the main, and the beans smelled fresh. He dropped his other clothes on the kitchen island, found two small porcelain cups and set them under the nozzle. Less than a minute later, black liquid adorned with a proper dark golden crema gathered in the cups, and the smell lifted Sal's mood even more. He grabbed the cups and walked back upstairs, not surprised that Enzo was still blearily sitting on the side of the bed.

"Any updates?" He offered Enzo the double shot, who knocked it back as if it were vodka or medicine. Sal grinned and drank his slightly more slowly, but not much.

"Left a message for the doc, license plates are in progress. What about Barsanti?"

"Still where we put him." Sal took the empty cup from Enzo's hand. "I'd say we'll do it in the bathroom. Less exposed."

"Yeah." Enzo looked back toward the bed. "Burn the house down when we're done?"

"Yes. When we're done." Sal was tempted to touch Enzo. Hug him or pat his shoulder, but they were now in that slightly awkward transition from what they'd done last night to how they normally were, and it would feel weird to get physical with each other while they set about destroying another man. Better shut down the more tender parts and let Enzo put on his killer self. "You good?"

Enzo snorted without derision. "No regrets. I don't do regrets, but even if I did, this isn't one of them. You?"

"I do regrets, but same." Sal headed back down. He

dropped the cups off on the breakfast bar, then went to the master bedroom. He took the lamp and bowl and put them on the bed, then moved the chair back where he'd found it, and unlocked and opened the door.

Barsanti sat exactly how they'd left him, and looked very tense even hooded and bound, from the way his shoulders were pulled up and his stomach pulled in as if he expected a punch or slap to wake him up or set the mood.

Sal took down the ropes, grabbed Barsanti, chair and all, and dragged him along out of the walk-in closet.

"So this is it," Barsanti said.

"Yep." He dragged the chair across the wooden floor and into the bathroom. He briefly checked Barsanti's wrists, but while the skin felt hot to the touch, he didn't seem to have fought particularly hard. He was likely in some discomfort—he smelled of misery and exhaustion, a metallic tang that was beginning to overpower his deodorant. One sleepless night wasn't enough to break a man, but it chipped away at his resilience. Another card stacked against Barsanti, and they'd all add up. And that was before he played any of the others.

The bathroom was a wide-open space that would be perfect for their purposes. The large Jacuzzi in the corner upfront, two sinks to the left, two shelves for towels, wicker laundry basket tucked away discreetly, then the huge walk-in shower to the front and right. A sheet of milk glass separated the toilet and bidet from the rest of the bathroom just so that there was no direct line of sight.

"Why the fuck do you hate privacy?" Sal muttered, not expecting a response. "Your house freaks me out."

"I spent a few years in a room sized six by eight feet."

Six by eight ... oh, prison. He'd known Barsanti had done time—he and the others had made the news. Being deprived of views for a few years made them precious even if the house's layout was still stupid. "About the same size of your closet. Any flashbacks?"

"My ..." Barsanti paused abruptly, then shook his head. "No."

Now Sal was somewhat intrigued. Barsanti seemed chattier than before, maybe due to the tiredness, maybe he was determined to enjoy the time he had left. "You should have done okay. All the prison pussy you could want."

Barsanti shook his head again. "It wasn't like that."

"Did your boss make sure you were safe? Nobody tried to take you down a peg? Good-looking guy like you?"

Barsanti laughed softly. "That all you care about? One of us reeks of sex, and it's not me."

Ooooh. Andrea's lapdog had found his bite. Sal walked up to Barsanti and plucked the hood off his head. Barsanti blinked against the light but fixed his pale eyes on Sal quickly, looking defiant, aware that his last comment was pure provocation. But that look also told Sal that Barsanti wasn't going to apologize, and that took some balls, considering how unevenly the power was distributed between them. "I don't know. I figure it could have gone either way for you. Nobody even took a shot at you? Never felt lonely? No buddy to lend a hand?"

Barsanti blinked a few times rapidly, thoughts racing behind his brow. "I had privileges."

"Such as?"

"My own cell. Guards making it pretty clear not to mess

with me. Some other prisoners who had an interest in winning favors."

"Not via blowjobs, but protection."

"Exactly," Barsanti said tersely.

Weirdly, Sal believed him. Enzo was the best example of how flexible "hetero" could be under certain circumstances. Though as a bisexual man, Sal himself might not have the wiring to understand how people would exclude certain groups of people as potential sex partners. Going years without touch because one's preferred gender wasn't freely available seemed stupid. Then again, Barsanti was five to ten years older than him—maybe it was a thing for Generation X. It wasn't a Catholic thing—from what he understood about the faith, Catholics could get freaky as fuck and were absolutely fine if they confessed before they died.

"As you mentioned, I'm not a monk." Sal remained in front of Barsanti, aware of his own naked chest and arms, but no bigot would ever make him stand down. Examining and accepting the urges he'd had since he could remember had been tough, and acting on them had been absolutely nerve-wracking at first. And at second. Becoming comfortable with his sexuality had taken hard work and Barsanti wasn't going to make him ashamed.

He noticed how Barsanti's gaze was fixed on his, and how he both didn't avoid looking at his chest and almost paid too pointed attention to it. Sal ran a hand over his pecs; maybe Barsanti didn't routinely get to see bar piercings through a guy's nipples. Or maybe it was the simple gold ring on the chain around his neck.

He turned and walked past Barsanti toward the shower.

The consigliere wasn't going to see much of him as he washed, unless he craned his neck, and Sal didn't expect he would. He shed his pants, dropped them on the pile with his other clothes he'd brought in from the kitchen, then stepped into the walk-in shower. The water started strong and hot; the dials indicated he had twenty options when it came to the spray, but he liked Barsanti's pre-sets, so he took a quick hot shower and used Barsanti's body wash and shampoo; mint and lemongrass, which was nicely refreshing after the night he'd had. He gradually dialed down the hot shower to cold to wake up fully.

He still couldn't quite believe Barsanti had lived such a sheltered existence in prison. His own instinct would definitely have leaned toward testing the man's mettle any way he could, had he been a fellow prisoner, and quite frankly, if not for all the baggage and history, Barsanti would have fit his preference easily.

He left the shower, grateful when he could towel down, and his body heat overcame the chill on his skin. But he was awake now. He dressed and heard Enzo approach as he was pulling down his shirt.

Enzo carried his tool bag and methodically spread out a large plastic sheet in the middle of the room. Barsanti's eyes closed, but Sal had caught that look of pure terror when he realized Enzo was setting up the kill site. As things were going, they'd wrap Barsanti's body in the plastic along with all the bits they would have removed and deal with him offsite.

"See," Sal said, "at least Enzo knows what he's doing. I can't say it will be pleasant, because it won't be, but he's a pro."

Barsanti didn't open his eyes, didn't respond at all.

"Changes one's perspective, doesn't it?" He cast a glance at Enzo who was lining up various tools, much like a medieval inquisitor would show the victim the implements of torture. Seeing saws and knives and claw hammers meant imagining what they could do. And Enzo had shifted entirely back into the capo who didn't mind the dirty work and regarded it as part of the job, the same way as dressing an animal was part of filling the freezer with game.

Something Sal had found in his own career was that intelligent men had good imaginations. They assessed, ran scenarios, minds constantly flitting into the past and future to understand and respond to the present. Barsanti was intelligent enough to realize his future had drastically shortened.

"Look at me." Sal stood close again, but Barsanti just sat there, breath labored, clearly terrified but still trying to maintain his dignity. "I said, look at me."

It took several seconds before Barsanti forced his gaze up.

"You're a smart man. So why are you propping up a fucker like Andrea? What do you owe him that you're willing to go through this to win him time? Because that's all it is. You're giving an asshole a few more hours. Big deal. We all know you're going to talk. So why do you want this?"

"No." Barsanti looked up, eyes blazing. "This is your choice. I've fucking offered you peace. I offered you help to take your share. But you give me nothing I can negotiate with. Why do you hate me so much? What have I done to you?"

Sal took a step back, surprised at the man's conviction. Seemed he kept digging up further reserves. "You, or Andrea, or somebody in your organization. You murdered my wife."

13

His *wife*? Jack was almost grateful that his mind had something to chew on to keep any panicked begging at bay. He managed to conjure up a name—Caterina Rausa, if he remembered correctly. Like most wives in their circles, she hadn't exactly kept a high profile.

The wife of a boss might be his advisor, but mostly she was the one who birthed and raised his children, and provided the home that her husband returned to between mistresses and business. Caterina had been mostly on Jack's radar because she was from out of state, but still part of their circles. Her family had been connected to the Marino clan, which had been wiped out in the biggest Mafia trial of the past two decades, with Stefano Marino handing his whole family, root and branch, to the Feds. The *pentito* boss, the one who'd recanted, lowest of the low. Scum. But that had been before their wedding. Still, Jack imagined the Rausa might have felt a bit tense when the trial had gone national.

Caterina Rausa. He faintly remembered a short, curvy

woman with shoulder-length black hair and a heart-shaped face, but otherwise he drew blanks. She'd never figured in his plans. The understanding among men of honor was to leave their women and children alone. Not everybody obeyed that rule; sometimes, mistresses and sisters ended up in the crossfire, but generally violence focused on the men.

Sometimes that might be a mistake—Jack had heard stories of wives running the business successfully while hubby did time. Petra Lo Cascio was mostly a moderating, not a steering influence on her husband, and Sarah Dommarco was primarily visible on the charity circuit. They had been the inspiration behind his ill-fated proposal to Beth—he was reasonably sure that he could have kept her safe.

"I thought ..." He swallowed because Rausa looked coiled up as if ready to punch him again. "I honestly thought she'd died in a car accident."

"You're fucking with me." Rausa's voice was flat and cold.

"I have absolutely nothing to gain from making you even angrier," Jack tried. "That's what I heard. Car crash. Didn't she veer off the road up around Black Hill?"

Rausa stared at him, then grimaced. "Yes, but she was dead before she even hit the bottom of the gorge." That same flatness.

"So ... it could have been an accident, except there's something that makes you think it wasn't."

"Sal." The blond man, Enzo, walked into view. "He's playing for time."

"Yes, I am," Jack said. "But if you're going to torture and kill me, at least tell me why."

Rausa nodded slowly, unevenly, like an automaton. "She

missed the hairpin turn halfway up Black Hill, went straight over the edge. Car kept rolling, broke her neck. When the autopsy came in, they found a rifle bullet in her temple. Quite unlikely some killer climbed all the way down to shoot her in the mangled car, so she was shot while up on the road. If you look at the scene, it's not an easy kill. But it was a rainy evening, visibility was low, and she would have crawled around that turn. He might have used night-vision goggles, I don't know." Rausa drew a deep, shuddering breath. "She didn't have enemies of her own. That was all on me."

Oh shit. Jack was still working through the information when Enzo placed a hand on Rausa's shoulder, who nodded and glanced at Enzo, but the gaze didn't make contact, didn't see anything on the outside.

"That was toward the end of the War."

"Yeah." Rausa blew out a few breaths, steadying himself and then slid out from sunder Enzo's touch. "The killing blow."

So that was the move that had pushed Rausa out of the game. Jack still didn't have the timeline completely straight, couldn't quite work out whether that was before or after Rausa had risen from underboss to boss, but those were mere details at this point. One thing he knew for certain, though—when it happened, he'd been sitting in a prison cell sixty miles from Port Francis.

Somebody had straight up assassinated Salvatore Rausa's wife, and even after all these years, it fucked with the man's head. Enough to not care if Port Francis burned. He'd turn the whole city into a pyre for her.

"I get why you think it was my family," Jack admitted. "It's not Dommarco's style. I don't see Cassaro ordering that, either. Both are too old-fashioned. Doesn't smell right."

Enzo shot Jack a baleful look, but Rausa nodded. The man's enormous energy seemed to pool and sharpen, and his attention returned to Jack.

"It also happened right after I'd landed a good blow against your outfit. You could say I'm not terribly interested in negotiating my rightful place with the fucker who murdered my wife." It came between gritted teeth, all white and sharp like a wolf's.

"For what's it worth, I didn't order the hit. I was still in prison, and this is the first I'm hearing about it."

"Then Andrea."

"Or his father. Or my predecessor, Vic Decesare. He smashed up so much shit during the War that it took me years to fix it." Jack remembered Cassaro's words when they'd sat down that first time, Jack sweaty in his suit because he half expected to be gunned down then and there, even though they'd rented a conference room in a neutral location. *Seems the Lo Cascio have switched from a war consigliere to one of peace. Is that what you are, Jack?*

At first he hadn't thought so. Consiglieri had to be able to handle both, but while trying to bury every hatchet that had been dug up over those war years, he realized that he much preferred peace. Maybe because the War had been so painful and costly, maybe because deep down he was a coward.

But talk about painful and costly.

He was under no illusion that all couples married out of love. Rausa was a good catch—attractive, rich, powerful. He'd draw his share of gold diggers based on that alone. But this simmering rage inside Rausa didn't feel like wounded pride. In Jack's experience, wounded pride didn't burn this hot. Those were more like flash fires that blazed bright for a few days or maybe weeks, and then cooled and were added to the ledger for later, when the time came to get even.

The expression he saw in Rausa's face warned him to not express compassion or condolences. From him, Rausa would consider it nothing but scorn or provocation. Now at least he knew two things: Rausa hadn't targeted him personally—he was after the whole family, and secondly, while it wasn't personal, it was inevitable. All he had to do was look at Enzo and his little collection of tools. The war had already begun, the first shots fired.

Rausa looked down at him, studying him with intent. Jack forced himself to meet the gaze, really look at Rausa, from his uneven hairline, strong forehead, deep-set hazel eyes, down to a stubborn chin and amply stubbled jaw. The hazel seemed more greenish tinged than Jack had noticed before.

"I'll ask again," Rausa finally said softly, no more than a quiet rumble. "Why are you supporting a man like Andrea? Do you think he's worth it?"

"You mean worth dying for?" Jack swallowed. "It'll have to happen at some point, right? Might as well be today." The truth was, he'd been on borrowed time, ever since that night on the bridge. By some miracle, he'd seen a sunrise again, and then another, and many more after that, but maybe death was like an illness that could go into remission and then return. As the saying went, nobody got out alive.

"Yes, I mean worth dying for." Rausa stretched out a hand and Jack forced himself to keep his eyes on him. When the cold metal of the claw hammer's head was pushed under his chin, he shuddered. "Especially dying like this."

"Nothing is worth dying for," Jack said. "But people die all the time."

Rausa dropped the claw hammer into Jack's lap, and, faster than Jack had expected, pulled the gun from the holster on his hip and pushed the muzzle hard against Jack's forehead, finger on or right next to the trigger. Jack's vision blurred and he blinked a few times, but then managed to meet Rausa's gaze again, even though his blood had gone cold. He clung to the thought that it would be a mercy if Rausa put a bullet in his brain, but it took every ounce of willpower he had.

His mind emptied of all thoughts except one: *A mercy*.

14

Barsanti was pale and tense, but not cringing in horror, as most people would have in this situation. Did he have that much loyalty? Or was he calling Sal's bluff?

Sal kept the gun pressed to Barsanti's forehead, and while Barsanti pulled back slightly, he didn't try to evade the pressure from the muzzle. Against his will, Sal was impressed. That took fortitude and conviction. He couldn't just blow Barsanti away, of course. But so far, no new cracks showed.

That was when a phone rang. The buzzing came from Sal's trouser pocket, and he quickly holstered the gun again and pulled out both phones—Barsanti's and his own. It was Barsanti's screen that was lit up with an unknown number. He tilted the phone so the man could see the screen while it was still ringing.

"Who's calling you?"

Barsanti's eyes flicked to the screen and there was some

recognition in them, then he shrugged and looked back at Sal. "It's not important."

"Not in your contacts?"

"No." Barsanti was terse enough that Sal called bullshit. The phone kept ringing. "Who knows."

"Want to take it?"

Barsanti lifted his shoulders demonstratively to indicate that he was still tied up.

The ringing stopped. Sal kept an eye on the phone, and it didn't take long for ping that there was (1) new voicemail. "Maybe it's your boss."

Barsanti shook his head. "No, I know his number."

"Who else?"

"Doesn't matter anymore." Barsanti's words seemed too carefully calibrated for indifference. He didn't even glance at the phone, as if by ignoring it, it could become invisible or inconsequential. Now, chances were, the call was from Andrea, or a capo or soldier who needed five minutes to agree to a meeting or confirm a job was done or request instructions. Nothing of any importance was ever entrusted to a phone, and nothing was ever clearly stated—with the recent infiltration of Encrochat, even encrypted networks were considered high risk in their circles. Considering Barsanti had already done time because the authorities had managed to piece together a case against him, he'd be doubly wary.

"Then maybe share your PIN with me?" Sal mock-offered Barsanti his phone. More ignoring. "Or the password to your laptop?"

Enzo moved into the background and after an exchanged glance, left the bathroom. Sal returned his attention to

Barsanti, but felt that the man had already reinforced his mental and emotional firewalls against that particular angle of attack. And, if he stayed with that picture, short of a brute force attack to blast through, Sal was out of options. If he'd had a few more days, he could ramp up the discomfort to the point where Barsanti would trip up, and with a couple of weeks, he'd break the man without so much as leaving a mark. He studied the swelling on Barsanti's temple. Too late for that, but the principle still held.

"It's funny, you seemed to believe me when I told you what will happen if you don't cooperate."

"I believe you. I do." Barsanti drew a deep breath. "But there's nothing I can do except this."

"Resist?"

"Wait." Barsanti's lips curved into a sad little smile and Sal was surprised how much that expression touched him. He walked around, tucking the phones into his pocket before curling his hands over Barsanti's shoulders. Sal tightened his hands around those tense muscles, then ran his right hand up Barsanti's neck, tips of his fingers brushing his Adam's apple. He felt him swallow again.

"Out of curiosity, any reason why you say you can't?"

"I still think the war can be avoided."

"It's not your choice." Sal kept his hands where they were, increased the pressure slightly, but then relaxed them. "The deaths won't be on you. And you'd be the first man I've ever met who wouldn't sacrifice the world to save his own life."

"It's not that easy." Barsanti cleared his throat. "You're still going to start a war and if I give you what you want, you're at an advantage. And I'll be the traitor who's responsible."

Sal leaned in until his lips were very close to Barsanti's ear. "I'm already at an advantage. Andrea won't expect me. This isn't a spontaneous thing. All my pieces are in position. So why are you making it hard on yourself? Pride?"

Barsanti shook his head. "Whatever happens to me, it sends a message that the Lo Cascio were weak in the first place. Andrea won't like it."

Won't like it? More likely enjoy it as much as getting kneecapped. Losing his consigliere, being aware that the enemy knew everything that the smartest guy in the organization had known, would be psychologically devastating. Enough to make rash and very damaging mistakes.

"You've seen Enzo, right?"

A small nod.

"If superior intel means I save the life of one of my men, it's worth everything else. That man could be Enzo, and he's important to me. He's a friend."

Barsanti released a breath like a sigh. "Shit."

Now that was cryptic. "Shit?"

Barsanti shook his head again and didn't say anything, but the tension in his shoulders was unmistakable. Sal patted the side of his neck and let him go, then stepped away to sit down on the rim of the Jacuzzi. The consigliere was completely withdrawn, back to that neutral place that spoke of resources being marshalled and rapidly deployed behind those high walls. "This ends with a bullet in Andrea Lo Cascio's head."

No response. Barsanti looked down at the floor between them, eyes hooded. Not the face of a man who was terribly worried about what would happen to his beloved boss.

"As far as I'm concerned, Enzo is worth more than your whole fucking organization."

There, a twitch around the eyes, a narrowing, like rebuilding his focus.

What was it about Enzo that made Barsanti respond more than talking about shooting Andrea Lo Cascio in the head?

"One of us reeks of sex."

Sal laughed. "Oh yeah, and we fucked last night, but I guess you knew that."

Oh. If that wasn't the closest thing to a full-body cringe. Sal half expected Barsanti to call him names or express his disgust. A dyed in the wool bigot surely wouldn't hold back, even in this situation, unwise as it was to provoke somebody when one's hands were tied. Sal was done with being judged —while he didn't exactly run around in fairy wings and rainbow outfits, what happened inside his bedroom—or that of others—was nobody's business. Not that Barsanti would live to tell anybody about this. As a general rule, corpses embedded in cement didn't gossip.

Barsanti did nothing, just sat there, tense and tight.

Enzo returned, finishing off a slice of bread in one hand and sipping coffee from the mug in the other. Sal reached out to pat Barsanti on the knee and left him there. He walked up to Enzo, who offered him the mug before Sal could take it from him. "Breakfast?"

"Yep." Sal followed Enzo to the kitchen, where Enzo had already prepared a plate with some bread and cheese and ham. Enzo poured himself a fresh mug and set both elbows down on the breakfast bar while he watched Sal eat quickly. He was actually ravenous.

"You seem in no rush."

"With Barsanti?" Sal shrugged. "We have the whole day."

"Sal." Enzo gave him that look.

Sal hesitated, knew that Enzo could see that, and sighed. "I guess I respect his conviction."

Enzo scoffed. "And I suppose how pretty he is, has nothing to do with your hesitation."

"No." He pondered that after his answer, but no. Barsanti was definitely attractive and played in a league looks and personality wise that Sal would definitely go for—if Barsanti were one half of his usual sexual diet of urbane and worldly mixed couples where one partner was bi or very solidly bi-curious. But that didn't matter here and now. He'd still turn that man into minced meat if necessary. "Just thinking, Barsanti might not give a fuck if I put a gun in his face, but maybe putting one in her face would make a difference."

"Taking her means there's a chance people will notice she's missing. Maybe even more quickly than him." Enzo wasn't appalled at the thought, just keeping track of all the potential collateral damage.

"Yes. I'd like to see if he chooses his girlfriend over his boss, though. Might even offer to let them ride off into the sunset together. Throw that in as a sweetener, since he's so into negotiating."

Enzo tilted his head. "And will you?"

Sal finished his last slice of ham and washed the saltiness down with the strong coffee. "No."

15

One glance at the number and Jack knew Beth had kept her promise. He'd doubted she would, but being proved wrong didn't come as a relief.

I can explain this better when I've slept. I'll call you, okay? Tomorrow?

And no, of course she wasn't in his contacts, for exactly this reason. Any connection to him exposed her to danger. If he'd had an alternative, he'd never have pulled her into any of this, though at least if she'd accepted, he could have made things official and extended protection to her.

The same protection that had failed Caterina Rausa.

The thought made his stomach churn. Some bastard had assassinated the wife of a boss or underboss. Who could blame Rausa for wanting revenge? If it had been a love match, Jack couldn't fathom the pain of losing a wife. Even if it hadn't been a love match, the level of disrespect couldn't be borne. It irked him that traditions thought a man's honor and respect more worthy than the life of a woman.

Too bad there was no way he could tell Beth not to call and not to come by. He could only hope she was too busy or that Rausa would be done with him by the time she showed up to check on him. Though she'd give him space for a week or so if he didn't respond—and by then, it would all be over.

And then that unexpected gut punch.

"Oh yeah, and we fucked last night, but I guess you knew that."

He'd *had* a strange sense of too much familiarity between Rausa and Enzo. The first few times he'd put it down to them being good friends or relatives, but there was a current between them that wasn't accounted for by those options. At first, he'd thought he was seeing things that weren't there, and pushed it all aside because it wasn't immediately important. But it had crept back every time Rausa laid his hands on Jack, which he seemed to do a lot of.

It was a display of power and of strength, but even knowing that, it raised Jack's hackles, especially because Rausa's hands felt good on his skin. His synapses had to be fried from lack of sleep and yesterday's bump on the head, because enjoying touches that promised pain and eventual annihilation nauseated him to his soul. He had to remind himself that Rausa wasn't touching him to touch him, but to control and intimidate him, and he still bristled at both.

From a straight man, such touches were definitely threatening, meant to belittle and provoke. But Rausa wasn't straight—Jack didn't imagine that fucking his capo was an option of last resort. Both of them could have their pick of people. Considering that being anything but straight got you killed in their circles, the open way he'd said it was yet another provocation. Rausa's defiance and courage made Jack heartsick.

He could imagine how Andrea would react if he ever learn about that. Not that he would, from Jack at least, even if by some miracle he survived.

When Rausa returned, Jack forced himself to meet his gaze. Rausa settled on the rim of the Jacuzzi and regarded Jack evenly. Enzo was nowhere in Jack's field of vision, and Jack couldn't hear any rustling steps on the plastic sheet.

"Let's try this again," Rausa said, sounding as reasonable as if he had come to a negotiation table.

Jack flexed his fingers. Even though the restraints weren't digging into his flesh, his wrists were sore and too warm, and his shoulders screamed for a stretch. His body ached and throbbed with deep and shallow bruises.

He was thirsty, but the most pressing message from his body was about his bladder. Rausa didn't seem like the kind of interrogator who'd allow him a toilet break, though.

Rausa smiled at him, and that hateful heat was tempered to something like warmth. Lines around his eyes betrayed that Rausa knew how to laugh, and Jack found himself momentarily lost in the cast of his strong forehead and nose. His profile was classic Roman, and hewn into that white marble, he could easily have been one of those murderous Praetorian guardsmen who'd knifed the emperor to take his place.

"You know what I want, Barsanti, or are you going to make me ask again? And I hear you. I know you want to keep the peace, but that's not on the table."

"You already said you'll kill me, and all that's on offer is you'll make it quick."

Rausa nodded. "While that's not very appealing right now, trust me, it will be."

Jack had no idea how long he'd hold out, or even if he would, but as much as the prospect terrified him, he couldn't overcome all his internal obstacles spurred on by threats alone.

"You've got heart, Barsanti, I'll give you that." Rausa rose and patted Jack on the shoulder, as if approving. Touching again, though.

"More a curse than a blessing," Jack offered.

"I still don't get why you would let yourself be butchered to protect a man like Andrea." Rausa stood to his side, keeping that heavy strong hand on his shoulder. "I guess he chose his consigliere well."

Jack lowered his head, processing that double-edged compliment. It was pointless to ponder what would have happened if Andrea had appointed someone else after his father's death—or if Vic Decesare had served a few more years. They wouldn't be here, for one. Maybe the War would have flared up again and more men would be dead. Including him.

"You don't seem to have a consigliere," Jack observed. "Why not?"

"I don't see the need to outsource."

"And no need to negotiate anything."

"No." Rausa patted his shoulder again. "We're readying for war. I need soldiers, not negotiators."

"And then? When you've wiped out the Lo Cascio? Attack the Dommarco next? You think they'll sit on the sidelines?"

"Depends what this victory costs me." Rausa leaned forward. "Whether I'm strong enough to take them next."

"What about the cops? The Feds?"

"As I said. It depends on what this victory costs." Rausa straightened and stepped aside.

"Boss." Enzo returned to the bathroom and handed a cell phone to Rausa, who paused and read whatever was on the screen. "Marty texted and said he's available."

"Okay. I'll head into town and get him." Rausa nodded toward Jack. "Keep him like that. Want anything?"

"No, I'm good." Enzo lifted the phone in his hand. "I'll forward you the text."

"Great." When Rausa left, Jack really didn't like the pleased look on his face.

16

Sal contemplated whether he should take the truck—Enzo would hardly need it for the moment, but when he stepped out of the door, Barsanti's silver Porsche was basically flirting, the way the sun sparked off it like it was winking at him.

The keys weren't hard to find, and the car might look sleek and compact, but Sal found it had a surprising amount of leg room. A quick search indicated that Barsanti was as obsessively clean and tidy with his car as he was about his house. No discarded receipts, food wrappers, or so much as a stray water bottle. Enzo's blue Nissan Rogue, by contrast, would allow someone to piece together every meal and all his shopping over the past week.

Barsanti had good taste in cars. At first, the steering felt sensitive, even skittish, but a few miles later, Sal realized that all it required was a lighter, gentler hand. The Porsche responded beautifully—what a marked contrast to its owner, who practically begged to be tortured.

So maybe it was slightly reckless to show his face in town driving Barsanti's car, but if Sal knew one thing, it was that their kind didn't rise early on a Sunday. He briefly played through in his head what would happen if he was spotted, or of the cops IDed him driving Barsanti's car just before his disappearance—all while taking the Porsche around the curves of the road cutting through the forest, using two or maybe three fingers at most. Great car for recreational driving, and he imagined that Barsanti must have gotten quite a bit of pleasure from it. The house, the food, the car, the coffee machine, the view—the man clearly liked refined and beautiful things. But he himself wasn't delicate or refined to the point of vulnerability. He took his beatings.

If Sal was spotted, fine. His men were ready for the inevitable battle. Enzo would deal with whoever came to the house to check on Barsanti. Besides, Sal would be there, and the doc would join him. Between them, they'd defend their ground. Not a problem—just an acceleration.

"Or sometimes, you need to show the world it can't fuck with you, Salvo, don't you?"

Yeah, that. Catia had been the first person in his life who *got* him. Hell, he'd fallen for her the moment he'd seen her, but he fell easily, he knew that much. They'd progressed at lightning speed, no masquerading necessary—with her family in the business and him an up-and-coming man of honor, the stakes had been clear from the start. He'd asked her later whether she'd bet on him like on a winning horse in order to secure herself power and standing.

"No, but what I like about you will definitely lead you to the top. And you're more of a challenge."

She'd liked those, and she went for the jugular if she

spotted so much as a flicker of insecurity or felt somebody else waver. He'd never forget that first time in the car, when she'd straddled him, kissing him wildly, and taken him right then and there, recklessly and breathlessly. Maybe it was weird to call it "taking", but that was exactly what it had felt like—she'd made it clear that she was in charge and he'd better comply. It was both electrifying and vaguely scary being with a woman with such a healthy appetite, who'd demanded sex right then, and that was even before the ropes and leather appeared in their bedroom. She'd thoroughly tested their compatibility before they'd married, he knew that now, but the real journey had begun over glasses of chilled white wine and a seafood dinner on the veranda of that honeymoon villa in Hawaii. Ocean breathing so close they could almost feel the spray, they'd had The Talk.

"I love you, Salvo. I always will. And I love how you are in bed. But there are things you need to know, and if I'm to fulfill those wedding vows to make you happy and you me, we can't have secrets between us. I don't want to go outside and get what I need from somebody else. And the same goes for you. Whatever it is you want, even your dirtiest fantasies, things you haven't done with anybody else, it's all on the table. Now, talk to me."

Of course, he hadn't been able to confess anything. It didn't seem necessary. She could be soft in bed, submissive, or take him the way she'd taken him in the car. He was pretty good at responding to her moods. Mostly, he counted himself lucky to have found a beautiful, smart wife who was just as horny as he was.

So she'd been the one to start it. Over another bottle of wine, they'd traded fantasies like poker players. Some things he was definitely on board with—hell, a second woman with her? Bring it. Others he was willing to trade for—she declared that if he wanted to take her ass, she'd do the same to his.

He faintly remembered two of his guys making a joke about anal sex and laughed with them mostly because they had no idea what mind-blowing orgasms they were missing out on. His men did notice he was eager to get home after business, and they grinned knowingly at each other—newly married, yadda, yadda. What they didn't know was that he couldn't wait to check the little blue-glazed bowl in the hall. She'd drop a hint as to what awaited him upstairs, or what role he was supposed to play when he came up.

They'd run through a whole catalogue of fantasies. Sometimes she was the barely legal daughter of a friend. The next night she was a bored businesswoman who'd hired an escort with clear and exacting requirements. Sometimes, she braided her long hair tightly, put on that makeup that made her lips stand out blood red, and that was when wanted the dominance games—leather, PVC, and corset included. He was never bored because he never had any idea of what awaited him, what toys or elaborate roleplay.

A couple years in, they hired a professional to explore her bisexual side. It had been his idea. Apart from the second-hand thrill of watching her with another woman, he genuinely wanted her to be happy, and she'd told him that being with another woman was totally different from being with him. Eventually, he encouraged her to look for a girl-friend to keep her company, whether he was there or not.

Two false starts, and then Julia entered their lives, though admittedly mostly Catia's. Julia went to college in town, collecting a range of STEM qualifications, and she'd first drawn Catia's eye because she was looking for a "Sugar Mommy". At Sal's dumbfounded expression, Catia explained that there were "Sugar Babies" out there looking for a Mommy or Daddy to pay the bills and spoil them and appreciate them, and these arrangements could, but didn't have to, involve sex.

When they met, the chemistry between Catia and Julia was thick enough to cut with a knife, but Sal also got to appreciate what a skilled huntress Catia was. How Julia resisted the onslaught of Catia's headgames and pure sexual energy was a miracle, but Sal assumed that her academic commitments kept her grounded enough. She was looking for something casual too—which was what she got, and also wasn't at all. But their relationship wasn't just about the sex. Catia was only four years older than Julia, but it turned out those four years could count for decades. Catia was strong-willed and also the head of a Cosa Nostra household, so she fixed problems and did it often with an invisible hand.

No, Barsanti, I don't have a consigliere because she was murdered, and I couldn't replace her.

Sometimes, a memory came back of them cuddling on the couch, Julia exhausted post-exams in Catia's arms, woolen blanket spread over both of them. He'd loved seeing them like that, so tender and strong. Weirdly, he'd never felt jealous. Sal felt he saw different sides in Catia when she was with her girlfriend, a softer, more feminine side, maybe.

The truth was, it took months before he even figured in their sex—Catia insisted they should get to know each other better first, but once the trust was established, Julia added a new dimension. And he wasn't always invited—or rather, he knew they spent time together when they left the city for a long weekend, or he was away on business. He was glad they had each other.

Since he knew it was one of her fantasies, he hired the best male sex worker he could find for one Valentine's Day. He'd spent a week browsing profiles, trying to guess what type she'd want. Also what type he wanted to see with her.

While she'd loved his Valentine's Day gift, she'd asked for the guy to give Sal a blowjob the morning after, which put paid to anything Sal had ever said about not being into men. At all.

The guy had blown the top of his head clean off and Sal had been both shocked and possibly embarrassed about how strongly he reacted. Getting pegged, sure, enjoying fucking his wife's curvy ass, any day and any hour, but touching a man and getting touched that way brought his walls crumbling down.

Not once could he have dreamed that he'd ever act on those impulses and attractions—he'd never felt anything was missing, but Catia reasoned with him after breakfast that he understood how she felt with Julia now because part of him needed the same kind of freedom. He tried to explain to her that it was different, because he was a man, at which point she'd reached over the breakfast table and tapped his temple.

"All that is just in your head. Let it go. You can trust me."

Unsettled over his own responses, he resisted a while longer, fought the desire to say yes because he was Salvatore Rausa and while he didn't fear anybody, decades of taboos and suppression couldn't be unmade with a blowjob. Of course, he gave his wife the freedom to do what she wanted, as long as none of his men got the sense that he was being cuckolded—and it turned out that Julia and Catia could get awfully affectionate in public with nobody picking up that they were more than friends. At the same time, he couldn't allow himself the same freedom. Partly because he didn't feel he was missing anything, partly because being too affectionate with a man was a no-go in his position.

Still, the same sex worker showed up again with a big grin and a clear set of instructions from Catia. And Sal might still have balked if Catia hadn't sat all three of them down with a wonderful meal and a few bottles of white wine, which Sal had started to regard as her secret weapon. Then she'd skillfully interrogated the guy—Chris?—about being a bisexual man. Sal remembered he'd specifically chosen Chris not just for his various attributes, but also because he was bisexual and specialized in couples, assuming it would be easier for a rented body if he didn't freak out if the husband was in the room, watching, or taking part.

They traded stories, and while they all drank wine, Chris answered Sal's questions in good humor and with easy laughter. Sal felt himself relax during that long evening. It was no different from when they'd met Julia those first couple times to get to know her first. Chris seemed relaxed about whether he got paid for an X-rated chat or X-rated events, but things progressed quickly that same evening. The fact that Chris seemed into both of them helped.

Ironically, having Catia there made it easier to tolerate a man's tenderness. She couldn't know how often he'd fought down the impulse to fight, to shove Chris away, not because he didn't want the closeness, but because he wanted it too much. He found himself wanting all of it, to taste the man's skin, to feel the silken heat of his cock in his hand, and discover the ways to make Chris groan and squirm. But he saw that knowing light in Catia's eye, and shivered when she touched them both and got the lube.

The morning after, Sal felt like he'd been stripped down to his soul, but also trusted that Catia would never regard him as anything lesser because he'd enjoyed everything that had happened the night before. She was right: he could trust her, and it *had* been all in his head, and she liked watching him with somebody else. With every step they took toward total honesty and openness, he fell more deeply in love with her. Nobody else had seen those weak moments, or even the ugly ones, but with her, he could be naked down to the very fabric of his being.

Enzo had been a different case. Sal had assigned him to keep an eye on Catia whenever she left the house, especially as the War was heating up and he felt uneasy about her being out in public but would also never restrict her movement. After a few days, she'd laughingly declared Enzo the "subbiest sub who ever subbed", and when he didn't believe her, counted on two hands, and then on two hands again, the instances when Enzo had followed her orders without so much as a blink or a hesitation, even if they were playful or a little cruel.

It could easily have been that clichéd story about a boss's trusted lieutenant getting too close to the boss's wife, but over the next few weeks she tested Enzo and got to know him, clearly analyzed his weaknesses and strengths. And Catia never set out to hurt anybody when it came to love and/or sex. She had a way of coaxing people to accept their own desires and follow their fantasies, and those she paid, she paid and treated well.

Sal had known they were moving onto thin ice. The moment they involved anybody they couldn't pay off, they were running a huge risk. And maybe he shouldn't have half-jokingly confessed that something about Enzo attracted him, but their relationship was so strong and flexible that he'd left Catia completely free rein. He trusted her judgment and her decisions.

Besides, he didn't feel his big fierce capo was particularly fragile.

In that, he'd been wrong.

Enzo proved a lot more brittle than Sal could have imagined, even when he'd agreed with Catia that Enzo responded well to a "firm hand". Between those two, the game was a lot less equal, because Enzo only wanted to serve and hand over all responsibility. He was lucky that Catia was both strong and caring enough to rise to that challenge. To Enzo's credit, when he broke, he accepted it and even offered up his weakness as a service and token of his submission. Whenever he joined them both in their bed, Enzo was game for anything, and Sal didn't catch on that Enzo wasn't nearly as bisexual as Sal himself.

But when he finally noticed, it was after the fact, and while he might have shrugged that off with anybody else, he liked and trusted Enzo too much to ignore it. He didn't feel guilty so much as worried that he'd pushed Enzo too far. Catia explained it to him—it all fed into Enzo's submissiveness. Enzo might not be very much into sex with men, but if he was if ordered to, or if it pleased whoever was filling the dominant role, he got off on it. It didn't compute for Sal, but he accepted it. He'd noticed that same obedience before and it all made sense, but he was definitely wired differently.

Enzo got pleasure and orgasms out of it, and also didn't want them to stop, so while some unease lingered, Sal did overcome it in the end, and accepted Enzo's different take on sex the same way he'd accepted his own.

At the same time, Enzo's chaotic life settled down. He had been erratically flipflopping between multiple girlfriends for as long as Sal had known him. Catia had probably ordered him to get his shit together. He took fewer risks, was less reckless, and, Sal noticed, less cynical. Old Enzo would have played Russian roulette if the stakes were high enough, and he'd insist on putting two more bullets into a six shooter. New Enzo was calmer, more cunning and better at anticipating the ultimate backlash.

Some of the guys had commented Enzo was "growing up", but Sal knew that for much of his time, Enzo was wearing a chastity device under his clothes that either Catia or Sal held the key to. Maybe it was that reminder, that very noticeable claim of control and ownership that made Enzo calm down. Maybe it was because he didn't want to be taken in by cops while wearing that contraption. Whatever the case, they'd been happy.

Till death did us part.

Sal took a fortifying breath at the thought. He was glad to catch a red light and take a moment to wipe a hand over his eyes. For the first couple years after her death, just remembering her hurt. Maybe that was the strongest indication that her guidance had made Enzo stronger, because while Sal fell completely apart, every bit of his strength washed away like the walls of a sandcastle annihilated by a storm-whipped sea, Enzo didn't. Sure, he suffered like an animal, but his prime goal had shifted from serving Catia to supporting Sal.

Enzo had been there those first few days when Sal was so numb and anguished and beside himself that anything could have happened. He accepted that Sal screamed at him, wrestled with him, and not in play, watched Sal when he raved and ranted, and was there when Sal broke down. Sal could not say in all honesty what would have been more likely—that he'd blow his own head off or go on a killing rampage because only blood could drown the sheer agony of losing Catia. The person who'd dug up layers of himself he'd never have dared to examine on his own, and made him okay with them. More than okay. She'd made him whole. The one person who'd loved him unconditionally even in his weakest, ugliest moments.

She hadn't deserved to die, surely hadn't deserved to be murdered, and identifying her body had been the hardest thing Sal had ever done in his life. After that, everything was child's play—the war that was now on the horizon meant little compared to that, except that it was his revenge for her death. And still, his current game moves were to protect himself from unnecessary losses. He wouldn't put Enzo's life at risk, for example.

He'd wade through the guts of a thousand Jack Barsantis for that.

17

Bethany Grace Howard. It had been Enzo's cop buddy who'd come through with the driver's license. The photo was definitely older—it showed her as a bleached blonde, and with the lack of contrast, she looked like a ghost except for her wide-set dark eyes. She lived in one of two apartments above a nail salon, front door toward the side-walk, which made it easy to observe from where Sal had parked a bit further down the road. Nearby were a dentist and a physiotherapist, and unless somebody paid him close and prolonged attention, Sal could have been a bored husband waiting outside for his wife or children.

He still had to wait too long, so he pulled his tablet from its padded sleeve and pretended to work.

It took only about an hour for Miss Howard to appear in the door with a bag slung over her shoulder. Her dark hair was gathered in an untidy ponytail, and she looked rushed and preoccupied. He dropped the tablet underneath the seat. Port Francis was pretty safe, but it was still the kind of city where some people might be tempted to grab a piece of tech if all it took was to bash in a window. The professional criminals would never touch a made man's car, but some amateurs might not be so wise.

He checked his reflection in the car mirror, but he looked fine. If his eyes were still slightly reddened, he could always claim allergies.

Sal stepped out of the car and locked it remotely, then walked parallel to Miss Howard on the other side of the street. She vanished into a supermarket on the corner, but instead of chasing her, Sal leisurely crossed the road and waited on the corner, peering at his phone like a dozen other people within sight were doing. Once he pretended to make a call, acting as if he'd been stood up, or whoever he was planning to meet wasn't answering the phone.

There she was again. She came dashing out of the shop, carrying a gallon of fresh milk in one hand, and a bag of sliced bread in the other.

"Excuse me?"

Sal slipped his phone into his pocket, forced to give chase because even though there were no people between them on the sidewalk, Miss Howard maintained a hectic pace. She either hadn't heard or was ignoring him.

He repeated, "Excuse me, Miss?" He carefully chose a more urgent, insistent tone in the vicinity of "you dropped your wallet", and that made her stop and look over her shoulder.

Bingo. It was definitely her. She probably weighed no more than a hundred twenty pounds soaking wet.

Sal put on his best smile, and added some "of course I know you, surely you recognize me" to his expression. Bullshitting had to get him past the fact that he had no reason to know her last name or any idea what Barsanti called her. "I do apologize. We have a friend in common—Jack Barsanti."

She froze, flashed a nervous smile, but it didn't linger. Clearly, she recognized the name. "Oh?"

He'd read that most people formed a first impression in about seven seconds, including whether somebody could be trusted. They were solidly into that short period now, and her gaze zigzagged over him as she assessed whether he was a threat. So he kept his smile in place and adopted a "not a creep" stance.

Sal made a big show of relief. "Sorry, I'm Sal. Jack's friend."

She kept her guard up—almost literally, because she drew that gallon of milk toward her chest and the hand with the bread defensively held onto the straps of her shoulder bag. Yeah, this wasn't working, but he kept his smile up as if he expected her to recognize him, already readying other strategies.

"Jack. Is he okay? He didn't ..." She interrupted herself, and Sal wondered if Barsanti had already given her the Cosa Nostra girlfriend briefing: don't talk to anybody. If you see anything weird, call me first. The police can't help you—I'll handle it.

"He's had a busy morning. Quite tied up with a few things." Sal almost laughed.

She gave a weak smile back. "Oh, well." She clearly wanted to say more, but suppressed it, then looked over her shoulder in the direction of her flat, telegraphing how uncomfortable she was. "Nice to meet you, Sal, was it?"

"Yes." Now was it Bethany, Beth, Betty or something else

entirely? "Sal Tomasi." Close enough, using Catia's maiden name.

She kept studying him. "Are you a colleague of his?"

"No, a friend." He lifted his eyebrows for emphasis.

She grew even paler and then flushed slightly, eyes wide. "Oh my God. Are you his boyfriend?"

The last two syllables were said in such a low voice that Sal needed a second to process the word, but in an impulse —because fuck it, why not—he nodded. "Yes. I am."

"Oh my God," she said again, voice shifting into a much higher tonality. She didn't seem shocked, more surprised. Immediately, her defensiveness broke apart and Sal was relieved. He'd made the correct call, even though his mind was still catching up with the unexpected turn of events. He'd been stalking the prospective girlfriend of one of his enemies, and she thought Sal was his boyfriend?

While she was clearly still off-balance, he pressed his advantage. "And what should I call you?"

"Beth." She still stared at him and he noticed her shoulders relaxed and her expression eased, which made sense because now he was gay in her eyes. Also, he thought he caught some veiled appreciation for how he looked too. Or maybe she was mentally positioning Jack next to him and decided they fit well together. What the fuck?

Beth. He could easily have chosen wrong multiple times and ruined his approach. With a sigh, he lifted his shoulders and dropped them. "I know it's probably weird, but maybe we can talk somewhere? Could we grab a coffee, maybe?" He nodded toward a shop that sat on the corner across the road.

"Uhm, sure." She seemed to only now become aware again of the things she was carrying and stuffed the bread at least into her bag. "But if you don't mind, maybe we could go to the independent one down the road? The chain place burns their beans really badly, and Jack wouldn't forgive either of us if we went there, right?"

Based on the Gaggia, Barsanti knew his coffee. "Of course. I figured it was closest. Please." He stepped to the side, gesturing for her to take the lead.

She did, a bit slower than her prior pace, but she still moved briskly. "Now I only hope we'll get a table." She shook her head at herself. "I'll look like a complete idiot if it's full and we have to go back to the place of Burnt Beans, right?"

A "complete idiot" for trying to get them decent coffee? Really? "Well, I'm easy. And we don't have to tell him."

She pushed through the door and a delicious waft of coffee and carby baking fumes from the waffle maker on the counter, welcomed them. She nodded toward the back where one table was being vacated. "I'll grab that one."

"Great. What can I get you?"

"A latte and a waffle, maybe?"

"You got it." He watched her navigate around the departing patrons and claim the table, while a girl wearing an apron and a dozen facial piercings cleaned away the cups and plates.

Sal then waited for a couple of takeaway customers to put in their orders before he asked for two lattes and two waffles, paid, and was assured he'd be served at the table. Of course, the whole interlude gave Beth time to relax and maybe question what it was he wanted from her. If he got nothing out of this but her phone number and being able to establish a relationship he could exploit later, that could still count as a win. Apart from that, discovering Jack was gay opened up a whole new dimension.

He joined her and glanced around as if to take in the surroundings, before he focused on her. "Didn't know this place existed," he admitted. It definitely hadn't been on his radar as anything more than a hangout of college students, but the patrons seemed more diverse, from shoppers having a break to middle-aged friends meeting for a catch-up.

"Best coffee and waffles and ice cream within walking distance for me." She was clearly pleased that he seemed to like it. "So, wow. You're the only one of Jack's friends I've ever met."

"Same." Sal chuckled. "For a guy as connected as Jack is, he doesn't seem very good at connecting people with each other. A dinner party would do."

"Maybe he needs time alone after work. Anyway, nice to meet you. And thanks for the invitation."

"Absolutely. So yeah, it's going to sound weird, but I was wondering if you could help me." Catia had told him once that asking people for help for something small and meaningless helped establish a connection, and he'd found that it actually worked.

"Is it about Jack?"

"Of course." Sal smiled again. "He's been ... off, I guess. I mean recently. The past couple weeks, definitely. And he's, well, guys like that, they don't talk about their emotions. It's not like I can tie him to a chair and force him to talk." It made him laugh, but a small voice in his head told him to not stretch that angle too far, as much as it amused him. "That would be wrong," he added, because she didn't laugh with him.

But her face seemed thoughtful. "Yeah. I mean, maybe not ... we don't talk that often. But we text and talk on the phone. Sometimes we meet up, but I know he's busy a lot with work, and sometimes he looks so tired I feel bad that he's gone to all that trouble only to check if I'm okay."

That last bit pinged something else in his brain. "And, are you okay? I don't want to bring all this stuff to you if you have your own stuff going on."

She looked up and smiled, a small, honest and somewhat shaky smile. "Thank you. I'm better. Jack helped me through a rough patch a while ago, and it took some time to get back on my feet, but I'm good now. Happy to help you both if I can."

He took a moment to taste the words and listened to the tone behind them. All right, so while he hadn't unearthed a kinky lover or girlfriend, she was a friend, and from the way she made it sound, Jack Barsanti's only one. And they couldn't be more different—this shy, pretty creature with her tender heart, and Jack Barsanti who believed everything could be negotiated, and that taking a bullet to the head for his boss was the expected end to his career. Basically, if they did have a real emotional bond, she was prime leverage.

"Did you notice anything? I might be imagining things, but ..." He shrugged in a display of helplessness. "He's got me worried."

She drew her bottom lip through her teeth. "I ..." She stopped herself, shook her head. "Sorry. I'm confused because some things make so much sense now."

"Such as? I don't mind if it's a jumble."

She looked up and Sal saw the pierced girl approach

from the side, so he leaned back in his chair to give her easier access to the tiny café table.

Beth pulled the waffle and coffee toward her. "That he's gay, for example. I always thought he was, from the day we met. It was so *clear* to me, even though we never talked about it. I thought he knew that I knew, so that was never an issue when we met up, and then yesterday ..."

... when she'd all but fled from the scene.

"Yesterday?"

"Promise you won't be angry with him?"

The fuck? "Did he make a move on you?" She didn't say anything, so he added. "Of course, I promise."

"Not a move, no. Though I guess you could call it that in a way ... he asked me to marry him." She was clearly upset, red spots dancing on her pale cheeks.

"And you said no."

"Of course! Firstly, I can't be a gay man's ... what's the word, beard? I'd do everything else for him, but I can't marry him. It'd make us both unhappy. He might think he wants that right now, but what happens a few years down the line? Can you imagine? If I meet his friends or colleagues and they think he's straight, and I have to keep up appearances, but we're both living this gigantic lie?" She angrily stabbed the waffle and Sal found her terribly endearing with her ruffled feathers. "But more importantly, he has to stand up to his people. This is the twenty-first century; he can't keep hiding from his family."

Oh, Beth. Barsanti hadn't meant that type of family.

Sal got it. He knew why Jack was hiding. For the most part, Cosa Nostra families hadn't emerged into the twenty-first century when it came to the rainbow crowd. "That's what he said? He asked you to marry him because of his relatives?"

"Yes." She put the fork down and folded her hands. "I guess his parents might be old and traditional, but he can't let them pressure him to marry someone he doesn't love. It'd ruin his whole life. And for what? Just so they're not disappointed? Next, they'll bring up grandkids, and I'm definitely not up for that."

"For the record, I don't think he'd 'ruin his life' with you, but the rest of your argument stands. What the fuck, Jack?" He focused on his waffle which was still warm and crispy on the outside and slightly moist on the inside. The richness of vanilla was clearly noticeable.

"Exactly. What the fuck, Jack?" She mirrored him, also eating her waffle. "So that's why I tried to call him this morning. And I got worried too, because he didn't answer. I'm sorry I disappointed him after everything he's done for me, but I'm also angry, I guess? I shouldn't be angry, but I am."

"Nah, your emotions are perfectly valid." One of the things Catia would tell her. "You thought you can trust him and then he's pulling that shit on you. That's not right."

"... but ..."

"It's not right, Beth. Trust me. Jack's a strong guy, he's tougher than he makes out."

"I hope so. Does hearing all that from me help you, though?"

"It's definitely a piece of the puzzle I was missing." That seemed to relax her again, and he leaned back in the metal chair. "He's not talking about his emotions, and I thought we were getting to that stage in our relationship where he could open up to me about what's going on inside of him, you know."

She nodded with enough force that he knew he was on the right path and that the Jack she knew was consistent with his fake boyfriend Jack. "Men."

"I know, right?" He laughed softly. "But I like him, so I'm trying."

A long pause, then she asked, "How and when did you guys meet?"

"Work thing. I was aware of him for years because my firm sometimes works with him, but we got closer at a wedding. Some alcohol was involved, and I was pretty surprised to see that other side of him."

"Are you in consulting too?"

Oh, thank you, Beth, for adding more puzzle pieces. "No, I'm in IT. Project manager, though I keep getting promoted. At some point, I'll run this whole damn city if they don't stop opening doors." He laughed into his latte.

"Do you want to?"

Her question caught him off guard, even though it seemed innocent. "Not exactly, though most of the time, when I see the infrastructure other people have set up, I think I'd do a better job. Plus, if I roll out WiFi, trust me, your download speeds would look totally different. No more fucking Zoom lag, that's for sure."

Nothing much changed about her expression, so she wasn't into computer stuff, and that meant he didn't have to keep up that charade. A lot of people in this city were IT professionals, thanks to a generously funded and very well-regarded technology-focused college, and multiple start-up hubs dotted around town. Settle anywhere with a laptop or a high-performance tablet, and you became scenery and practically invisible.

"Maybe you could work together on a project? Maybe if you spend more time together, he'll open up?"

"Strictly speaking, he's currently consulting for the enemy. My outfit and his have 'history'." He added scare quotes. "Anyway, how did you two meet?"

"Oh." She took her cup and held it with both fingers. "He saved my life."

"Pardon me?" Wow, that came from left field. It wasn't even in the same stadium, maybe the same sport anymore. Above all, it was her tone that gave away that she meant this literally. "I mean, wow. Will you tell me?"

She hesitated. "As I said, I was ... going through some stuff. Stupid boyfriend stuff. That, and some other things, and I couldn't see a way out anymore. I know that sounds dramatic, but I thought maybe I didn't want to be around anymore." Her voice was now flatter, and she looked very subdued. "And that night, when I ... was going to do something about it, he was already at the place, and he was standing there." She swallowed. "I was glad I wasn't alone. He didn't ... do anything much, at some point he gave me his coat. But it's even harder to do something when a human soul cares about you. Even if he's a total stranger."

"Shit, sorry. I shouldn't have asked."

"No, I think it's important to talk about it. It helps. If you're too much in your own head ... thoughts can take a wrong turn and suddenly doing something terrible seems like the best solution. Even if there's a better way. That's my five cents, anyway." She shook her head.

"Are you better now?" Weirdly, he found he actually

wanted to know. Though in his experience, people who were close to a breakdown didn't talk about it so openly. Silence was the killer, not weakness.

"Yes. Much better. Thank you." She smiled warmly at him. "I didn't ask at the time, of course, but since then, I've wondered why exactly he was alone on that bridge that night. I guess as far as meet cutes go, ours sucks. Yours is better. Weddings are a classic."

Sal nodded and had to force himself to concentrate. He had pieces of the puzzle that could help Beth understand Jack Barsanti. Shit, he'd come here to secure leverage, and maybe find a weak point in the consigliere's emotional armor, a way to get to him. She'd given him so much he could turn Barsanti inside out if he wanted.

"You know what Jack needs? A therapist."

She nodded. "It really helps. If he's worried about seeing one, I can tell him what he can expect. Maybe he can work through his family stuff with them. I feel he's focused on the wrong solutions. Maybe you can help him understand that?"

Unlikely. "I'll see what I can do. Wow, that got pretty heavy for such a nice Sunday." He finished off the waffle and watched her eat too. "Thanks for telling me all this. It helps me understand what's going on."

"He's lucky to have you. You seem kind."

"Doing the best I can." Sal checked his phone. "I need to call a friend. Maybe we can exchange numbers and keep in touch?"

"I'd like that." She gave him her number, and he texted her to make sure he had the correct one. Yet another thing Catia had briefed him on. "And can you tell him to call me?"

"Will do. First, I'll have to have a somewhat difficult

conversation with him myself, but you can have what's left over when I'm done." He winked to indicate he was joking.

"Oh my God. Please be gentle? He's a good guy." She, too, said it jokingly, but he still nodded.

He left her at the table, dialing the doc's number before he got to the door.

18

The "doc", or Marty Russo for everybody else, was only half-Italian if you rounded up. Sal himself didn't rate that requirement too highly; much more important to have the family connections and be aware of the culture, but overall ability counted for a lot in his book. From what Sal understood, Russo had largely joined the Army as a "fuck you" to his family, which hadn't guaranteed he'd thrive in that environment. Evidently, he hadn't. And regarding that discharge, Sal had an inkling it had to do with Russo's at times disturbing interest in and talent regarding pharmaceuticals.

More importantly, the doc had been the friend of a soldier who'd caught a belly full of lead during the War. Said soldier had been lucky since Sal didn't mind breaking every rule of the road when a guy was bleeding out next to him. It'd been a hellish night anyway, so bad that Sal had simply shut his emotions down. Fortunately, the doc had agreed to meet them minutes later at Sal's place and did what he could to save that poor bastard's life. Sal had learned to respect the doc's coldness under pressure, how his hands never shook while cutting into a writhing body, and how at dawn he'd unwound with a bowl of homemade carbonara right after chasing bullets through what had looked like a hell of a lot of intestine.

Sal waited in the car outside the unassuming house. He'd quartered the doc here in one of his own properties, not far away from the town center so that no landlord would come calling about muffled screams or blood, though of course they'd always tried to keep medical procedures off site.

The door opened and the doc emerged, backpack on one shoulder, a large medic-type bag in one hand. To Sal it looked like a messenger bag with multiple extra pockets. With his paunchy wrestler's build and muddy brown hair well past his shoulders, the doc looked like a somewhat older student, maybe even faculty, or your average gamer nerd who'd also once upon a time spent a lot of time lifting weights and then given up in favor of a lifestyle involving more weed and chilling.

Sal leaned over and opened the passenger door for him.

"Nice ride!" the doc said. "New?"

"Borrowed."

He dropped the backpack on the seat behind them, but kept the medic bag between his feet after he'd fallen heavily into the seat, noticeably rocking the car. "You going to give it back?"

"Maybe." Sal grinned. "Thanks for making time, doc."

"No problem. Enzo already said you have a tricky customer on your hands."

"Yep. If there are any issues with your Hippocratic Oath,

we'll pick up a coffee at the drive-through, and I'll let you out again."

"Enzo said 'enhanced interrogation'."

"That about nails it. Though it's me who'll do the interrogation, or, fuck it, call it torture. I gotta break a guy because what's in his head can save lives."

The doc didn't blink at the term. "You're worried I thought I'd have to get my hands dirty?"

"I don't know you well enough to know what your lines are. Just saying it's necessary and I have my reasons, and I need you to keep him alive or bring him back." Sal had both hands on the wheel, but let the car idle. "Mostly because he can't check out before I know what I need to know."

The doc grinned briefly but sobered. "Thanks for checking."

"Yeah, well." Sal opened his hands on the wheel and dropped them. "That's what's going on."

"Any conditions I should know about? How hurt is he?"

"He's not. At least not yet."

The doc clicked the seat belt in place. "I got all the gear I need. Let's go."

They spent the drive back up into the hills with bursts of small talk that didn't feel forced or awkward. The doc wasn't the kind of person to chatter away, but was perfectly happy to express an opinion about anything, and ask about how Sal had been doing.

As far as the doc was concerned, a war like this seemed to be mostly a logistical exercise—where to bring the wounded, if any, where he should be when things kicked off, that sort of thing. Overall, he seemed to regard the future with the same mix of anticipation and readiness as if he would watch the progress bar while downloading a game he was eager to play.

Sal envied him that; as the man who would send the troops into battle, he was much more directly responsible for those who'd end up with the doc's hands on them, digging for bullets or trying to staunch the bleeding.

Enzo opened the door, looking relaxed.

"Did anything happen?" Sal stepped to the side to let the doc walk past him.

Enzo shook his head. "I didn't talk to him. He didn't seem in the mood, either. Any success?"

"Plenty. I found his friend."

"And?"

"She's nice." Sal shrugged with a fair amount of irony. "We had waffles."

Enzo looked quizzically at him, but Sal left him with that. He'd tell Enzo the whole story when they had the peace and quiet for it. "Let's get the patient ready."

19

Jack had argued back and forth with himself about whether to attempt striking up a conversation with the blond capo. As the man who'd dragged in a whole pile of claw hammers, saws and drills, Enzo was unlikely to be the friendlier one of the two. But Enzo was playing with his toys so much that Jack couldn't resist. Later, he blamed his tiredness.

"Robbed a hardware store, I see." Just a quip because the clanking was getting to him, but not the way Enzo likely thought.

He hadn't expected the reaction he got. Enzo's eyes narrowed, he dropped whatever he was toying with, and kicked him so hard against the chest that Jack lost his breath and then his bearings when the chair twisted and overbalanced and Jack hit his head again. Second time in so many days, but this one seemed worse—it came with searing, splitting pain high up on his forehead, and Jack tried to blink his vision clear and held onto consciousness, but just barely. He smelled blood, and felt it run into his hair and ear.

Enzo crouched before him. "Sal thinks you're smart, but that was pretty fucking dumb."

"Agreed." He didn't have any more than that.

Enzo grabbed the chair and using a foot to ensure the chair legs couldn't skid away, hoisted the chair and Jack into his original position. The blood now ran down the side of his face and into his shirt collar. Jack focused on blinking and keeping it out of his eyes.

Movement and voices refocused his attention.

"You said he wasn't hurt?" A long-haired man in his late twenties walked up to him and cast a long glance at Jack's forehead.

"That doesn't count." Sal crossed his arms in front of his chest. "Enzo?"

"I wasn't in the mood for sass," Enzo stated.

Rausa looked at what had to be the doc, and shrugged with a "See?" expression.

It took all the concentration Jack had to make sense of the interaction, but he had to. Everything depended on him assessing the situation and the players. Nothing had changed. The doc crouched by Jack's side and checked on his wrists. He then stood and studied Jack's face with interest, specifically the aching side, and prodded his upper arm.

"I see you're working out. Any heart conditions?"

"What?" Jack lifted his head. "No."

"Asthma? COPD? Any other pulmonary issues?"

Mistake. He hesitated, head pounding too much to think fast enough. If he managed to pull off a lie, surely they'd have to go easier on him.

"He's fine," Rausa said. "Trying to weasel his way out again."

The doc turned to Sal, and only then did Jack fully compute what was going on. Shit, he was definitely getting slow and careless. Seemed he'd been medically cleared for something?

Rausa nodded grimly, unfolded his arms, and Jack noticed he'd taken off his shirt again. He stepped up to the Jacuzzi in the corner and opened the tap. The noise of running water went straight to Jack's bladder, and he gritted his teeth. Not the time or situation to ask for that toilet break. Rausa's jaw muscles tensed and relaxed, tensed and relaxed, while his fists remained clenched.

The doc took position near the windows, leaning against them, while Enzo completed the uneven triangle with the long-haired guy and the Jacuzzi at the apex. The hairs of Jack's neck rose under all that attention from three men who were going to hurt him. Well, hurt him more.

The water kept gushing into the Jacuzzi, while several minutes passed. Then Sal set himself into motion. "Remember, you can stop this at any time."

"Same goes for you," Jack said.

"Oh, I know." Rausa vanished from his view and stood behind him. "Break's over. Now we'll work."

Suddenly a pressure against the plastic ties around his wrists, and his hands were free. Jack swallowed and noticed that Rausa was also freeing his legs. "Get up. Slowly."

He couldn't have moved fast if he'd tried. His muscles were tight, his body exhausted and tense from the restriction, balance hard to maintain from hitting his head yet again, but above all, one against three was never going to work in his favor. He briefly rubbed his wrists and rolled his shoulders, but Rausa already took his arms again and put fresh ties around his wrists.

"Let's go."

Jack realized with growing horror that Rausa was pushing him toward the Jacuzzi, and pushing him hard so Jack struggled to climb in because his balance was so off. "Kneel."

"You sick fuck."

Rausa grabbed him by the arms and pushed him forward and down. The water was lukewarm and quickly overcame shoes, socks and climbed up his legs. Rausa stepped into the Jacuzzi with him, also almost fully dressed except for his shirt. "I said, kneel." He pushed Jack forward and kicked him in the backs of his knees so Jack went down with a splash, knocking his shoulder against the rim of the tub. He watched the water rise further in dread. Right now, it only reached halfway up his thighs, but thanks to the very nicely specced Jacuzzi, it was climbing rapidly.

Rausa grabbed him by the neck and leaned closer. "You know what's going to happen, so why don't you just talk?"

"Fuck you."

"Not an answer, but we'll get to that," Rausa said in a low tone. He grabbed Jack's neck harder, and then pushed his head down. There wasn't enough water to completely cover his head, but plenty enough to push his face under, and now Jack fought, thrashed in a helpless panic, aware that he was burning precious oxygen and lost breath, screaming into the water that was reddening with his blood. He lost control of his bladder; he simply couldn't help it. More hands were held him down now, but the white-hot panic seared all other thoughts away. He desperately kicked and squirmed, trying to free himself.

He was just getting dizzy when Rausa grabbed him hard around the arms and pulled him up. Jack straightened, gasping and gulping air so fast that he breathed in some water and broke into a nasty coughing fit. He caught a glimpse of the doc checking his wristwatch. When he nodded, Rausa grabbed him and shoved him under again.

Jack had had no time to recover or even take a deep breath, choked off by coughing. Panic swallowed him in an instant, his body out of control and fighting like an animal.

He tried to push back against Rausa, tried to move forward or to the side, wildly seeking any open space, but Rausa held him and further hands pushed down on him, folding him effectively in two, which put pressure on his lungs and kept them from fully expanding. Again, the water and bubbles and cream-colored ceramics blurred with spots dancing before his eyes, and his vision rapidly darkened and narrowed. If he'd been panicked when Rausa had choked him out near the gate, this was a thousand, ten thousand times worse, lungs burning, while he was swallowing water, and they kept him like that for an eternity of horror and fear.

And then Rausa pulled him up again, one hand gripping his arm, another against his throat. "You already pissed yourself. Let me know when you're fucking done, because I have plenty more of this for you."

At least this time he had a chance to gasp in air before Rausa pushed him down again. The Jacuzzi was a lot fuller now, pale yellow water well past his belt, and it kept climbing until Jack was submerged to his chest, but Rausa kept pushing him all the way down. Maybe they hadn't put that hood back on him as a small kindness, because being blinded and drowning was maybe worse, but considering everybody around him simply rolled with it, from the long-haired guy checking his watch and timing it all, to Enzo standing there, half kneeling on the rim, just as drenched as Jack or Rausa, categories such as good or bad simply ceased to exist. All that counted was getting that next breath, or recovering some of the oxygen he'd been robbed of.

And that was the mistake. He couldn't—wouldn't live at any cost, and even then just a little longer. Borrowed time. All of it, everything, had always been on borrowed time. One way to go out on his own terms. He felt nothing but the thrashing fear of his body, but inside it and beyond it, he recognized something hard and cold, like a decision. He'd carried it since forever, but he'd first become aware of it that night on the bridge.

Yes, I'm done.

As if he'd managed to step outside of himself, he regarded his body, that bruised, thrashing, scared flesh with an odd mix of compassion and acceptance.

Just a little pain, and everything's going to be okay.

When he went into the water this time, he forced himself to breathe in. He swallowed water first, and fought the cough that gnawed on his lungs, but finally managed to inhale. And despite the pain, it wasn't unlike that attack down at the gate. He was aware of uncoordinated movements, and then his vision greyed, dimmed and narrowed, his lungs stung, but a calm settled in his mind. Choosing his path more than twenty years ago had led to this end, and it was all right.

20

Something was wrong. It wasn't one specific thing, perhaps just Sal's instinct that picked up on it. Sal had been wrestling for years and honed his instincts for shifting tensions or a redistribution of weight to anticipate the opponent's next move. Maybe that awareness made the difference. He knew something was wrong with Barsanti even before his frantic resistance suddenly shifted into something else. Something about his breathing pattern.

The doc took a rapid step toward the Jacuzzi, and then Barsanti stopped fighting. Surprise, disbelief and then alarm crossed over the doc's features, and in an impulse, he reached out, which was when Sal let go of Barsanti.

"He's drowning!" The doc grabbed Barsanti from almost under Sal. His quick and precise movements would have been surprising if Sal hadn't seen the man work before. He helped the doc get Barsanti out of the Jacuzzi by grabbing his legs, and laying him flat on the tiles. The doc was already reaching for his bag, and Sal noticed Barsanti's skin had a decidedly blueish tinge.

Shit. What had the whole timing thing been good for, then? Above all, Sal couldn't wrap his head around the fact he'd pushed it way too far. If it had been just about killing Barsanti, that could have been done much easier and much faster. This had never happened before, not to Sal, not to anybody he knew. What exactly had he done wrong? Had Barsanti suffered a stroke? A heart attack maybe?

He balled his fists and became aware of how his clothes stuck to his skin. He was drenched; water dripped from his hair, but he only tore his gaze away from Barsanti's lifeless body on the ground and the doc administering CPR when Enzo stepped in front of him with a towel. Sal nodded and forced himself to turn away. Surprise seeped out of him, and a mix of guilt and resentment flooded in. They'd been so fucking close, and he'd ruined it.

Fuck.

He was no use in the bathroom now, and found it impossible to look at Barsanti and the struggle for his life. He didn't want to witness it, feeling deep down that it would fail. It was over, all the work was lost and now they had a high-profile dead body on their hands and nothing to show for it. He'd fucked up.

Towel in one hand, he left the bathroom to dry off and get rid of his wet clothes. But the moment he was upstairs in the guest bedroom, he heard coughing, retching and then the unmistakable sounds of somebody vomiting.

He changed in record time and hurried back down, taking two steps at a time.

While Barsanti was white as a sheet beneath his tan, he

was no longer blue, and he was breathing again. Well, "breathing". It sounded raspy even to Sal's ears, and even though his breath was fast and shallow, that was still enough to make him cough, and those came from deep inside his lungs. He'd rolled onto his side, knees drawn up, arms hugging his heaving chest.

The doc crouched next to him and had a hand placed on Barsanti's shoulder. "Try to relax."

Barsanti didn't respond, not with a quip or even by trying to pull away. He was wholly preoccupied with just taking in oxygen and suffering through wracking coughs.

The doc brushed his hair back behind his ears and straightened, then made eye contact with Sal.

"What happened?" Sal asked.

"I think he did it on purpose. He tried to drown himself." The doc's face betrayed his surprise, so Sal wasn't alone there. He couldn't even feel relief that it hadn't been his mistake and that Barsanti was alive.

"That's not supposed to happen."

The doc glanced back at Barsanti as if to check he was still breathing. "Now I don't even want to know who he is, but that was one for the family album. Metaphorically, not actually. Of course."

"Good job bringing him back." Sal patted the doc's shoulder. He tried to imagine what it would take to override one's own survival instinct and failed. People could be driven to extreme places where they might jump out of a high-up window to escape a raging fire, but this was a totally different caliber. All the other instances where Barsanti had resisted paled into nothing, could have just been driven by pride. This though ... "I guess we can give him a little rest and then put him in there again, just more carefully."

"Not a great idea. He's not out of the woods. He's aspirated water, so there's a chance the difficulties he's having with his breathing will get worse. Secondary drowning is no joke."

"What do you mean?"

"If this was a different situation, I'd send him for observation at the hospital, but with things being as they are, at the very least I wouldn't let him anywhere near water. And keep an eye on him. Respiratory distress can get nasty very quickly. Drowning victims definitely need twenty-four hours to recover, forty-eight hours is better." The doc shrugged with an "at least that's the rules" expression.

"And in the meantime? Hook him up to a car battery?"

"I wouldn't recommend it. That was a close call."

Okay, so Sal had fucked up, but it wasn't irrecoverable. Fine. They didn't really have that much time, but they'd lose more if they had to go with an alternative plan. Barsanti was still the decisive factor, and Sal wasn't going to accept that Andrea's consigliere had bested him.

Not permanently, not from a position of such weakness.

Watching Barsanti cough and suffer there on the floor, Sal wanted to punch something, somebody, and the adrenaline from earlier began to turn into acid in his veins.

Belatedly, he noticed Barsanti's hands were free, but even so, the consigliere posed as much of a threat as a half-drowned kitten. He couldn't tell whether those were tears running from the man's closed eyes or just water, but if they were tears, they might be from purely physical misery. Barsanti didn't even attempt to wipe them away.

Both the doc and Enzo looked at Sal expectantly.

Sal took another one of those blue-grey towels from the shelf, where they were stacked as tidily as for a photo shoot, unfolded it and placed it on Barsanti's hands. The man didn't respond, too trapped in what Sal assumed was either exhaustion or distress, or maybe both.

Sal could still feel the echo of Barsanti fighting him with the desperation and single-minded focus of a landed fish, and only now had a good idea of the man's raw physical strength.

He'd wrestled others for fun and for sport, was a pretty competent grappler, when it came to that, but there was a metallic tang to Barsanti's battle against him. He must have been sweating adrenaline, and maybe Sal felt a little guilty about how part of him had almost enjoyed this—not the fear, not the agony of drowning, not the coughing, definitely not. He wasn't a sadist—blood and cruelty left him cold.

The part he had enjoyed was feeling Barsanti's power, the tension in his muscles, and the terrible intimacy of near-death. The water hadn't exactly been warm, so the heat from the man's struggling body had felt good against his own, and taking off his shirt had been a mistake, because he'd felt it more keenly, unfiltered. In fact, he'd been glad for the doc's presence, which kept him on task, kept his timing on track, and also that the doc had stepped in when Barsanti's act of desperation hadn't just changed the game—it had flipped the table on which the game was played.

He walked over to the liquor cabinet in the living room, which held only a few but expensive bottles, mostly old whiskey. Sal didn't have the palate for it, so he simply chose the bottle that had the least, reasoning that it might be a favorite, and added two fingers of the golden liquid to two heavy tumblers. Not the time to go easy. He tossed the whiskey back in one gulp, and appreciated the sharp, mellowing burn all the way to his stomach. And another sense memory of Barsanti bucking underneath him. *Fuck.*

He poured himself another finger of the whiskey and chased right after the first one. He should eat something more solid than coffee, whiskey and a waffle, but his hunger came from something else and he knew it.

"It's not because he's pretty?"

Shit, if Enzo asked him that question again right now, his answer wouldn't be so glib. Worse, it'd lack conviction. Though it wasn't because Barsanti was *pretty*. In this town and within driving distance, he could have any number of pretty faces, all ranges, all types, all genders. Most came for free, the others were within his budget. Pretty didn't cover it. Pretty was skin-deep. Pretty didn't mean a damn thing.

He'd known the game had changed when Beth had spilled Jack Barsanti's secrets to him in an attempt to help his "boyfriend" understand him better. What he hadn't anticipated was that it added another layer to his growing respect for the man.

"Meh. Straight guy rubbing one out. Not exactly thrilling stuff."

Except Barsanti wasn't straight, and was proving to be far more thrilling than Sal could have predicted. Maybe he shouldn't, but he took Beth's word for it. If Jack were straight, his restraint around her was impressive; she was hot in a vulnerable, sweet way that absolutely wasn't Sal's type, but he could see Barsanti with his cultured tastes developing some kind of Pygmalion fantasy around her.

Whatever Barsanti's orientation was, he was apparently looking for a bride due to "family" pressure. So, had he committed some kind of indiscretion? Anything that made someone among the Lo Cascio think the consigliere wasn't up to requirements? Was someone trying to blackmail or backstab him, and he sought to head this off at the earliest opportunity? It had to be something like that.

So, Jack, they'll crucify you for what you're sticking your dick into but you're still willing to die for those fuckers?

He drew his shoulders up in a deep sigh, drank the last few drops that had gathered in the glass, then put it down in the kitchen on the way back to the bathroom, where Barsanti was now lying stretched out on his back, clutching the towel Sal had given him. The doc seemed to be finishing up an inspection of his wrists, and then stashed the stethoscope he'd used to check Barsanti's lungs earlier.

"Anything, doc?"

"No damage to the wrists." The doc stood and stepped aside. "Smart to tie him behind his back. Doesn't seem like you pulled them too tight."

That had been more of a habit. Catia was no longer there to rip into him, but she'd taught him proper restraint safety, and that recreational skill came in handy in his line of work.

What would she have made of Barsanti? Everything aside, if she hadn't died, and if Barsanti weren't who he was, would she have focused on Barsanti and fully analyzed and then repaired him like so many of her gallery of broken toys? "I know my restraints."

Enzo coughed, and the doc looked up, eyebrows quirked.

Laboriously, Barsanti changed position, every movement sluggish and clearly taking much more effort than normal, but just that he was stirring seemed to be a good sign. His breathing was the only sound in the room as he managed to sit up into a cross-legged position. He remained that way as if not quite trusting his balance.

Sal tapped him on the shoulder and handed him the glass. "Drink."

Barsanti glanced at him and for a few heartbeats, Sal expected him to ignore it or slap it out of his hand, but then he took it and drank the whiskey quickly, before handing back the glass. No "thank you", though Sal didn't begrudge him that.

"We still got business, you and I. You should change out of your clothes. Guys, I'll handle it. Take a break."

Enzo nodded to the doc and they both left. Sal crouched before Barsanti, who still sat there, looking a little more focused and clear-eyed than before.

"Handle what, exactly?" Barsanti's voice was raw from the coughing, but Sal was oddly relieved that he'd found some of his attitude.

"Getting you changed." Sal noticed Barsanti's head wound had also been looked after. He'd probably just split his scalp there.

Barsanti stared at him, now more cautious, even lightly alarmed.

"Believe it or not, that was the nicest option I had."

"Right. 'Nice'." Barsanti shook his head.

Sal grabbed him under the arms and pulled him up. Barsanti's movements were somewhat uncoordinated and came with a noticeable delay, like those of a drunk, but he helped. "I'm going to be even *nicer* and let you rest a while."

In truth, Sal also needed more time to think. If not for

the doc, he might have attempted torture again to pry open that crack—surely there was one when a man tried to kill himself. Nobody came out of a near-death experience without taking something emotional and deep from it.

"All right." Barsanti walked mostly under his own steam, while Sal guided him to the master bedroom, the only room in the whole damn house where there was some measure of privacy and Barsanti likely felt safest. He let go of Barsanti once they were past the door and crossed his arms, and broadened his stance while remaining in the doorway.

Barsanti moved like a much older man, and the coughing was near constant. He shed his shirt first and dropped it on the floor at his feet. Then the undershirt, revealing a body that Sal had already admired, if in a purely calculating way. Now that view had grown teeth and claws that dug into the animal parts of his brain. Barsanti was hot, in a "wholly unapproachable but unable to defend himself now" way.

Hands on the button of his slacks, Barsanti paused.

Sal pretended ignorance and kept his gaze fixed on Barsanti's face.

Eventually, Barsanti pulled down his trousers and boxers, kicked off his shoes and stepped out of his wet clothes, then pulled off his socks. He sat down on the bed, not a stitch of clothing left on him, and regarded his wrists, prodding the reddened, swollen areas. "While you're being so nice, can I make a phone call?"

Probably Beth. "Maybe. Going to say goodbye?"

Barsanti looked up. "There's a thing I need to fix, and ..." He lifted his shoulders and dropped them. "Ultimately, it won't matter, of course, but ..." He cleared his throat.

"Get dressed."

Barsanti shook himself and got up again, then walked to his closet, opened it and dressed after wiping himself down with a towel right there. Boxers, socks, undershirt. He didn't seem to have any truly casual clothes except workout stuff— just the same type of clothes he'd taken off, the same grey tailored slacks, the same black socks, black boxers, white undershirt and tailored white shirt. He ran a hand through his hair, too short to get untidy in anything but a fashionable way, then walked up to Sal and offered his wrists again.

Sal resisted the impulse to grab them and pull him closer. "What are you doing?"

"I didn't think you were going to risk my hands being free."

"Sure, but let's talk first." Sal had other angles of attack he hadn't used yet. He reached into his right thigh pocket and pulled out a fresh zip cuff. "What does Andrea have on you? Were you planning to take his place and he found you out? Why are you willing to kill yourself?"

"It's not about Andrea, and no, I don't see myself as boss either. I'm not like you."

"Huh. I think we're not that different, Jack."

Barsanti almost jumped when Sal said his first name. "I gotta say, you being 'nice' is even scarier than you pushing me under water." If that was a joke, it fell flat because his voice shook.

Can't imagine why. Sal placed the plastic loops around Barsanti's wrists and tightened them, again, leaving about a finger of space in either loop. "Bed?"

"I guess." Barsanti walked over to the side of the bed he apparently preferred and lay down on the covers. A quick inspection revealed two ways to tie him to the bed. To the side using one of the legs of the bed, or above his head using the frame underneath the headboard.

Sal chose the more comfortable option. Barsanti ended up lying on his side, tied hands fairly close to his chest, and the ties connected to the leg of the bed. It wasn't foolproof —but enough to ensure Barsanti couldn't escape in his present condition. As long as they checked on him regularly.

Sal sat next to Barsanti, noticed how the man seemed too exhausted to even try scooting away, though the restraints limited how far he'd be able to get. "Do you need anything else?" He surprised himself with that question, which would be more fitting in a wholly different context. Despite himself, though, he'd begun to respect Barsanti, and he'd decided to set Barsanti at ease for now while he took the time to think through his other options. But even though on a certain level it felt like a twisted kind of aftercare following rough play that had blown past the limits, it definitely wasn't a peace offering.

Barsanti closed his eyes. "No, just sleep."

Sal lingered, but Barsanti was shutting down while he watched. He cleared his throat or coughed a few times, but then his breath came easier and deepened, so Sal stood and left the master bedroom fetched his discarded wet clothes from upstairs, then dumped everything into the dryer before he joined the others in the kitchen.

The men sat at the breakfast bar, polishing off bowls of what looked like fresh tortelloni with green pesto.

"I hope you've left me some," Sal groused.

Enzo put his fork down and went back to the stovetop to pour more steaming tortelloni into a third bowl, then placed it before Sal along with a fork. Sal pushed himself onto one of the stools and focused on eating.

"How's the patient?" Enzo asked.

"Tied to the bed and sleeping. I'll keep an eye on him."

"This whole thing have anything to do with that master-plan of yours?" the doc asked.

Sal glanced up and then back onto his pasta. "First step. Trying to limit how much work you'll have to do. Avoid you having to do triage when things get hot."

"And what was that about restraints?"

"Recreational use." Sal grinned and reached for the large glass of water that Enzo had poured. "Give me a good length of rope and I'll wrap you up nicely for Christmas."

The doc chuckled but raised his hands as if in defense. "Not my scene."

"Don't worry. I'm not recruiting." Sal took several large gulps of water. "I thought we'd lost him for good. Army trained you well."

The doc gestured in a kind of circular motion. "These things can spin out of control. Had a hazing incident at the base where ... somebody got damaged more than was intended." He relayed it as a matter of fact.

"You involved?"

"No. Heard the rumors, though." The doc sighed deeply.

Sal left it at that. Everybody around this table and in this house had their secrets. He concentrated on his tortelloni and then placed the bowl in the sink. The combination of whiskey and carbs was already taking the edge off.

"I'll go check on him."

"Coffee, boss?"

"Later." He returned to Barsanti's bedroom, where he

settled in a corner on one of those designer chairs. The room darkened around him while he thought and waited. He shouldn't have worried about Barsanti, either. The man was out like a light. And for a while, all he did was listen to the man's raspy breathing. He'd never have thought that he'd pay this much attention to a sleeper's every inhale, every twitch of discomfort, every exhale, and then the moment of stillness that allowed doubt about the cycle continuing to creep in—this stillness could feel like the smallest of deaths, before the next gasping breath returned the sleeper to life.

21

Pure exhaustion pulled Jack under like a heavy, warm wave of nothing. He didn't, as a rule, remember his dreams. When he did, they were anxiety laden and all about having to be somewhere, but nobody had told him where, and the geography around him kept shifting until nothing made sense anymore. If it had been that dream again, that would have made sense, since that had bizarrely become his reality. But no.

Instead, his subconsciousness served up a gallery of hazy erotic scenes, and all the particulars evaporated when Jack awoke with a start, convinced he heard water sloshing around him. Being awake and aware meant being in pain again—his lungs felt as if they'd been scoured with barbed wire, and his chest and throat ached as though he'd been punched multiple times.

Rausa sat by the side of the bed and looked like he'd been there for a while, which gave Jack goosebumps. He tried to move his hands, but the ties were too short to do anything useful with them, so he rubbed his face. It was dark outside, the house calm and gloomy. The only illumination from the lamp on the far nightstand, and some golden light pouring in from the living room.

When he stayed here, Jack did his best to sleep in the middle of the bed, but the previous owners had liked their space—or maybe their orgies—and it was simply impossible to fill out a king size all by himself, especially since the bed he used most in town was a normal double. If felt like there was too much space that he had never claimed and didn't know how to. Not a problem he'd continue to have, though.

"If I let you make a phone call, who would you call? Beth?"

Jack tensed—had she called again? Rausa shouldn't have been able to answer it without the PIN, but maybe he'd figured out a way into his phone. Maybe he'd somehow accessed the voicemail. Shit, maybe he'd called her? How much did he know?

"She's a friend. And she isn't part of any of this. She's just a friend." Shit, he was babbling. But seeing Rausa's face so close, and almost feeling the heat from his body, maybe babbling was natural. He should just have mercy on his vocal cords and shut up.

"A friend or pet?"

"What?"

"Answer my question. What does a guy like you have to do with a woman like that?"

"You talked to her?"

"I did." Rausa cracked a half-smile. "And I'm curious."

Oh God. "I helped her out. She attached herself to me, God knows why. I don't mind her. We've become friends, but she knows nothing. She thinks I'm a consultant."

"Shit." Rausa chuckled. "You're pretty good, but clearly addled."

"Did you threaten her?"

Rausa stood. "After we played submarine, you scoffed at the idea that it was actually the nicer option. But it was, because the alternative would have been to send a couple of men to pick up sweet little Beth at home and bring her to a nice, quiet place with good soundproofing. Then transmit the video for us to watch together live. Four or five mean guys can break a woman like that down in a couple hours at most."

With her history, one guy could break her down in half an hour or less. Jack's stomach clenched so hard he felt ready to throw up at the suggestion, and his face grew numb. "You don't have any fucking idea what she's been through."

"Life's a bitch, Jack. We both know that better than most."

Yeah, maybe. They surely weren't good Samaritans. Neither of them would have gotten where they were without stepping on people to make money. Both of them needed to be respected, and that could easily involve teaching some-body to be respectful who hadn't been so inclined at the start. But people like Beth weren't a threat to anybody. The best Jack could have done was help her back on her feet and then cut off all contact. And yet not even twenty-four hours before, he'd been willing to pull her into all this darkness. Where she would have met sharks like Rausa. And all to save his own neck.

Jack gathered himself, breathed deeply a few times to test his lungs. It hurt, and there was a tickle in his bronchi, but the worst of the coughing seemed past. "But you're right. I'd rather you do this shit to me than to her."

"What? You want to spend a couple hours getting gang-raped?" Rausa said it jokingly, but there was calculation in his eyes.

Jack swallowed. "You know exactly what I mean."

"I do. But you should remember that, yes, I'm playing nice right now, but not for a lack of imagination or resources." Rausa reached for his belt, freed the multi-tool from its holster and unfolded it.

"Why play nice? I'm a dead man, surely. And we both know I'm not going to haunt your conscience. Especially with all the dying that's going to happen on both sides when your war starts. The dying you're apparently itching for." Shit, he was getting angry, and he was way too exposed to backlash. "Listen, you can still turn around. You can still stop this."

"And you'll sit across from me at the negotiation table and remember how I almost killed you a few times?" Rausa placed one side of the multi-tool precisely against the zip cuff that held the restraints around Jack's wrists. "And pretend nothing happened?"

"If that's what it takes." Jack tried to meet the other man's gaze, but couldn't quite. He had no idea how he'd live in the same city as Sal Rausa after everything that had happened. If he survived this in spite of the odds, the first thing he'd do was call Beth and tell her to leave Port Francis and the state, to change her name and her appearance and never try to call or contact him ever again.

The second thing he'd do was activate Plan B and prepare his own retirement. It would involve some play-acting for Andrea's benefit and the rest of the organization, and a couple days in a hospital to recover from a "heart attack" or similar—he was pretty sure he could talk to a friendly doctor about how to appear unfit for work. That way, Andrea wouldn't think he'd sold him to the Feds or worse. Except of course, Plan B looked shaky at best now.

"Maybe I've come to respect you, Jack Barsanti. You're old-fashioned as fuck, but you're smart and strong."

Jack blinked, shocked that Rausa would say such a thing. Then again, he could be magnanimous because he held all the cards. Easy to talk up an enemy you could dispose of. It meant nothing. Still. Maybe he could use it somehow. "Leave Beth alone. Please. Even after I'm gone. Leave her in peace."

"Dying man's wish?" Rausa snapped the plastic in two places and picked up the cuff when it fell. He stuffed it into his thigh pocket, but kept the multi-tool in one hand.

"I guess. When you kill me, obviously I won't care anymore, but—fuck, please. She's never harmed anyone." Appealing to Sal Rausa's softer side felt like begging a tiger, but maybe that "respect" he claimed to feel gave Jack a foothold.

Rausa's eyes darkened. He holstered the multi-tool and pressed the metallic button down with a soft click, then sat down on the bed and placed a large strong hand flat on Jack's chest, fingers splayed. "You can take this the wrong way, Jack, but you're really fucking hot when you beg."

For a few heart-pounding moments, Jack was completely speechless. Nobody had ever dared touch him like that. Well, not true. There had been an incident when a man in a bar in Las Vegas had groped him—luckily he'd been alone, so all he'd done was turn around and push the guy away. There had been other unsubtle moves from a number of men over the years, but Jack treated them with the same indifference as he'd always responded to women. Though with women at least he didn't have to worry about witnesses thinking he'd somehow invited the attention. If any of his men had doubts about Jack's masculinity, it'd never been whispered loud enough to hear.

This now, this ... he didn't have a frame of reference for this. The same man who'd threatened the one innocent on the planet that Jack cared about, the same man who laconically called drowning "playing submarine" and promised to kill Jack after all of this was over, just touched him like this, demonstratively, provocatively. More than that, he'd halfway untied Jack before he did it. The same who casually told him he fucked his capo but also shook with rage when he'd talked about his dead wife. As cunning as Rausa was, his emotions were ... raw. Pure. Powerful.

All his life, Jack had learned over and over again that emotions were a weakness. The old consigliere had offered only one piece of advice: don't ever blink. And in prison, if he'd shown fear or weakness, or just how much those walls had been closing in on him, everybody in there would have seen it, smelled it on him. And the same back when he'd been a capo. Had he lain awake at night and tied himself in knots about making one of his big plays, the gambles and schemes that had recommended him as consigliere in the first place? He sure as hell had. Other made men could fuck and snort and drink that tension away, but Jack had always known the moment his senses blurred, and his control slipped, that darker truth about him could come out, so he never let it happen.

"You're really fucking hot when you beg."

Ears ringing, he rolled fully onto his back, hands lifted so they didn't touch Rausa's. It was hard to breathe underneath that touch. His body responded to the contact, the heat, the promise of pleasure, even though Jack tried to hold onto the fact that "the promise of pleasure" was really only an absence of fresh pain right now. If he did invite more of this, exploited what seemed like attraction from Sal Rausa, could he gain any control of the situation? He knew from his job that a lot of men got themselves into trouble for sex.

Sal Rausa was attractive, and Jack's own body was interested; there was no need to fake anything. But would he be able to ignore the fact that Rausa was his torturer, maybe his executioner, and get past the fear of him? Could he loosen his self-control enough to allow himself to use sex as leverage? Exactly how he was meant to do that when he'd never used sex for anything? How to seduce a man when all of this was new territory? His experience so far was comprised of *resisting* any attempts at seduction, so not much help there.

What if Sal Rausa turned the tables on him and humiliated Jack further? If Jack tried this, he was committed, and there was no way to back out. Rausa would then have the power to hurt him in totally new ways. It didn't matter. If Rausa wanted to fuck him, he would, whether Jack was willing or not. But Jack couldn't resist the hope to gain just a scrap of leverage.

"You want to hear me beg again?"

"Yeah." Rausa gave him a lop-sided grin, a dangerous glimmer in his eyes.

"Please leave Beth alone. She's not—"

"Enough. Stop talking about her. It's messing with my boner, Jesus." Rausa chuckled. "Sorry, but she's not my type. You don't fuck small birds that have fallen from their nest. You just don't."

One thing they could agree on, Jack assumed. "She's had it pretty rough."

"I said, stop talking about her." Rausa's voice was low and held no edge, but the authority was still there. Interesting to witness Rausa wield a much quieter power than brute force. "We both know you don't want to fuck her. Or any other woman."

Jack swallowed and said nothing. He couldn't imagine how Rausa knew that. Maybe because a red-blooded male responded differently? He should shove Rausa away in anger, insult him and his lineage, but he found himself quite mesmerized by that single point of contact.

Rausa winked at him. "And always thinking. You're never not thinking."

"Not thinking is dangerous," Jack said quietly.

"In the big picture, you couldn't be in more danger than this." Rausa slowly moved his hand to the side, to cover Jack's left pec, brushing over his nipple. The sensation was a sharp dart through his body, soothed by the slowly moving heat.

Jack should use his elbow to push the hand away. This touch was more than a simple squeeze of his ass, or a wink, or a number scribbled on a paper napkin. Strangely, now Jack wished he'd been more reckless in the past, so at least he would die knowing what it felt like. But even more than that, he hadn't realized how much he'd longed for touch—a friendly one, or a deliberate one, rather than an accidental or threatening one. The intensity of this caress was unbearable—Rausa this close, watching him, maybe truly seeing him.

"You're never not thinking."

How ironic, maybe, that of all people in the world, Rausa would be the one to recognize him.

"Does Andrea know about you?"

Jack tried to keep his face neutral, because the whole trajectory of the conversation was disturbing, yet he couldn't think of a way to change it. "Know what?"

Rausa squeezed his nipple between two fingers and Jack jerked involuntarily. "I can't quite figure out what you are, Jack Barsanti, but you're not straight. And not quite vanilla either."

"Are you fucking saying I enjoyed drowning?"

Rausa regarded him with amusement and a strange heat in his eyes. "Anger. Always good. You heard what I said."

The truth was, Rausa was possibly right. Jack found himself unable to tear himself out of this situation, and, heaven help him, he liked the touch too much. The mix of pleasure and that lingering fear of death had twisted his brain and slowed him down.

"Where do you think this is going?" Jack asked.

"Unlike you, I'm following my gut." Rausa slowly moved his hand across to Jack's right pec, and the deliberateness made Jack nearly squirm. He was glad there were two layers of cloth between Rausa's fingers and his skin—without those, he'd be losing his mind.

"You must have a plan?"

"Big picture stuff right now." Rausa grinned at him. "Though, honestly, I wish I had more time with you. I'll be annoyed to have to smash up a half-solved puzzle box."

Annoyed. That was one way of phrasing it. He'd be *annoyed* when he killed Jack. He had to focus on that. Death. Not Rausa's touch. Rausa was mocking and manipulating him, using that one weakness against him, and what a weakness it was. The old consigliere had been right— emotion and losing his nerve were the two things that could unmake him, in more senses than one. But dragging himself back from the precipice took everything Jack had and he wasn't even sure why he should. Falling could be so easy.

If he could let himself do it, maybe he could reverse this situation, get under Sal Rausa's skin, though that seemed like a terrifying place to be. But with death so close, there was no point denying himself one selfish pleasure—feeling what it was like with a man, feeling all of it, hunger, need, hell, even desire. Everything else was decided, everything he'd sacrificed that part of himself for was gone now, stripped away.

Rausa re-centered his hand on Jack's sternum, and then slid it further down, to where the hard cage of bones ended and only muscle protected him. From here, angled upward, a knife would stab him right in the heart. Judging by the gleam in Rausa's eyes, he knew that too.

"I can't tell whether you're turned on or scared or both, but your heart's racing like hell."

Jack swallowed but didn't dare to look away or close his eyes. "I got no answer."

"It wasn't a question." Rausa chuckled and that slight vibration went right into Jack's chest. His hand traveled lower, and Jack's muscles tensed. He had to stop this, needed to stop it, but Rausa knew, damn him.

Rausa moved to straddle Jack's knees without removing his hand. He was momentarily unbalanced, and Jack might have been able to kick him away since his legs were free, but he couldn't move. Didn't want to. His tied wrists were almost tucked under his chin, an awkward compromise between avoiding touching Sal's hand and making himself more vulnerable by placing them above his head.

"Do you ... do you this to everyone after tying them up?"

Rausa laughed. "My God, so coy. If I thought you did that on purpose ..." He put the other hand on Jack's hip. "I'd say you were doing it to turn me on."

"Coy? Fuck you. You tortured me."

"Yep, I did. And this is different." Rausa's hand moved to his groin, but his touch became lighter, using just a couple of fingers to trace the outline of Jack's cock. Jack squirmed, torn between outraged and *not nearly enough*. He'd briefly entertained doing this as leverage, but the truth was that Rausa had the upper hand in this game too. He could do whatever he wanted, fuck him, rape him, ask his two friends to join, hell, call a few more friends while he was at it, and Jack had nothing.

"This isn't a fear erection, Jack. I'm not going to flatter myself and think this is specifically for me, but right now I'm the only guy who can do something about it."

"What are you ... what's your game? Humiliate me before you put a bullet in my head?"

Rausa's features darkened. "Is that all you're feeling? Humiliated?"

Exhilarated, scared, turned on, embarrassed. To start. "You're going to kill me. I've accepted that. So it's really fucking hard to get into this, if that's what you want. You're just torturing me again." Jack realized he was nearly panting.

22

Humiliation. Sal was happy to give it to people who craved it. He sometimes did it to others to make a point, but he didn't sleep with those people.

But Jack Barsanti had moved onto a kind of twilight edge, somehow. This wasn't purely business anymore, but also not personal. Barsanti wasn't one of those tech millionaires in their thirties or forties that Port Francis was good at producing and which, whether married or not, formed part of Sal's sexual diet.

Fuck, drowning somebody wasn't keeping their dignity intact, either, yet Barsanti somehow clung to at least erotic self-determination. Hands tied, physically restrained and controlled, and this was the hill he chose to die on? Yes. In a matter of speaking.

Sal was so tempted to brush that resistance aside, because while Barsanti's head battled him, his body didn't. He wouldn't put up a real fight, and maybe Barsanti would play ball better if teased and turned on enough. Sal was patient like a rock when it mattered, and if the reward was big enough—he could tease and edge Barsanti all night and only fuck him when the man was begging him for it. And how much fun that would be, if only it were possible.

There was something very compelling about making a guy like Barsanti come apart like that, and it would undoubtedly be hotter than hearing him beg to protect somebody else.

If Sal had been younger, brasher, he'd have continued. Before Catia taught him that self-control was even more important than controlling the other. And Barsanti was in the twilight space where some of those rules should apply. If Sal wanted to look at himself in the mirror later, anyway.

Meeting Barsanti's eyes, he kept his hands where they were. If Barsanti told Sal what he needed to know, Andrea would either have him executed the moment it was discovered, or there would be such a large price put on his head that Barsanti would have to run to the ends of the earth. Even if nobody caught up with him, he'd be a hunted man for the rest of his life. Killing him here, after extracting the information, could be considered a kindness. He'd never killed anyone he'd fucked before. He wondered if he could.

"To answer your question, Jack, and because I'm in a nice mood, yes, I sometimes tie up my lovers. What about you? Any fuzzy handcuffs in your life?"

Barsanti looked more bewildered than ashamed. "No."

How a man who looked like Barsanti seemingly had such a narrow range of experience mystified Sal. How could every single past lover have failed to dress that defined physique in chains or restraints? With that skin tone and the light eyes, he'd look stunning in electric blue or maybe bottle green ropes. Wine red was out—that was Catia's color.

"Sal?"

Sal turned his head and saw Enzo standing in the door. Not admonishing, not scandalized or in the least disturbed. "What's up?"

"Just checking in."

Yeah, as much fun as this had been, he needed to focus. After his nap, Barsanti seemed to have recovered some of his sass, but Sal was no closer to getting the answers he needed. "I'll join you guys in a few minutes."

He waited for Enzo to withdraw, then ran his hand back up to Barsanti's sternum. "Let's say I'm going to forget that Beth exists, what's it worth to you?"

Barsanti's eyes closed, and tension returned to his body. "How can I trust you?"

"Is trust a luxury you can afford right now? Besides, as I said, I talked to her. She's nice and her death could lead to complications. Not enough reason to take her off the table as leverage, but I'm not going out of my way to machinegun puppies."

"Six eight ... two three." Barsanti opened his eyes. "That's the phone."

"And the laptop?"

Jack nodded. "Capital ... T, small p, number two, small p, small i, small h, underscore." There. That was it. The crack and the leverage to widen it enough that he could slip into Barsanti's resistance.

"Repeat that."

"It's the first letters of a sentence. Christ."

"What's the sentence?"

"'The path to paradise begins in hell'. 'To' replaced by the number."

Sal chuckled, immensely pleased that he had something to work with and it made him feel a lot more generous. "Aren't you a deep guy."

"It's Dante's *Inferno*." Delivered in a tone as if he didn't expect Sal to be a big reader or know who Dante Alighieri had been.

"As a password, it's not too bad, but it's too short." Sal squeezed Barsanti's shoulder. "All right, that's sweet little Beth saved. Good job. But next I'll have questions about your organization. Andrea. The capos. The soldiers. I'll need to know everything."

And again, Barsanti shut down, but not before Sal noticed the despair and loathing flashing across his features. At this point, Barsanti had more reasons to spill the rest than withhold it, but it seemed his pride was rearing its head again. With anybody else, Sal would have applied pressure, administered another beating, or gone back on his word and brought Beth back into play, but some part of him wanted to make this last part as easy on Barsanti as possible under the circumstances. Maybe it was the attraction, maybe it was respect.

Sal dismounted from both man and bed. He tied Barsanti again, then left the master bedroom. He briefly wondered what Enzo had made of Barsanti's state of arousal—he'd likely noticed. Maybe he'd thought Sal was playing his usual games with the enemy. Enzo was intimately aware that arousal and power were both very complicated indeed.

The doc sat in the living room jabbing and poking at his

phone as blips and music came from the tiny speaker. Enzo stood near the window, staring out into the darkness.

"Hey, doc. I need to ask him some more questions. He seems to be breathing okay, but maybe you have something more elegant to get him to talk?"

The doc put the phone down and straightened. "How clear does he need to be?"

"Pretty clear. He needs to remember things." Sal shrugged.

In his experience, some men were physically strong, some intellectually, others emotionally. Or spiritually, whatever one wanted to call it. Barsanti was physically strong, and clearly intellectually too. Spiritually—he had no truck with that. If Barsanti had any issues with God or the saints about what he'd done in his life, Sal had no idea how to exploit them. He'd end up in the same circle of hell, no doubt. Emotionally—Barsanti had shown cracks. Sal could have made good on his threats, but Barsanti already feared him, hated him most likely. And maybe that bothered Sal a little, and not just because Barsanti was hot. In a different life, he could easily imagine caring about how Barsanti regarded him—caring about whether he respected him too.

The doc nodded. "Yeah, I got something. What do you reckon he weighs?"

"A hundred-seventy-ish. Ten to fifteen percent body fat, I'd say."

"That tallies with what I thought." The doc dove down to dig around in his bag and straightened with a small black case in hand. Sal had seen similar ones in the hands of diabetics, but when the doc unzipped it, it held a couple syringes and two small medical vials. "Can you immobilize an arm for me?"

"No problem." He motioned Enzo to come along, and together, they returned to the master bedroom, where Barsanti lay exactly as Sal had left him.

Barsanti seemed oddly complacent, considering he had to know what it all meant. And now that his mind had gone there, those zip cuffs struck Sal as crude and painful. He could easily have tied up Barsanti much more elegantly, without so much as reddening his skin. Though Barsanti wouldn't appreciate the offer to use braided rope instead of that sharp-edged plastic.

"Gonna help you out, Barsanti."

Barsanti tensed up and gritted his teeth. "'Help me out'."

Sal grinned back and freed Barsanti's left arm, pushing the shirt sleeve up before pressing his arm flat against the mattress.

The doc walked in, drawing a syringe from one of the vials. He checked the amount of liquid in the syringe, then tapped the needle and knelt on the floor next to the bed. Deft fingers traced and found a vein, rubbed a piece of gauze along the skin, then gently and precisely pierced it with the needle. He hesitated. "I should ask about allergies to painkillers ..." and then he grinned.

Barsanti snorted and it could almost have been laughter.

"I guess he's fine." The doc emptied the syringe into Barsanti's arm, then pulled the needle out. He stashed everything in a small black case he pulled from a trouser pocket. There was a spark in his eyes. "That's my type of 'recreational', you'll see."

Sal ran his hands along Barsanti's arm and then released it. "What is it?"

"House mix." The doc tilted his head and looked at Barsanti, who made an odd sound, a kind of release of breath, but not quite a sigh, not quite a groan. "Intravenously, it's instant. Also kicks like a mule with a grudge." The doc seemed genuinely delighted.

Sal chuckled and freed Jack's other hand. "You freak." With fascination, he watched Barsanti's shoulders relax and sink into the mattress as tension drained away. He was so tempted to run his hands over Barsanti's chest and the rest of his body. Some men didn't even flinch when you damn near chewed their nipples off, but Barsanti was sensitive there. A touch had been enough to get his attention. "You said it's instant."

"Yep. Look." The doc waved toward Barsanti.

Jack Barsanti's breathing was deeper and easier, shoulders and arms relaxed, knees opening a little, though shudders passed through him, and one of his feet twitched restlessly. Damn, that change was something to behold. His eyes were open, but his lids seemed heavy, and his gaze was turned inward.

"Shit. That's a nasty fucking mule."

"Trust me, he's having fun," the doc said.

Enzo cleared his throat. "Might be a good way to kill him if you don't want to use a bullet. Make it look like an OD. Lo Cascio would freak if his consigliere turned out to have been a junkie."

"And it's strong enough that people get the dose wrong all the time," the doc agreed.

Sal looked at Barsanti, twitches in his face betraying

something, though Sal had no idea what. Was he fighting for clarity? To speak? Or responding to two guys plotting his murder out loud?

Sal rolled his shoulders and sat down on the side of the bed. "Do you hear me, Jack? I need names, addresses, and passwords."

He needed to know everything Barsanti knew about every single member of the Lo Cascio ... where they lived, who they fucked, what cars they drove. And where Andrea was hiding his money, everything about his bank accounts, his shell companies. Everything. And he would get it.

23

Jack couldn't decide whether he was feeling light and dizzy, or warm and heavy. Both. The injection had poured liquid heat into his arm, from where it rapidly spread through his whole body, and he could feel and hear his pulse thunder in his ears. An unfamiliar feeling of joy bloomed in his brain, in his heart, a sense of complete happiness and sparking euphoria, as if he could shrug the restraints off and walk away, unharmed, through a hail of bullets. He'd never felt so strong and at the same time so peaceful in his life.

And yet, when he opened his eyes, his surroundings felt unreal, though he couldn't work out whether they'd changed. They must have, their outlines alternately blurred then sharpened, though lacked depth. The wood paneling seemed too bright, lit from within. The pain in his head was gone. He felt no pain at all. The lightness changed, and with it, he could no longer figure out where his body was, or what position it was in. He thought his arms were lying at his sides, but he couldn't perceive them, and his clothes caught on his skin as if it were sandpaper. But then his body simply faded, like a lever slowly pushing down and with it, any awareness of heavy or warm or restrained or throbbing diminished and then completely ceased to exist.

A good-looking man—Sal Rausa—sat next to him, but he, too wasn't quite real. Jack blinked, couldn't figure out how long he'd looked at him. Hours? Time had stopped. Nothing to keep track of.

"Listen to me, Jack. Tell me everything you know about Andrea's business operations." His voice was too loud.

There was a reason to not answer, but it didn't seem real, didn't seem important at all. He could have been watching a TV show, but he wasn't the audience. He was watching the audience that was watching. Not quite a dream. It took forever between wanting to move his mouth and doing it, and the lag disoriented him even more. He couldn't move, didn't want to, and couldn't grasp onto any thought—his head was simply empty, and somehow that was a tremendous relief and a heavenly pleasure.

When he spoke, he had the distinct feeling he was rambling, and as if he were losing track of what he was saying. He had no control of the words. They appeared on his tongue without first hitting his brain.

Was Rausa repeating the same question? Had they talked about this already? He couldn't remember.

Rausa spoke. Questioned. Touched his face, though the touch was far away and happened to somebody else.

Jack wanted to curl into him. He believed Rausa had been in this room with him for their whole lives and there was nothing outside of it. The brightness increased. Light outside. Sun. Slowly, slowly, Jack's body returned to him as if melting out of wax, though for an eternity he was convinced that all his joints were put together wrong so he couldn't move them, but that feeling faded as well, and he slowly regained an understanding of where his limbs were.

He basked in the total relaxation and warmth in his body, and the maddening pleasure of breathing and looking into the sunlight, glaring as it was.

Sal Rausa leaned over him, took his face in his hands and placed a kiss on his forehead. "Unbelievable, Jack. You're phenomenal."

A trembling passed through him at the touch and the praise. He lifted his head from the pillow, bleary, struggling to focus. "Do ... do that again."

Rausa raised an eyebrow, but took his head in his hands and kissed his forehead again. "Feel good?"

Sal grinned and stroked over Jack's face with his thumbs. "Fuck, you're still so out of it."

"It's good. It's really good."

Sal turned away and talked to the other two men who'd been in the room, left, and then came back a few times, if he remembered right. "Enzo, get in touch with your buddies. Use what we have to refine the plan. Doc, do you want to go home?"

"Probably for the best, though I can grab another nap on the couch."

"We're done here. I don't think we'll need you again. Not for this."

Sal touched Jack's face again, skin rough against his stubble. And his chest, almost too intense, too much. "Fuck, I wish I could ..." Sal said.

"I need to go to the bathroom." As blissful as it was, just lying here, his bladder kept nagging him.

Rausa paused. "Can you move?"

"I'll try." Sal helped him up, and despite knowing that somehow his limbs were detached and mismatched, his body mostly obeyed, though his sense of balance was shot and he leaned too heavily into Sal, who walked him into the bathroom. He withdrew somewhat while Jack wrestled with his clothes and then managed to sit and do his business. Sal only assisted again when Jack stood and headed for the sink, offering him a towel.

The way back to the bedroom took too much effort so Jack shuffled to the couch in the living room and sat down. But even sitting up took too much focus, so he stretched out sideways.

Sal looked down at him. "I can't quite tell whether it's a comedown or a second phase."

"I feel good."

Sal knelt next to him and ran a hand over Jack's chest. Jack lifted a hand and placed it on top of Sal's. As his body returned to awareness, so did the pleasure of that touch, and he wanted more of it, so he pushed Sal's hand under his shirt and onto his bare skin. He pushed Sal's hand down as he tugged his shirt up, until he felt the fingertips slide down across his stomach. A thousand small sparks lit up, and Jack groaned with the pleasure. He tried to unbutton his shirt but failed. "Help me."

Sal carefully unbuttoned his shirt and pulled it off, and Jack managed to shed the undershirt next. Sal regarded him with an unashamed hunger and arousal that lit up every inch of Jack's skin.

"All right, I'm opting for a second phase," Sal said. "And I guess it no longer makes a difference, right, Jack? Whether I'm the one to touch you or someone else does."

"No." Jack directed Sal's hands to his body and squirmed beneath the caresses. Sal ran his fingers over every inch of his exposed skin, explored and stroked every muscle, every line, every dip and hollow. Not enough. He pushed Sal's hands lower and was pitifully grateful when the man opened his belt and worked his pants and boxers down over his cock and past his balls. He'd imagined what being touched like this would feel like, had dreamed about it, but now that it was happening, he felt elated and reckless and sexy in his own skin. That Sal was the first man to touch him was fitting and oddly wonderful, though his hand around Jack's cock made him gasp—the heat and roughness of that grip was altogether breathtaking.

Sal took his hand away and Jack was about to protest when Sal shushed him. "I'll make it better. Back in a second." He stood, walked away and Jack took that moment to pull his trousers and boxers down further, though it seemed impossible to get past his feet. Fuck it.

Sal returned and knelt down again. His hand was slick now, and that same slickness then covered Jack's cock. The grip was strong, though the strokes were slow and intense, the slick palm adding a slight twist that was different from how Jack did it himself but completely mesmerizing. He closed his eyes because another man's hand stroking him was overwhelming, but also because he wanted to focus on the sensation, of friction and tightness and heat and slickness. When Sal sped up, he was ready to come, pushing up into the man's hand, but then Sal slowed down again, and

Jack balled his hands into fists. Though it felt so good when Sal squeezed his balls in the other hand. "Please."

"Say 'please Sal.' I have a name."

"Sal, please."

"All right." Sal began jerking him faster again, oh so skillfully, timing those strokes just right, and when orgasm began rolling in, tightening every muscle in his body, Sal's mouth suddenly covered his.

Jack was too breathless for a kiss, overwhelmed when his orgasm hit and he came over Sal's hand, but the kiss wrecked what was left of his mind—a greedy, openmouthed, hot, wet affair that was as dizzying as it was new. Even once his orgasm was over and he came crashing down, heart pounding almost painfully in his chest, Sal still kissed him. Jack couldn't think, just mirrored Sal's kiss, and soon lost himself completely in the taste and heat that was Sal Rausa.

24

Jack Barsanti was a fucking mess and Sal loved it. Whatever stuff the doc had shot straight into his blood had changed everything. And despite how fucked up Barsanti was, he still remembered everything. Every detail. Every name. Numbers—fuck, the guy had a mind for numbers and could recite passwords, phone numbers, account numbers and even balances down to the cent. At first, Sal had been skeptical that a man, who at times looked around with rolling eyes as if struggling to recognize where he was, could correctly recall account numbers, but when he looped back after an hour and asked for that account again, he got the same answer.

What kind of man kept the really important information exclusively in his head? This one did. And, well, it made sense. It was a place the Feds would find a lot harder to raid, because to Sal's knowledge, the Feds relied on leverage that didn't come in a small glass bottles.

What impressed him most was how Jack's words

remained understandable throughout, though he could get vague and muddled and wander off the point, adding details that seemed to come so far from left field that he and Enzo had looked at each other, puzzled, but the doc seemed less surprised. Same with the pauses he needed before responding—they seemed a little longer than even for a thoughtful answer, but again, whenever Sal grew impatient, the doc told him that was to be expected.

Jack seemed drunk or overly tired to Sal, except for that sharpness of recollection, and the mix was weird.

"That's quite the truth serum."

"Nah, it's a happy side effect. He could still lie, but lying is a pretty complex process, and we derailed him a lot. Also, after that first session, the question is if he would still want to lie. So vote's out."

"What's in that shit?"

"Based on ketamine. Ketamine is fun, you should try it."

"I can't for the life of me understand why you'd want to get so fucked up."

"It's really intense and pleasant."

It seemed to help with the guilt and hesitation to sell his whole damn organization out, and also with whatever loyalty he felt to Andrea. What was interesting was the flatness with which he responded to questions—none of that tension or the constant attempts to out-think and out-race Sal, but also, it didn't come with any suffering.

Sal felt his own exhaustion as the night pushed on; some small bites from the kitchen and shots of coffee could only do so much after all that intensity. While the doc offered to give him what he called an "upper", he'd declined, because he needed his judgment intact and, frankly, seeing Jack

ALEKSANDR VOINOV

Barsanti coming totally apart after an injection was another counter-argument. He needed his wits about him and while he liked the doc and was more than happy about the man's contribution, he wasn't going to trust him or offer his arm.

Any last lingering doubts that Jack was much more together than he pretended to be fled when he had to help him walk. But how they'd got from there to Jack insisting that Sal touch him and all but begging for sex was a mystery. And that resolute statement that it didn't matter whether it was Sal or anybody else—it almost made Sal laugh, because after all that coyness and composure Jack had displayed, this was new. It was refreshing. And maybe, after everything he'd put Jack through, he owed him a handjob. It wasn't like he wasn't getting anything out of it. He loved the moment when the barriers came down, instinct took over, and urges ran the show. It made him feel alive and needed.

But that kiss. Yeah, well, he was a kisser. He also kissed Enzo, though never casually or outside the bed. Jack wasn't in a state to push him away, but he'd gotten really into the kissing, and it had been Sal who'd turned away in the end because he was too close to losing control. Jack on the couch, smelling of sex, blissed out and blurred around the edges and still uncoordinated hit several of his buttons—he could have lain down next to him and rested until they'd slept or recovered or both. Or he could have stripped him to the skin, pushed up his legs, and fucked him then and there. Or he could have rested first and then started again, seduced him and take that last bit of him that Sal wanted.

Control.

But he wanted Jack to feel it.

Alcohol, drugs, all of that could be good fun with a

206

partner you knew well, but Sal wanted Jack Barsanti clear-eyed and with a clear mind. He'd ripped through the man's defenses for information, but when it came to sex, that moment of surrender, of yielding was so much better if it was a choice. It already felt weird that Jack had been so startled by the kiss, seemed so tentative, so hesitant in those first few moments. It seemed *he* wasn't a kisser.

Sal drew a deep breath while he watched Jack drift off, then shook his head. It would be at least two hours until Enzo returned, and unless he wanted to tie Jack up again, he couldn't afford to sleep yet. Still, the man didn't pose a threat now. He'd given up everything. He could possibly attempt to escape or fight back, though Sal didn't expect him to do either.

A knife or gun was a great leveler, though, so better safe than sorry. Which meant the idea of having a cold shower to shock him awake was out. Too bad. His banked arousal made him restless, especially with Jack spread out temptingly.

He forced himself to sit down with Barsanti's phone and laptop, and typed "6823" into Barsanti's phone. Interestingly, its content was pretty bare, and intentionally so. The mail app held about fifty emails in total—mostly confirmations of services Barsanti had booked, such as dry cleaning, or reservations for tables in restaurants, though he didn't seem to entertain a lot. There were a couple bookings for two people, but it seemed Barsanti mostly ate alone. Meanwhile, the "Sent" folder was empty, and so were the ones for junk mail and deleted messages. An investment app told him that he had "new documents", but it didn't include a link, and Sal wasn't that interested in how much Barsanti had in investments. Living in this kind of house and driving that kind of car outside, it was clear the man was comfortable. Some made men blew everything on sex and drugs, fast cars and mistresses, but Barsanti struck him as more circumspect.

No photos. Browser history cleared. Call history empty. Seemed Jack Barsanti relied entirely on that phenomenal memory of his. A text message from a number that was likely Beth's: *Tried to reach you, please call me back.*

Sal called voice mail and listened to her. "Jack, this is Beth. I hope you're well. I've had some time to sleep on it, and I think we should talk. I'm free tomorrow, so let me know. Please take care. Call me!"

She did sound worried but also tried to hide it, likely for Barsanti's sake. Sal assumed Barsanti didn't have the slightest clue how much Beth worried about him. While she obviously couldn't know that her worries were more than justified, maybe some part of her did catch how serious the situation was. She seemed good at interpreting emotions.

A reading app, but flicking through the books didn't flag anything special that would have attracted Sal's attention. Seemed mostly business related. Barsanti's music app had rock and pop music, a few jazz compilations, and again nothing special.

And, despite all of the many apps he could have had, not a single dating app. No hook-up apps, not gay, not straight, nor those that catered to both. Huh.

The extensive collection of Queen albums was possibly the only truly gay thing on that phone. Barsanti had been willing to die to protect this? Maybe the clues were on the laptop.

He opened it and typed in the password.

The background desktop was tidy, making him expect

the worst, but while the mail app was synched to the phone and thus held nothing of any value, there were spreadsheets and text documents, though all of them were locked. Painstakingly, Sal had to match every single doc and spreadsheet to the long list of passwords Jack had given them. It was a long fucking list.

There they were, Andrea Lo Cascio's business activities, at least one of the things they'd come for. These seemed to be only the legal businesses, or businesses made to look legal—whether they actually were was a different matter. But in any case, after a quick skim of the spreadsheets, Sal estimated Andrea Lo Cascio's various interests were worth mid-eight figures. A lot of income would be cash, other inflows looked legal because the Lo Cascio would obscenely overcharge to account for their "fees" and "consulting". There were letters to various lawyers about contracts and ongoing activities.

All of this would be useful when it came to picking the meat off the bones after neutralizing the Lo Cascio. Some of these cash flows would be redirected into Sal's pockets, others would be leverage.

A while later, he closed the documents and opened the browser. He didn't expect much going through the few bookmarks, but then scrolled down and hesitated over a familiar link. More than familiar. So, Barsanti didn't use hook-up apps, he didn't even like any YouTube videos, and wasn't subscribed to anything, but that one saved link went to a large porn site. Mixed porn, so not in itself a problem.

Sal clicked on "log in" and was taken to a login screen. This was one of the sites that made him a pretty penny each month, and he now had access to Jack Barsanti's email—and yes, it seemed Jack had used that one to register, because sending a password reset link to the man's inbox worked.

Jack, Jack. You use a throwaway for that kind of thing.

Such a Generation X mistake to make.

Probably not such a big surprise that Barsanti had subscribed. The team had plastered Port Francis in virtual advertising, in part because it had tickled Catia to, as she'd put it, "walk incognito in Port Francis as its God-Empress of Porn." As the site had grown, so had the money inflow, and then it was network effects all the way down. After the War, with his family suffering and on the retreat, Sal had doubled down on this site and others. The benefit was almost nothing about online porn or online high-stakes gambling and poker required any kneecapping. Without that money, going invisible would have destroyed his family, and Sal had dealt with those dinosaurs who'd disagreed with his strategy.

Sal reset the password and logged into Barsanti's account, but this was where his lucky streak ended. Barsanti had cleared his browsing history, which should have been the end of it.

Would have been for anyone else.

But Sal pulled his tablet closer and switched it on. He went into Barsanti's account details and pulled his user ID. Then he used the tablet to log into the site's back end and fed the customer number in.

The site had started as Catia's side project and was successful because the algorithm that suggested "what you might like" was top notch, all powered by a sophisticated tagging system. The system quickly learned a user's preferences and ranked new content so it was almost impossible to miss out on anything that fit a specific kink or practice or body type, among many other criteria. After his big restructuring following the end of the War, most of Sal's biggest cash cows now grazed happily and one hundred percent in cyberspace.

The back-end analytics functions were razor-sharp and originally meant to ensure they got enough of the most popular content, though users were probably not aware how much data they were giving the algorithm. Barsanti didn't "like" or comment on anything, so the social features of the site were completely lost on him.

He visited very regularly at what Sal assumed were his bed times, stayed for ten to twenty minutes at most, and logged out. Sometimes he visited early in the morning, but there was no regular pattern to it.

Going by the tags associated with Barsanti's profile, his tastes ranged widely, with a distinct lack of hits toward the heavier and exotic kinks on the spectrum.

Solo performances, couples and threesomes of a mix of body types and skin colors, though Sal felt there were very few twinks in the mix. It seemed he preferred the kind of ubiquitous and interchangeable, clean-cut muscular types, though he didn't seem peculiar about age. Flavors ranged from sweet to harder, scenarios from seduction, gay for pay, straight "first times" (yeah, right) to "you scratched my car, now suck my cock". He had about thirty most-played videos; the engine called it his "heavy rotation", and Sal clicked on his most watched one.

It started without any preliminaries, both actors already naked. Both were dark-haired, in their thirties and forties respectively. It was one of the semi-professional offerings, which had both amateur charm and higher production values than two out-of-focus bodies slapping together in a badly lit motel room. Sal actually knew the couple—they were pretty prolific and made a decent living. Part of their appeal, beyond their nicely muscled bodies and sizeable cocks, was how clearly they were into each other. One of them, older and more tattooed, was kneeling on the bed in profile, lubing up his cock, while the younger partner scooted back. Then the fucking started, by turns slow and gentle and more passionate, with the older partner grabbing the younger guy's throat in a show of possessiveness. He didn't squeeze or choke him, just rested that large, powerful hand on his lover's arching throat. Very sexy, especially when coupled with their noises and groans, and all their passionate kissing as they moved together.

Sal cleared his throat. Again, he couldn't fault Barsanti's taste.

If he'd had any doubt left about Barsanti's sexuality, he now knew that Beth's gaydar had been spot on.

And this explained so much about the man's prodigious self-control and composure. If Barsanti had had to hide such a fundamental part of himself for so long, while the other men around him partied and snorted coke off the tits of their various mistresses, all that Barsanti could conceivably do was learn how to grin and look relaxed.

"You should have done okay. All the prison pussy you could want."

And Sal had prodded and harassed Barsanti mostly because he'd blinked and he'd thought Barsanti was so bigoted that riling him up about gay prison sex would make him come out of his shell.

You pushed a gay guy around out of a sense of self-right-eousness, Mr. Open-Minded Bisexual Boss.

Weirdly, Sal felt worse about taking jabs at Barsanti's sexuality than about drowning and then drugging him. No doubt he needed his fucking head examined.

All of this kept Sal from falling asleep, even though an ache settled in behind his eyes that told him he was overly tired and needed rest because caffeine was no longer going to cut it.

After a while, Jack stirred next to him on the couch and cleared his throat.

Sal looked up and noticed that Jack was making an attempt to sit up and pull up his trousers. Was this going to be awkward?

"Shit." Jack fought his trousers and nearly fell back, but he managed to get dressed, gripped the seat edge and an arm of the couch for balance.

"Where are you going?"

"Kitchen. I need ..." He gestured, but Sal couldn't parse the gesture. "Water."

"I'll get you a glass. Anything else? You hungry?"

"I can't even tell." Jack let himself sink back down.

"All right." Sal stood, closed the laptop and slipped his tablet back into its sleeve. In the kitchen, he found a large glass and filled it with water, then added one of the ready-to-drink protein shakes from the bottom of the fridge and brought both over to the living room area, reasoning that the latter would be easy calories that didn't require fine motor skills. Jack was checking his arm and prodding at a small bruise from the injection.

"Here." He handed both to Jack, who sat up to reach for

the glass first and placed the protein drink on the couch next to him. He'd pulled down his undershirt, but the dress shirt over it was open and still looked great on him.

"Thank you." Jack must have been parched because he emptied the glass in seconds. "What in the devil's name did you ..." He gestured again.

"Doc tells me it was mostly ketamine. Though he put his own spin on it. Real boutique stuff you were treated to. How are you feeling?"

"Dizzy. Might be lack of food, though. Headache. Could be caffeine withdrawal." He put the empty glass down on the table and opened the plastic bottle. "Light's still glaring." He nodded toward the gigantic windows opposite.

"Want me to close the shutters?"

"Please."

There was no real need or urgency in that word, but it brought back memories of when there had been. Sal stepped up to the windows and adjusted the shutters, turning the bright day into a pleasant gloom inside.

For a while, Jack did nothing but sip his protein stuff, but he was starting to look a little livelier, a little clearer.

"I have to say one thing," Jack said. "Your brand of compassion is among the weirdest I've ever seen."

"You mean the handjob or that you still have all of your fingernails?"

Jack paused, either thinking about it or taken aback by the language. Surely not? "Both. Was that ... what you wanted to do last night? When you touched me?"

Sal scoffed. "For starters, yeah." He turned fully to face Jack and had to hold back from grabbing him, kissing him, making him squirm every way he knew how. He wanted to see that tight, defined, strong body take his cock, open up for him, and cling to him.

"Jesus." Jack shook his head and laughed tonelessly. "That's so ... wrong. Everything about this is wrong."

"I don't give a fuck about your old-fashioned morality bullshit. I know you're gay. You know I'm bisexual. I basically started our conversation with that."

"'Conversation'," Jack echoed. "Right."

"I needed what was in your head. To protect my people."

"And destroy mine," Jack shot back.

"Your people? The same people who'd kill you and chop you up if they knew you fuck men? Fucking listen to your-self." Now he did walk up to Jack, who sat up straighter to offset at least some of the height advantage.

"And how's that different from what you're going to do?" Jack's face softened and he rubbed his temple with one hand. "Besides, I don't."

"Don't what?"

"I don't ... fuck men." He moved his lips like it was a sharp word that hurt his tongue. "Or let them fuck me. I don't."

What? None of that made sense. "Explain."

"Well, you know everything else now, so why hide it?." Jack swallowed visibly. "I never ... I don't have hook-ups. Nothing ... casual or committed. When I realized what I am, I decided to never take that risk. Because I might decide it was worth dying for, or lose everything because I couldn't control the temptation. It didn't seem worth it."

Fuck. *And I called you a monk.* "Are you telling me you've never had sex? I mean, sex involving another person? You're, what, in your forties?"

Jack hesitated for a long time. "I'm just not like that. I'm different."

"Different in what way?"

"I just don't constantly look at people pondering whether I want to have sex with them. That seems to be the normal way? From what I've observed about others. I try not to think about it too much. I'm busy with other things."

"Okay. I ... I think I get that. But you get turned on."

"Yes. It's ..." Jack sighed and shook his head again. "And you're the first person in the world I'm talking to about this. It's not constant, like it seems to be for others. I'm still ... when I'm into something it's ... men, but I'm not constantly into something or someone."

Okay, those were some unusual wires, but Sal had learned to take pretty much all sexualities in stride, from Catia's "anything goes with anybody" to Enzo's submissive flexibility and his own fantasies and kinks. When he initially met up with one of his couples, the conversation invariably turned to what everybody was into, and Sal was usually happy to play along with whatever came up. He'd quickly learned to go to those meetings with a mind so wide open it was more of a landscape.

"You were okay with what we did, though?"

"It confirmed what I suspected." Jack looked up with a crooked little smile. "That, yes, I'd take unreasonable risks for it, and that maybe I made the wrong decision to keep it all locked away. I ..." Another deep breath. "I can't help but wonder what it might have been like."

Might have been. He was thinking about death again. Sal tried to imagine a life without touch, whether sexual or intimate, and couldn't. Being a consigliere was already a burden because of the responsibility and the power that came with the job. While it made Jack less vulnerable to attack since he didn't have the weakness of a partner—like Sal had with Catia—who could betray him to his enemies or sell him to the Feds in return for WITSEC, it also meant he'd never had anybody to lean on, nobody to trust on that most fundamental level.

Did that make Jack Barsanti the most resilient man Sal knew? To get where he had without support or avenue for release, was unimaginable. He certainly had to be the loneliest fucking man on the planet.

25

Considering how quickly Sal Rausa bristled and how volatile he was, it was strange to see him calmly take in what Jack had confessed. Because it was a confession—if he was going to die, that wasn't something he wanted to take with him wherever he'd go, if there was a place to go to. Better to leave it all behind with the one man who'd wrestled all his other secrets from him. Sal hadn't been after these private secrets, but it seemed only fitting that he should have this one too. It was too heavy for Beth.

And it was nice to not be judged for his choices or for what he was. He could see easily how Rausa had maintained his position at the top. That kind of acceptance went a long way toward building loyalty among people. Made men were as complex, fallible, and weak as the rest of the population, so giving them support and not sweating the small stuff helped making it all work. In every way, Sal was the direct opposite to Andrea.

Jack finished the protein shake and capped the bottle again. He was already feeling less queasy, though the headache was lingering.

"Can I ask a question?"

Sal sat down on the same couch and nodded. "Sure."

"Did your wife know about you?"

Sal's eyes darkened, but his smile was soft and tinged with sadness. "She made me the man I am. Emotionally. Sexually. Before her, I figured the best sex was wild and passionate and hot and wherever and as often as possible, and only with women. I was probably compensating for the stuff I was suppressing, though my method was different from yours." He absentmindedly rubbed his chest. "She was bi, like me. Kinky, like me. Man, she could take you apart and put you back together without all the shit you were carrying. She could make you stronger. Better. She wouldn't accept lies ... and gave you the courage to figure out who you were, sexually. As a person. I miss her every day."

That raw emotion was in his voice and face again, a mix of love, pain, fondness and longing. Jack understood the yearning, though his was different. His was for something he'd never had, and he envied Sal that he'd known those emotions. And now Jack would never have a chance to feel the same. He reached out and touched Sal's arm. "She sounds very special."

"She was my best friend. My advisor. My soul. My heart. I'd have died for her in an instant. I didn't think love like that was even possible. Until her I was nothing but a boy dabbling in crushes. I had no idea how close you can become to a person. That thing they tell you in church?

About becoming one flesh? Having and holding each other? She taught me that that's the truth and the goal." Sal's eyes filled with tears, but he blinked them away, and he cleared his throat. "And since then … I've made do. I've had my hookups. I try to be honest with my lovers, all of them, and act in a way that she would have approved of. Those lessons can't be unlearned. I'm not like her at all—I'm not leaving my lovers better than they were before, but I do my best."

Jack reeled at the sheer amount of vulnerability Sal displayed, and his heart hurt, imagining what it might have been like, having something like that and then losing it. So young, so unnecessarily. He'd seen and felt the anger, but this was what fueled it. That intense pain, from an inseparably deep, apparently selfless love. "I'm truly sorry for your loss."

Sal pressed his lips together, but also didn't push Jack's hand away.

"I could help you find out who did it." It was a flash of an idea, but if anything, Jack had much better chances to get to the bottom of it. And it might just buy him his life. Here was something Sal surely wanted, and that no amount of drugs or torture could give him, because for that, he'd have to capture and torture those who did know. Jack remembered Sal had asked him while he'd been drugged, and he also remembered his response: I don't know. But at least that meant that Sal knew now that Jack had had nothing to do with it. "If it was one of ours, I can find that out."

"To head off the war and save Andrea's miserable fucking hide?"

"No, to help you put your demons to rest." Sal's eyes

flashed, and Jack added quickly, "Or at least calm them down. I have no idea if revenge actually does help—I've never been in that situation, but I understand that you have to do what you have to do. Find the guy who gave the order, and the man who pulled the trigger."

"To prevent the war?"

Yes, ideally. Kill two or three men, instead of risking all-out war that could cost all of them everything. But he'd tried that argument multiple times before and had only hit granite and rage. If he managed to divert all that rage toward the parties that were actually guilty, maybe Sal would no longer feel the need to burn Port Francis to the ground and salt the earth on which it stood.

"Make that decision later." Of course, it was still a breath-taking betrayal of the Lo Cascio.

Sal bared his teeth in a not altogether friendly smile. "You're still not giving up."

"Let's focus on the cause. You want revenge; I'll give you the murderer. Take it from there."

Before he could push Sal to consider it, the door opened and Enzo walked in. Sal's focus returned to his capo, and he stood. "Any news?"

"Well, yeah." Enzo locked the door behind him and shed the jacket, only pausing briefly to hang it up. "Time to make that call?"

That question seemed to sober Sal and refocus him the same way as it might if it were a reminder to call in a bomb threat or deliver a blackmail or ransom demand. He glanced at Jack, features sharpening again, then walked off, picked up his phone and left through the front door.

"The call?"

Enzo gave him a quizzical look, as if asking, *We friends now?* But shrugged. "Next step. Now that we're done with you."

Yep. They were done with him. Now everything was truly out of his hands.

26

F uck, it was a chilly day, and possibly felt chillier because Sal was exhausted and wired at the same time. While he could cope with the frustrated arousal, the emotional fatigue pulled on him. But they were dealing with schedules that were only partly in their control, thanks to timezones, so he dialed the number he'd saved years ago.

He'd only ever called it a handful of times since Catia's funeral. Gianbattista Falchi had approached him after everything was done and Sal had been so sore and broken inside that somebody could have cut his throat and he wouldn't have lifted his hands to defend himself. Not that the old man still did the dirty work himself. Sal didn't remember much of the conversation, except that Falchi told him he'd "liked Caterina very much indeed", and wished to "extend every possible assistance and help to her widower".

It had taken a long time for Sal to get over the word "widower" as if it had been some kind of deliberate move to test his reflexes, his bite, whether he was going to come back from the ashes and ruins. Falchi was cruel and cunning. Some said that was the only way he'd survived that long. He didn't offer his support to just anybody. So Sal had assumed Falchi had an interest in avenging Catia for his own reasons.

A year after the funeral, Sal had finally dialed the number on the card Falchi had given him. It'd felt like a pact with the devil. He liked to take care of his own business, and asking for help was always a sign of weakness in their circles. But Falchi couldn't have been more pleasant, asking him how he was faring, "all things considered", and Sal felt that Falchi remembered the anniversary.

And then that question: "Did you mean it? Can I count on you?"

"You'll find, Salvo, that I don't make frivolous promises. How can I help with your interests in Port Francis?"

He hadn't exactly consulted with Gianbattista Falchi on every step since then; it hadn't been necessary because he was simply better placed to lead the re-organization of his family. But now that he was going to do the same to the power structure of Port Francis, he could definitely use some support, if only to increase the force he could bring to bear to settle matters once and for all.

The unfamiliar call tone of an Italian cell phone. Sal shifted his weight back onto his heels and waited.

"Yes?" It wasn't that harsh "pronto!" that awaited a caller from Italy, so Falchi knew he was calling from abroad.

"Gianbattista, this is Salvo. Port Francis."

"Salvo, how nice."

"'Nice' doesn't cover it. I've been pretty busy here." Falchi would know exactly what he meant. "And I'm getting to the stage where I'll need help." No point making pretty words about it. He was outnumbered. The main thing he had going for him—aside from an absolute fuckton of intel and data that the Feds would never have been able to gather in years of observations and wiretaps—was that the enemy didn't see it coming.

"But of course." Sal could almost hear that smile. "Now?"

"Yes, now or as soon as you can make it."

"I'll send help. He's been on business on your side of the Atlantic, so could be there tomorrow."

"I can have him picked up. Whatever he needs, it'll be available. I'm well supplied here."

"I'll trust you with the details. I'll text you the flight numbers and a contact number. You liaise with him, and of course he'll stay as long as necessary. I'm also going to look into more local assistance, but that will require a few more phone calls and some horse trading."

"I hope it's not too much trouble."

"Oh, no. I have favors outstanding locally, so I'll make the calls today. I'm sure they'll come through."

So genteel, and yet Sal knew what Falchi was capable of. They didn't call him *Il Gentiluomo* for nothing. Fuck, he'd thought Barsanti was reserved and classy, but Falchi in his prime had pretty much rewritten the rulebook that Jack adhered to. Jack would no doubt freak out if he knew Falchi played on Sal's team.

And if that "he" Falchi had alluded to was the man Sal thought, then Port Francis would have a very interesting war. Legend was that Falchi's free-roaming chief executioner had played a major role in the fightback against the Russians—before Stefano Marino had turned *pentito*.

"Thank you. It would be an honor to host you over here if you felt drawn to our little corner of the world."

"You know, I might. It would be good to catch up, Salvo, once you have more peace of mind."

Peace of mind. Quite the turn of phrase there. Sal had wanted to express that he hoped Falchi would let him know what his help would cost—he didn't believe Falchi was all that concerned with money anymore. The man traded in secrets and favors. One day, he might call and ask Sal for payment.

"But I should leave you to your preparation. Do call me when you have more time—I'd be interested to hear how things went."

"Will do, thank you, Gianbattista."

Sal ended the call and felt a weight slipping from his shoulders. Maybe the spiritual people were right and Catia was out there somewhere, watching over him. Even in death, she strengthened and supported him.

He glanced down the driveway, but nothing had changed. While the sun couldn't completely defeat the chill in the air, it was a beautiful day to be outside, to soak up the brightness and wide open skies. If Falchi's guy did arrive tomorrow, the schedule still seemed doable. He could shower and change and then select whatever automatic handgun and rifle he liked from their friendly supplier, sleep a few hours, and then have a briefing and discuss targets. Including the inevitable cleanup to keep it under the radar, the whole thing was going to be over before the month ended, and that thought alone made him half excited and half impatient to blow it all open already and charge into battle.

When he returned, Enzo was in the kitchen, jacket off, his gun holster openly displayed at the hip, eating a handful of grapes. He glanced at Sal and nodded toward the living room. "So he's now moving around freely?"

"He's given us everything we need. And still coming down."

Enzo didn't seem completely convinced but shrugged. "Your decision." He dropped the last few grapes into his mouth. "How'd it go?"

"He's sending assistance." And considering the hitman's body count, he'd be useful.

"At least he's on your side, not Dommarco's or Cassaro's." Enzo opened the fridge and gave it an up-down glance. "When are we going to finish here?"

The plan had been so simple—grab the consigliere, torture him for information, kill him, make the body vanish, and strike before Andrea Lo Cascio even missed his right-hand guy. But as they said, no plan survives enemy contact, and it had all become far more complex than originally expected. And Jack's offer haunted him. The plan had been to kill everybody in the Lo Cascio, knowing that some people might still escape. But pinpointing who'd pulled the trigger on Catia meant he could make doubly sure the killer didn't escape retribution.

When Sal didn't answer, Enzo glanced over his shoulder, then moved his jaw around a few times, which he tended to do when he was thinking. "You seem to like him. Looked pretty cozy when I came back."

"Doesn't make you happy, does it?"

Enzo closed the fridge door and turned toward him. Mostly, he appeared to be a little baffled. "Dunno, boss. You tell me. You say the word, I'll put a bullet in his head, chop him up, drive him to the other side of the bay, get a burger on the way back. Or not. But what keeps him from calling Andrea and telling him everything?"

"I'm just not like that. I'm different."

"He's gay, and Andrea wants him to marry and probably breed soon. Seems his boss caught a whiff that Jack here has been playing cards with his prostitutes, but remained fully dressed." He had no idea if that had actually happened, though Jack Barsanti wasn't the first man to hide strategically in obvious places to prove his manhood. Sal believed him when he said he'd never had sex—somehow, Jack didn't strike him as the kind of man who forced himself to sleep with a woman for the benefit of others. He'd be the type to wave a bundle of money and flash his natural charm rather than humiliate himself that way.

And Jack's situation *was* hopeless. He couldn't afford to be found out—made men still got killed for that, and while a queer associate might be tolerated or beaten up and warned off, Andrea was unlikely to accept a gay man that close to him. Not a consigliere. Just the loss of face would drive a man like Andrea absolutely batshit. And even if Jack somehow managed to find a woman and did manage to father children (by whatever means), once these suspicions were out there, they never went away completely. Even if Jack Barsanti fathered a score of children and paraded around with several mistresses in tow.

"Maybe I made the wrong decision to keep it all locked away. I can't help but wonder what it might have been like."

And having had a taste of it, would Jack seriously remain celibate when it came to men? Forever rely on second-hand, but hollow pleasure, watching in secret, but never truly feeling a man's hands on his skin? He'd kissed Sal too eagerly for that, too passionately, too breathlessly, even with his split lip and bruised face. Had wanted—so clearly—for Sal to touch him. Sal didn't pretend to himself that he was special somehow—Jack could have gotten off with anybody in that state—but Jack had also been too clear-headed to simply ignore it had happened. In fact, he hadn't even attempted to flee into denial afterward.

A minute risk remained that Jack's defenses were only temporarily down, that once he recovered them he'd go running to Andrea. Jack did have a good chunk of their plan —enough to allow Andrea to brace himself for the attack, prepare, and fight back harder than if he'd been surprised. It would counterbalance part of the reason why they'd done this whole thing in the first place. But all that it would do was buy Jack a few more weeks while Andrea was more preoccupied with fighting a war than with his doubts about his consigliere's straightness. That problem wouldn't go away.

"Do you figure there's such a thing as reverse Stockholm syndrome?" Sal asked.

Enzo scoffed. "That what's going on?"

"Not sure." Sal blew out a breath. He'd been fooling himself for most of the weekend. He wasn't going to kill Jack, and wouldn't give the order, either. He'd never ask Enzo or anybody else to do something he felt incapable of.

He couldn't put his finger on when things had changed— maybe when Jack hadn't been as expected. Maybe when the man had stared at him, scared and tense, there, tied up on the bed, exhausted and yet clearly turned on. Maybe it was the fact that Jack Barsanti was queer—and what it had taken emotionally to hide for so long, Sal couldn't even imagine. They were more alike than either of them was ready to admit. Except Sal had been lucky with Catia, while Jack had been turned into a sharp, pure diamond under all that pressure. Working and cutting a diamond took another diamond.

He'd gotten under Jack's skin, but in the process somehow cut himself open too in some strategic places. Jack might not be aware of it, he probably still thought Sal was playing a version of good cop, bad cop with him, but Sal knew the openings existed.

On the one hand, he couldn't wait to drown the Lo Cascio in their own blood. On the other, he could have happily locked himself away for a week with Jack and a couple 30-foot coils of rope, and figure out what Jack liked, and where his limits were. But the latter wasn't an option—he had a war to fight and surely Andrea would eventually call and ask his consigliere whether he knew why his capos weren't answering their phones.

Another option was to make Jack "vanish" first, and Sal had no qualms about stashing him away in a safe place with a guard until the dust settled.

"Ah, fuck." Sal walked toward the fridge, almost shouldering Enzo out of the way who belatedly stepped aside, opened it, and pulled out the orange juice. While he busied his hands with taking a glass out of the cupboards, and pouring himself juice, then drinking it, Enzo stood too close to be polite.

"I know it would be smarter if we killed him. I know that."

"So why not? Just trying to understand it."

"I think he's on their side as an accident." He rested most of his weight on his knuckles on the work surface. "And I know that's bullshit. You don't become consigliere as a fucking accident. Vic Decesare would have advised on that. He must have been a very good capo."

"Right. And if you leave him alive, the Lo Cascio can recover. He could become boss or lift somebody else into that position. Then we'll have the same problem in a couple of years."

"Kingmaker? Jack?" Arguably, though, he'd find the one guy in the family who could actually do a decent job. Sal didn't relish the thought of having a skilled opponent who had the same level of insight into him that Jack had now. Peace negotiations would be easy, though, as long as it involved pulling Jack's clothes off.

"You got that grin."

"Yeah, sorry. Trying to figure out how to remove the last bit of risk without killing him."

Enzo took the carton of orange juice and took a deep sip, standing close enough that Sal could smell him, and that didn't help his hormones. Enzo was already available, could always be switched into submissive mode, like a kitten went slack when grabbed by the scruff.

"Saw something on TV once. You know what the Triads did? They might still do it, not sure."

"Enlighten me."

"They'd kidnap people and hold them for ransom. Family gets pictures, pays up, prisoner is released, everybody's happy, right?" Enzo shrugged. "Except not. While they have the prisoner, they'll rape them or force them to have sex with like guys, or women, or animals, and they keep those photos. And when they need a favor or some extra cash, they'll send a reminder. You get grabbed once by the Triads, they own you forever. And with everybody trying to keep face, the shame is worse than death."

Sal laughed. "Gotta love the Triads."

"Think about it. Fuck Barsanti, get it on video, and threaten to upload it to all of your sites. With his face, one of his guys, or someone who knows him will eventually stumble across it. That would end him—Andrea or no Andrea. Especially if he enjoys getting a cock shoved up his ass."

Sal swallowed at the image. "You'd even shoot the video."

Enzo's lips tightened in a small, somewhat malicious smile. "And warm up the lube if that helps."

"I'd put a gun in my mouth and pull the trigger." Jack stood barely inside the kitchen, legs spread somewhat apart like those of a newborn foal that wasn't quite sure yet how to use them. "Saves you work but doesn't answer that other question Sal has."

Enzo pulled away, mostly to keep Jack in view. Jack looked disheveled, his shirt was hanging open from his shoulders, and Sal studied the contrast between sunkissed skin and white cloth for a long moment.

"Enzo's got a point. If I let you live, who tells me you won't return to heel?"

"My secrets are all I have, and what respect I have, I've fought for. You do that to me, you destroy everything." Jack moved slowly, hand outstretched, clearly dizzy, and made it to the breakfast bar, where it took him several seconds before he managed to climb onto the stool. "I'd have nothing to lose, so I'd end it myself before Andrea sends somebody."

Not empty words from a man who'd intentionally breathed in water.

Sal stood, undecided, but not because the idea appealed to him. It did appeal on the level of pure fantasy like he'd perfected with Catia, where she'd play a role and he'd play a role and they'd both get off on it. He could even see it as a video—though it was more likely to be special content for those who paid for it than a wide release. Part of him wanted to go over to Jack and see if he was okay, but another part was increasingly resentful over keeping his urges and impulses on such a short leash.

And, hell, feeling Jack tremble under his fingers, the small sounds he made, and the tensing of his stomach muscles before he'd come. He could easily have turned all of that into a weapon. In fact, Enzo probably hadn't gathered all the cameras around the house yet, and despite the window blinds, maybe they'd recorded the handjob, or enough of it.

"Question remains, Jack. If I let you live, who guarantees you won't turn around and tell your boss?"

27

W ho even knew what the "right" strategy was anymore? That particular train of thought hadn't just departed, it had jumped off the rails, rammed a mountain side and exploded. Search crews in high-vis jackets were now combing through the wreckage.

In some ways it was easier to just accept death. But, like that night on the bridge, he'd met an unexpected fellow traveler on the way to hell, and that changed everything. Strangely, Sal Rausa understood him better than Andrea or anybody else ever had, and he didn't seem to judge Jack for any of it.

"I know you're not interested in negotiations." The way Sal's shoulders immediately squared and he lifted his chin confirmed that. Jack smiled tiredly. "I understand. If you let me go, I'll find out who killed her."

Sal grimaced, baring his teeth. "Only difference that makes is that I'll know which corpse to piss on."

Sal was lying, though. It meant a lot more to him than he

let on. He fell back on his gruffness when he felt his position weaken. At least that was Jack's working hypothesis. Jack rubbed his face, tried to clear his head more. He was getting better, feeling less hung over, less heavy and drugged with every minute that passed, but he was nowhere near back to his usual sharpness. He needed forty-eight hours of restful sleep, several bottles of water, a good, hard run, and a couple sessions in a sauna to work the last vestiges of the drugs out of his system. Not for the first time this month, he felt every year of his age. Twenty years ago, he'd have let this weekend wash over him and emerged completely dry and ready to fight.

And then there were the other issues. How to survive the war. How to deal with having failed so spectacularly at keeping the peace, the one thing he'd been good at. How to avoid the impression that it was him who'd sold everybody out to save himself. He'd have to leave town, the state, and ideally the country, in case somebody came calling to collect on that debt. Without the Lo Cascio, he had no protection.

And all that because he couldn't suppress those distracting emotions and needs? Didn't that confirm that men like him couldn't be trusted? That he was, on the most fundamental level, flawed and weak?

No. He'd seen enough men make terrible decisions because of money, drugs, or ego. Sometimes all three. He was no worse, and also no better. He'd tried for decades, and none of it had made even the smallest difference. He'd gone into the life willingly and with open eyes. Part of the draw had been that his father, who always found fault with him, had failed to get made. And, yes, he'd rubbed it into the old man's face when the money started flowing. Because money was a language his father understood. The only one he spoke.

What mistakes Jack had made had nothing to do with his sexuality, because he'd spent so much energy on suppressing it and excelling in everything else. He'd worked so hard in part because he didn't have to deal with demands from lovers or spouses or children. *"You're a machine",* his old capo used to say, part proud, part exasperated.

No, not a machine at all.

Sal Rausa came around the breakfast bar and placed both his hands on his shoulders, as he'd done right at the start, but now Jack's body only welcomed the touch. It was firm and strong and warm, and with a sudden flashing heat he remembered that touch on his bare skin. All those pretensions—his role, his duties, his past—had bled away, and he had been no different from any other man, just as vulnerable and brittle as any other human being experiencing such intense pleasure.

If he could have that again—if he could strip away everything that had separated him from being just some man, just anybody, whose deeds and decisions ultimately meant nothing, had no lives or power riding on it … If he could even conceive such a life, maybe he could start again. Start better. Far away from Port Francis. Maybe he'd find somebody for himself, somebody who accepted him as he was, somebody he could lean on as much as he himself was willing to support. A relationship of equals, without lies and subterfuge. If he found that, it could be the kind of love that made Sal's voice break when he spoke of his wife.

"Finding out who killed Catia … is that the only reason you can give me to keep you alive, Jack?" It was said almost with affection, and Jack swallowed. If he could have, he'd have scrambled to pull the comforting blanket of that drug back over his mind and emotions, because feeling those things while sober was too damn intense.

"I got nothing else. Andrea would have me killed if he knew what I am. That cat is out of the bag. There is no hiding now."

"You could. Plenty of guys leave the closet, and plenty go back inside." Those hands tightened on his traps, and all Jack could remember was that heated kiss and the taste of another man.

"It'd take even more rope than last night to keep me there."

Sal gave a low chuckle that made the hairs on Jack's arms stand up. "I'm pretty handy with a length of rope. Try me."

Try me. Jack looked up and saw Enzo watching them, looking alert, but not surprised. If anything, there was a hint of amusement around his lips. Something in Jack's perception had clearly changed because he could see easily why Sal would be attracted to Enzo, and vice versa. Maybe his brush with death had opened his eyes, or he now allowed himself to contemplate masculine beauty without a deep-seated terror that that alone might condemn him to death. Enzo was objectively very attractive, although Jack didn't feel any erotic charge. But Sal Rausa was stunning, metaphorically and literally.

Jack half-turned to meet Sal's eyes. "Let me think about it. I'll get back to you on that."

"Something distracting you?"

"Yes."

Sal laughed and stepped back. "Enzo, I'll go grab a shower."

"Understood." Enzo leaned against the kitchen counter and watched Sal leave the kitchen, then re-focused his attention on Jack. "You guys seem to be getting on well."

"I guess." Jack rubbed his face. "I don't know. That horse tranquilizer makes thinking hard."

"Thinking's overrated with Sal." Enzo flashed him a smile. "Want to hear what I'm thinking?"

"Do I?"

"He's turned on. You're pushing his buttons, and that shower is so he can clear his head." Enzo looked very relaxed now.

Jack blinked but it wasn't mockery, not a joke.

"He's turned on."

Well, made two of them. The touch had been intense while his head hadn't been clear, but if he understood correctly, there was an opportunity for some more of that. Maybe he didn't need to wait for that new start—provided he'd live to get the opportunity—to find out what he could feel if he gave himself that freedom. Of all possible men in this world, Sal Rausa had to count among the worst for a test run. But Jack might never get another opportunity to experience this if Sal did decide to kill him. Maybe this was the only chance he'd ever get in his life, and he already had more than his share of regrets.

"You're pushing his buttons."

And that was the thing. He didn't normally feel this way. There had been two men in his life he'd felt attracted to, and both had been friendly first and foremost. The first had been Tony, a fellow soldier, made just a few weeks before Jack, and they'd spent a lot of time together trying to come up with schemes to make money. And while Jack laughed one day about a scheme that was getting more and more hare-brained, he'd suddenly realized he wanted to kiss his friend. And now, thinking back, he thought Tony might have had a few such moments of temptation too, even though his success with dating was further bolstered by the way he flashed cash around. Jack had told himself that closeness was because their capo had leaned hard on them, but he'd still realized it wasn't just about the easy comradery. You didn't daydream about a friend.

The second man had been the physiotherapist who'd looked after him when Jack had managed to rip his ACL during a skiing trip. The aptly named Dr. Walker had advised him and helped him stabilize his knee with exercises. The man had been a good ten years older, well-groomed, patient, ultra-competent and silver-haired.

They'd hit it off well from the start, and Jack remembered how Dr. Walker had complimented him on his muscle tone and overall fitness and asked him whether he was a professional athlete or model. During the final check-up, he'd suddenly realized he wanted those competent hands everywhere on his body. But he'd pushed the notion away, and ignored what Jack now thought had been coded messages, such as the man indicating he'd gone on a trip to Mykonos with "a few friends" and he could recommend the "sights" on that island.

It was years later when Jack discovered that Mykonos was a famously gay-friendly island in the Mediterranean. Code was lost on those who hadn't been handed a code book to decipher it. A few times, he'd considered finding Dr.

Walker to confirm his suspicion, but he'd never followed up on it, and by now he was likely retired.

Nothing would hold him back this time.

When Jack stood, at least he no longer felt seasick; he was a little unsteady, but he could control his legs enough to walk in pretty much a straight line, though he didn't dare turn his head and cast a glance at Enzo because his balance was too tenuous for that.

He followed the sound of running water to the bathroom, and saw Sal Rausa's naked, wet form beyond the glass. His clothes lay in a pile on the chair to which Jack had been tied, shoes thoughtfully placed on the rim of the Jacuzzi, socks stuffed inside.

He noticed how Sal's dark hair was plastered to his scalp, how his hands moved quickly and efficiently over his skin, and soap suds travelled down those long legs that were solidly braced against whatever the world might throw at him. And where Enzo was pleasant and dangerous to look at, well, Sal was in a universe all his own.

On socked feet, Jack walked across the plastic sheets and headed straight for the door of the shower. He opened it enough to slide under the soft, dense, steaming spray behind the man, and place a kiss between his shoulder blades. Jack was massively overstepping, and there was always the danger that Rausa would explode into more violence, but he was serious about having nothing to lose now.

Sal seemed to laugh tonelessly if Jack read his breathing correctly. He lifted his face into the water and reached behind himself, grabbed Jack by the hips and pulled him closer. "Didn't even get undressed?"

"It seemed too much."

Sal glanced at him over his shoulder. "Still hedging your bets, Jack? As the saying goes, there's no such thing as safe sex."

"Never heard that." Jack found himself breathless and struggling for oxygen. He hadn't thought further than the need to touch Sal, but of course it wasn't Sal who was the blushing virgin.

"If you'd have ever joined us, my wife would have told you that good sex goes down to the soul like a damn knife."

"Is that ... is that what we're doing?" Jack felt how Sal guided his hands, and his mind overloaded with the sensation of heated, slippery skin and shifting powerful muscle. Seeing it was dangerous. Feeling it—was far too much. How did people stand it? He placed another kiss on Sal's shoulder, tasted the water on his lips, and moved closer to a kind of awkward and almost unbearable embrace. He felt Sal take a few deep breaths, his hands still on Jack's. Nervous about his erection pushing against the wet cloth of his trousers, he wasn't sure what he'd come for exactly. He had only a theoretical understanding how things would develop, what was even possible, what was wanted.

"I don't think I have to tell you how fucking hot you are," Sal ventured. "But that's not why I don't want to kill you."

Jack drew back instinctively, but Sal pushed his hands harder against his own naked skin, holding him in place.

"Why then?"

"You have heart." Sal pushed back against him. "I respect you."

"You'll be the only one in this town."

"Yeah, but they're wrong." Sal laced his fingers with Jack's and squeezed. "Fuck them. My town, my rules."

It wasn't that easy, though right now under the shower, Jack might be able to fool himself long enough to bask in that wholly undeserved level of trust. He rested his head in the crook of Sal's neck and shoulder, kept one hand where it was, and let the other one slide over the tensing muscles of his stomach. He felt strangely anchored by how solidly Sal Rausa stood, like nothing could move him if he didn't acquiesce. All that Sal's hand on his did was give him confidence, because he certainly didn't guide him.

When he slid past the belly button, Sal's breathing pattern shifted, and he trembled very slightly when Jack's fingers slid over trimmed, wiry hair and closed around his fully erect cock. Sal's breath was much shallower now, and Jack kissed his neck. "Tell me if I do it wrong."

"There's no wrong, Jack. If I get a chance, I'll show you how many right ways I know." Sal chuckled again. "Though I'd really like it if you were naked."

There was no way he'd break the contact now, though, certainly not to deal with pulling wet cloth off his body. He was far too fascinated and aroused by touching another man's cock. It felt both familiar and very much not, in his hand. If anything, Sal's was slightly thicker than his own as he ran his hand along the length first teasingly and carefully. He felt the tension in Sal's body and ultimately it seemed like payback after what Sal had given him on the couch.

With every stroke, Sal's muscles tightened, and Jack belatedly noticed that Sal's ass was pushing back against him, definitely an invitation to push as well. It was dizzying, especially when Sal's free hand deftly slid between them, and squeezed Jack's cock in his trousers before opening his belt. He let Sal's chest go to help him open the button and zip, and push the fly apart enough for Sal to slide his hand into Jack's boxers. Then all control fled and Jack became a reckless, not always perfectly coordinated mess of movement and breath and pleasure. It was good, but awkward enough that Jack couldn't quite come. And apparently he wasn't great at handjobs, because while Sal seemed to enjoy himself, he also didn't come and eventually turned around.

His eyes were positively glowing in his flushed face when he grabbed Jack's head with both hands and kissed him deeply, passionately, wrecking what breath Jack had left. It didn't matter anymore how dressed or undressed Jack was, though the next thing Sal did was nearly rip the shirt from his chest and push his boxers down to free his cock.

Sal bared his teeth in a dangerous grin, then winked and kissed him again. He pulled Jack closer against him, taking both their cocks in one hand, which was so intense Jack's knees felt weak. Between the open-mouthed, heated kiss, and all that skin against his own, Jack lost himself in the pleasure. It was nothing like he'd ever imagined, nothing like what he did by himself—he'd never relished getting off, just considered it something of an annoying pressure valve he had to regularly release. Another part of a normal mainte-nance routine of sensible diet, good hydration, regular exer-cise. Sal Rausa blew all of that out of the water with the same abandon that he'd wrecked the rest of Jack's life.

He felt Sal thrust along his cock, watched him move in the rare moments when they broke the kiss, which now involved tongues and teeth. Sal nipped playfully at his lips, and then Sal's mouth travelled to the soft skin between Jack's chin and throat. The sucking kisses and scrapes of teeth pushed him over the edge. Sal's movements grew harsher, faster, and Sal came right after him, his hot semen mixing with Jack's and the water.

Jack rested his head against Sal's shoulder and felt Sal move again, this time releasing him after a few last strokes. Embracing him tightly so they stood under the water, both breathing heavily, Sal held him up as Jack's knees shook and his skin tingled all over from the sensory overload.

"Tell me when you're ready to move," Sal murmured in his ear.

"No."

Another silent laugh. "Fair enough."

28

Maybe the most surprising part of the whole thing was how little Sal had felt the need to set the pace or call the shots, though at some point it had been clear that Jack had no idea what he was doing. Still, his inexperienced exploration was enough to light Sal on fire and make the lingering erection damn near unbearable.

He hadn't expected Jack to join him in the shower—it wasn't Enzo's style (though he'd come if called), but at the same time, Sal hadn't thought even once that the man joining him was anybody else but Jack. Which seemed meaningful, especially after the exchange in the kitchen.

"Is that the only reason you can give me to keep you alive, Jack?"

Strangely, he didn't think Barsanti had done this to give Sal a reason. Not with how much value the man put on his dignity. Holding him here, clearly shell-shocked from an intense orgasm, Jack wasn't dignified in the least. Nobody on the outside would ever understand what had happened, but

Sal did get the feeling this was the first time Jack had willingly and consciously given up control. And what a lover could he become if given time and opportunity ... he was attentive, gentle, eager to please and willing to be swept off his feet. Seemingly, Jack had nothing to prove sexually, wasn't playing dominance games and didn't hold back either. All things that Sal liked.

He gently moved away and pulled down Jack's trousers and boxers all the way. Jack lifted first one foot, then the other to step out of them, and Sal pulled off his socks as well before he opened the door to toss the sopping wet clothes into the nearby Jacuzzi. Then he kissed Jack's throat. "Ready?"

"Maybe." Jack looked at him still with that wonder and even awe in his eyes that made Sal's heart ache. That same expression told Sal that nobody had made Jack feel this way before, and what a crying shame that was. A guy like Jack deserved a whole lot more than a couple semi-rushed handjobs.

At the same time, Sal was grateful Jack had come to him like this. He'd normally have jerked off quickly under the shower, which was the original plan, because the arousal was messing with his head and emotions too much to simply ignore it. Enzo would have been up for taking care of it, but Sal didn't want to have both of them distracted while Jack was rapidly recovering his mind.

Not that it had done him any good when it came to getting rid of the sheer attraction. Instead, it had added depth underneath and layers on top of it.

Sal ran his hand over Jack's back and made himself avoid the man's ass, because he could quite easily build up enough arousal to want much more than had already happened. He'd end up dragging Jack into the master bedroom and taking him every way he knew, and he could easily lose the night doing that.

Because that was another signal; when he contemplated letting the other man fuck him. He didn't have any particular hang-ups about bottoming—there were quite a few bi and bi-curious husbands out there who had no idea that one of their claims to fame was that they'd fucked an incognito Mafia boss up the ass. It was a thing Sal did when he was in the right mood. Other guys he'd slept with considered him an exclusive top, because that was the kind of chemistry he had with them. Somehow, he'd contemplated for a few moments how it would feel to have Jack's cock push between his ass cheeks, either to fuck between them until Jack came all over his back, or change the angle and push inside him, or try to, at least.

And he'd liked the idea enough that it had surprised him. Maybe it was because he truly enjoyed Jack gaining confidence when it came to sex, maybe it was because he was experienced enough that a virgin's unskilled love-making couldn't possibly hurt him. He could get off easily on how much his partner enjoyed themselves, even if it took Sal a while to get into it too.

He felt Jack's fingers touch the bar in one of his nipples. "Did that hurt?"

"Hurt is the wrong word." Sal brushed wet hair from Jack's forehead. "I'm definitely too kinky for something as simple as hurt." He touched his head to Jack's, but avoided the area where his scalp was cut. "That's just how I'm wired."

And then Jack's fingers touched the chain around Sal's

neck, and Sal felt the metallic slide of the ring against the chain. It was done reverently, and didn't feel painful—if anything, Catia would have agreed with Sal that Jack was hot and would have welcomed him in their house. If not for some unfortunate associations.

"Let me find out who's responsible. Even if it doesn't make a difference."

"Why?"

"Because now I want to know." That response destroyed the very last remains of any suspicion that Jack might have been involved. It sounded completely honest and was even tinged with a kind of outrage.

"And if it's Andrea?"

"Why are you asking?"

"He's your boss."

"If he could see me like this, he'd shoot me himself. He's … he already thinks I'm not quite right. That he might not be able to … trust me with his kids."

Sal turned his head to look at Jack's face. "I call that too stupid to live."

Jack chuckled and kissed the place right above Sal's collarbone. "I think I'm good now." He reached out and shut down the water, then slid from Sal's arms and left the shower. He walked barefooted across the plastic sheets and grabbed one large fluffy bathrobe and offered it to Sal, but Sal shook his head, took it and wrapped Jack in it instead, which seemed to genuinely surprise him, but it added a puzzle piece to the overall picture.

"You like to serve, don't you?"

Jack froze, as if caught. "I guess?"

Sal dried him with the bathrobe and enjoyed tying the

belt in a loop that could easily be pulled open. Now, that would make sense. Unlike Enzo, Jack didn't feel like a sub; that tendency to please was different, but he'd pushed for that handjob on the couch while giving himself over to the sensation. In a twisted way, he had to get something out of serving Andrea, who apparently was a bigoted asshole even to the one man he had to unconditionally trust. There were other dimensions to it, and they were somewhat obfuscated by Jack's sheer inexperience.

"Nothing wrong with that. I like to serve others too." Sal reached for the large towel he'd spotted earlier and began drying himself off. "During sex. I get off when my partner gets off."

"Or you don't ... not when ..." Jack gestured in the general direction of the living room.

"I'm no longer sixteen." Sal grinned at him. "I also like delayed gratification and the build-up. I like fucking people's minds as much as their bodies, but if I can do both ..." He nodded slowly. "I'll do both."

"That's a fact," Jack said, and smiled, shaking his head, but he sobered visibly. "I still don't have an answer for you."

"Yeah, about that." Sal set about dressing himself, while Jack stood there in his bathrobe and watched him. The decision was both hard and too easy—and he full well knew that while Jack might be open and honest with him right now, the man might regroup and convince himself of the exact opposite of what he professed now.

There was too much at stake for him to be resolved with two orgasms. Sal knew he could turn a lover inside out if he found the right buttons to press, and while Jack might be overwhelmed right now by everything that had happened during the past thirty or so hours, he was old enough to be set in his ways. He could easily return to old patterns.

Sal slipped on his boots and straightened. "Don't get on my wrong side, Jack. You didn't like being there, you won't like it if you get back there, all right?"

Jack swallowed visibly. "You're considering letting me go?"

"Looks like it." Sal drew a deep breath and studied the man's face. "I have to make calls, get ready. If you're smart, you stay at home and wait until it's over. But if not, I'll tell my guys to not hurt you. That's void if you raise your hand against any of them, understand?"

"I do." Jack's shoulders dropped first and then he sank down onto the rim of the Jacuzzi, but the tension around his eyes softened.

Sal pulled himself together. He couldn't linger anymore, because otherwise he'd stay for the rest of the evening, and then the night, and after that, the cards would be reshuffled. "Got a burner phone?"

"In the car."

"Great." Sal gave him his number. "Remember that, if you need help." He didn't want to leave, but he took a couple backward steps.

"Sal?"

"Yeah?"

"Be careful."

Sal's heart clenched; one of those things Catia would say, sometimes in jest, when he was pushing too far, sometimes deadly serious. Jack now sat there, deflated, or so relieved he couldn't think clearly. "Same. If this doesn't go as expected, you need to get out—leave the city, definitely get the fuck away from Andrea, hear me?"

"I will."

Sal believed him. He managed to turn around and strode back into the kitchen, where Enzo offered him a cup with very strong espresso.

"You good?" Enzo asked.

"Yeah. Let's go."

29

On the way out, Sal paused and briefly ran his fingers over the gleaming silver Porsche Cayman. Apparently he was giving it back after all. Could have been easy to take it "hostage", as it were and slow Jack down a little longer. If the man was brave and stupid enough to leave the house and get involved, that is. Sal thought he'd given a strong enough warning, but there was no guarantee Jack would follow his orders.

"What are you thinking?"

"Pondering if I want one."

Enzo shot him an ironic look. "Weird, I didn't think silver was your type."

"I don't know. It's classy, understated, fun to drive."

Enzo huffed laughter. "And we're no longer talking about the car."

"We were talking about the car?" Sal pretended ignorance, but he didn't fool Enzo. And the car was so tied up with Jack that there was some kind of connection. *Fun to drive, indeed.*

"Can I ask a question?"

"That's already one." Sal winked at him, but nodded. They'd had that exact exchange a couple dozen times, and for the first dozen of those, Enzo had responded with exasperation.

"What happened in there?"

"One of two things." Sal shrugged and stuffed his hands into his pockets while they walked down the driveway toward the busted gate, gravel crunching under their shoes. The shadows were noticeably lengthening and the chill deepened as the humidity climbed and became more penetrating. In one version of events, he'd have walked a bound and blinded Jack Barsanti along the same path, and then into the virgin forest to a place without too many roots. Or dragged bags with his pieces along, blood sloshing in the construction-grade plastic. Instead, he could still feel the ghost of Jack's tentative touches on his skin. "Either I've gone soft and lost my touch, or we've made an unlikely ally."

"I call bullshit on both." Enzo pushed the gate open and waited for Sal to walk through. "First, you didn't exactly go soft on him." Enzo groaned when Sal raised an eyebrow at him. "I mean, not that way, but sure, okay, you got off with him. Means nothing, right?"

Means everything, apparently. Sal stopped walking and looked at Enzo. "He wasn't out, Enzo. Can you imagine getting to that age without ever ..." He gritted his teeth. "Living with that fear?"

Enzo had stopped as well, reaching out to touch Sal's shoulder. "So what? You spared him because he's gay?"

"Looks like I did. Fuck." Sal drew a deep breath and shook his head. "Definitely losing my touch, then. It doesn't make sense. We can't afford a war with the Lo Cascio if they know it's happening. Andrea on his own will make mistakes. But Jack is a real asset."

"We'll manage," Enzo said grimly. Sal had worried that Enzo might lose respect for him, which would pose problems for all aspects of their relationship. Seemed his capo was still rock solid.

"I thought you'd be pissed."

"I'm not." Enzo let his arm go and looked him up and down. "Want me to be completely honest?"

"Yeah. Though you might regret it."

Another one of those well-worn exchanges, but Enzo smiled only weakly. "For the record, I checked he wasn't going into the bathroom to attack you, but I left you to it once I saw he wasn't a threat."

"Him grabbing a kitchen knife might have been a giveaway."

"You know what I see? I see some glimpses of the old Sal, the guy you were before fucking Lo Cascio ripped out your fucking heart, okay? God bless you, Sal, but it's been hard these last few years. Some nights I didn't think you'd make it all the way through to morning, but in there ..." He didn't point at the house or even glance at it, "You were who you were before all that. I have no idea whether that's some psychological hacking from fucking Barsanti, or whether he's played you and he's going to backstab you. If he does, I'll find him and rip him apart."

He drew a deep breath, and Sal thought he might be

done, but then Enzo continued. "And maybe I'm getting all stupid now, but I missed you."

Sal stood stunned, then closed the distance between them and embraced Enzo. It made sense—their relationship had changed after Catia's death, it had lost most of the lightness and joy, but Sal hadn't had even an idea that Enzo felt that way. He'd thought they'd both been drowning men clinging to each other—now he realized he'd used Enzo as a life raft. He kissed the side of Enzo's head while he held him so tightly he felt the man's heartbeat. "I'm sorry."

A halting, shuddering breath. "I love you, you know that, right?"

"I do. And I love you too. In an almost heterosexual, manly way."

Enzo laughed and pushed his head against Sal's. "Yeah, and you're full of shit. I couldn't give a fuck about Barsanti. He wastes that second chance you gave him? He's dead. I only give a fuck about you, and I'll do what it takes. Whatever needs to be done."

"I know."

"Good." Enzo patted the back of Sal's shoulders. "Let's get moving."

30

Nothing said "close call" like being spared while sitting in a room that had been prepared as a kill site. The tools were gone, but the plastic sheets remained. The chair was still where they'd put it. Sal's discarded towel. And even though the house's temperature was perfectly set, Jack shuddered relentlessly. He didn't know whether that was the tension leaving, or the moisture trapped in the bathrobe cooling around him.

Breathlessly, he rose and cast a glance at his wet clothes in the Jacuzzi, remembering viscerally how they'd ended up there. Everything still echoed with Sal Rausa's fierceness, his rage, his pain, the violence in every turn of his head, every flash of white teeth. And still ...

Jack should probably feel shame, guilt, but he didn't. Even when he dug deep down for those feelings, because surely he deserved them, didn't he?

He went looking for his phone before he remembered

that Sal had taken it, and that was the last he'd see of it, or the laptop.

He did own a burner phone—just in case—but right now he couldn't face leaving the house. Instead, he walked to the master bedroom and the walk-in closet to get clothes. For the first time in his life, he didn't like what he saw. He stared at those nice suits and tailored shirts—all the same color because he'd never wasted time making such trivial choices first thing in the morning. Or at least, that was what he'd told himself. In truth it made him look the same, day in, day out, as if that could protect him from too much attention. He'd hidden behind inoffensive grey, and off-white and black, and accessorized with one of a small, restrained collection of expensive watches. And who even wore watches anymore?

His sudden aversion didn't matter though. He didn't have any other clothes here, so he put on a suit, then walked into the bathroom to look more closely at his face. Yeah, there was no hiding the bruise; it was a swollen blueish purple where his cheekbone and temple had hit the floor, and the location didn't lend itself to covering it with sunglasses or something similar. The doc had dealt with that cut high up on his forehead, and while the area was sore, and he could feel some swelling, the bruise was much more dramatic. And then there was the split lower lip. Any attempt to cover up his injuries would draw even more attention and raise questions as to why he felt he had to hide them.

Thankfully, the medicine cabinet held some untouched Tylenol, so he washed two of those down against the ache in his head, pocketing the rest. He brewed an espresso and had another protein shake, and by the time those were drunk, he felt slightly more settled and left the house.

The Porsche didn't stand where he'd parked it, but the phone was still in the glove compartment. He went back into the house to charge it, and once the screen showed signs of life, he dialed Beth's number. No response, so he sent a text.

Hi Beth, Jack here. Sorry, new phone. Call me?

The phone rang less than five minutes later. "Jack, Jesus Christ. I thought ..." And then she caught herself and the vehemence faded and died. "Thank you for finally calling me. No wonder I didn't manage to get through. What happened to your phone?"

"Drowned it. It's sitting in a bag of rice right now. Kind of a shame about the nice risotto." He took an icepack out of the freezer and placed it against the side of his face. "And admittedly, I've had a bit of a weekend."

"Yeah, Sal said."

Jack's blood froze.

"Enough. Stop talking about her. It's messing with my boner, Jesus."

Sal had told him he'd talked to Beth, but it still hit him like a hammer. The two parts of his life that should never meet. He could only hope to separate both completely and forever and repair some of the damage.

"Jack?"

"Yeah, sorry. I still can't believe you guys talked."

"He was really nice. You could have told me about him and introduced us yourself."

Oh God, Sal, what have you done? "Sal's kind of new in my life."

"I understand. But you know ..." She audibly steeled herself. "Look, I don't know him that well, but he cares about you, Jack. I don't know where you guys are in your relationship, but could you try talking to each other more?"

Sal, you utter bastard. "Right, well, we did that, this weekend. Talk. We talked a lot more than we ever have before."

"And? I mean, if you want to tell me."

"We worked thing out, I guess." Keeping it vague so he could assess the amount of damage that Sal had done to the whole façade Jack maintained for Beth.

"So ... your proposal?"

"It was a mistake. I'm sorry for confusing you. I guess I freaked out and ..." *It no longer matters.* "I'm sorry I pulled you into all this." *And put you anywhere near Sal Rausa's damn radar.*

"Oh, thank God." It came out as one single toneless breath. "I mean, I get that your family isn't okay with your sexuality, but we can't live the lives that our families want for us, even if they mean well."

Mine really, really doesn't. And how utterly bizarre to discuss his sexuality with the very person who knew the least about the real him. "I'll always have to be discreet about it, but I'll find a different way to go about it."

"I didn't mean you should grab Sal, saddle a unicorn, and ride straight to the altar. But you shouldn't let your family come between you, either. He cares about you, Jack, that's worth so much. And listen to me talk, Miss Guaranteed to Find the Biggest Asshole in any Room and Move in with Him."

Despite himself, he laughed. "Yeah, next boyfriend will get vetted very carefully." *And I'll be quite happy to give him the Dating the Mafioso's Sister or Daughter Treatment.*

"Same," she said with an edge of seriousness. "But I like this one."

Let's not even go there. "Good. I'm glad. So, what are you up to this week?"

"The usual." Which was too vague. He'd started the call with a notion of getting her out of the city, but more erratic behavior on his part would set her on edge again. Andrea didn't know she existed, and Sal wouldn't hurt her. Neither would Enzo. Any other danger would be due to a freak accident, not intention. But the war hanging over their heads made him want to personally drive her to the airport and send her off for a month or two to Hawaii or Alaska, and only let her come back when the dust had settled. He didn't know whether he would still be around when she'd come back.

"Good. That's good. Listen, I have to make a few more calls, but I wanted to make sure we're okay."

"Definitely."

He ended the call and rested his head against the door of the fridge. In a nightmare scenario, he'd imagined her banging against the door, two cops in tow. If Sal had opened it, it would have been "sorry to disturb, Mr. Rausa", and "no, we don't care about the bleeding man in the background, please continue, and have a nice Sunday, Mr. Rausa", or at least that was what his fevered imagination had produced.

See, that can happen when you get people involved who don't know the rules.

31

J ack hoped the shop assistant in the local Apple store earned a commission, considering she'd remained perfectly helpful even though he'd squeezed in ten minutes before the shop closed to replace both the laptop and his phone. He'd waved her off when she'd offered to check whether their "broken" predecessors were still under warranty.

He dashed to his house in Port Francis proper. With its barely 1,300 square feet, these days it would be pitched toward two young working adults on moderate salaries looking for their first home. Jack had bought it because it was close to some business interests at the docks and was only a fifteen-minute drive to the much grander residence Andrea's father had bought for his family. Besides, the neighborhood appealed to him—both old and young were unfailingly polite if he encountered them on the street. It wasn't because everybody knew who he was (though the Sicilians certainly did), it was also just that kind of place where some old people kept an eye on strangers or cars they hadn't seen before.

In turn, Jack kept an eye on the neighborhood. He'd single-handedly headed off attempts to build a huge modern apartment complex right in the center of it, and had instead pushed for the vacant lots to be turned into a community space with a park and a mini golf. Ever since then, he'd never had to worry about mowing his own grass out front, or cutting his hedges—it all got done quietly and invisibly, and nobody ever presented a bill. Jack suspected the retired couple next door.

In any case, it was a place where he could safely leave his car parked on the street. He still locked it and hurried inside.

After he'd dumped his various gadget packages on the kitchen table, he quickly plugged everything in. The devices walked him through the setup process, though it took effort to focus on it. He did need access to his files, and a way to be reached, and he urgently needed to safeguard as much money as he could.

With a sigh, Jack touched the tender side of his face, and prodded the bruise again to confirm it still hurt. He was tempted to grab a suitcase of clothes and vanish to the North Pole while Sal ripped the city apart. The best-case scenario would be a decisive victory—whichever way the dice fell. The way these things had played out ever since the three families had taken hold of Port Francis, the Rausa and the Lo Cascio would weaken each other, and the Dommarco would swoop in. Nobody had ever managed to take over completely. The closest they'd come to changing the landscape was when the Rausa had withdrawn into obscurity. Turned out that wasn't permanent, and the expression "with a vengeance" came to mind.

At the same time, his own hands were tied. Jack assumed Sal had more important things to worry about than Jack, but for now, in his kitchen, he could appreciate how merciful Sal had been. He could have simply killed Jack right there in his own bathroom and left it at that. Jack didn't believe his execution had merely been postponed, but that didn't mean that Sal would necessarily spare or even protect him.

He could try to hide here and extend his "break", pretending ignorance, claiming nothing had happened. But he somehow doubted that would be enough to protect him. The only real option was to meet Andrea and keep doing his job, and then act once he knew his options and could more accurately gauge Andrea's response.

He could even claim that somebody had stolen his laptop and phone and indicate that Rausa was going to make a move. Would that be enough to get him in the clear? Probably not. Worst case, Andrea wouldn't buy it. Best case, it made Jack look weak and pathetic—and Andrea's first response to weakness wasn't compassion or extending a helping hand. Plus he'd have questions about Jack's bruises.

He typed Andrea's number into his new phone, then tapped "Call". No response. Jack didn't leave a message, but sent a text: *New phone. Jack here.*

Restlessly, he downloaded all his files onto the laptop from his Apple account. His memory was hazy, but he didn't think Sal had asked him for his own, personal accounts. He still checked them for recent transactions and changed all passwords. Then he did what he could to secure the family's money. He needed to maintain a façade of normality for a few more days. That way, he could prepare his exit while making good on his promise. If he stayed calm, he could pull off both. His main worry was that Andrea had already tried to call him and was pissed that Jack hadn't answered.

He toyed with the burner phone and tapped it on the surface of the kitchen table, trying to decide. Finally, he typed Sal's number, and his heart beat up into his throat while he listened to the ringtone.

"Yes?" Short, snappy.

"Jack here."

A few moments of silence, enough for Jack to ask himself what the hell he was doing, and begin convincing himself that he'd misread Sal's signals, and that Sal Rausa didn't particularly care about collateral damage such as a compromised consigliere.

"I'm listening."

"Have you started your war yet?"

"Anybody with you?"

"No, I'm alone."

"Right." Sal sounded tense. "Why are you asking?"

"Because I'll have to talk to Andrea soon, and I need to know what kind of situation I'm walking into."

Sal hummed softly, and the sound somehow hit Jack low in the gut, but in a sweet, sensuous way. "What will you tell him?"

"You worried I'll tell him you punked me?" The prison term sounded harsh in his own ears, but the alternative was to ask whether Sal was worried for his safety. The deck had been reshuffled so thoroughly over the past few hours that Jack found himself reeling. "It's not an option. He'd take me out like trash."

"Good. And ... we'll talk about this, Jack. With time, and once this is all done. I owe you an apology and a few explanations. Shit, you could come over and stay here."

Crawl into the protection of the one man who'd made that protection necessary. Tempting, but no. If not for his inability to pretend to be normal, or drag Beth into a life of misery and fear, or strike a deal with a woman who'd take the money in return for playing his doting wife—because he could already see a hundred ways that would only stall the catastrophe—Jack would never have become so vulnerable. He'd brought this upon himself, he needed to deal with it. At the same time, those considerations somehow didn't mean a thing when he closed his eyes and remembered the feeling of Sal Rausa's naked skin against his own.

He wanted that, wanted more of it, and maybe something was seriously broken about him, but he couldn't hate himself or Sal for it.

"Jack, you listening?"

"Yes. I'm thinking."

"I'm serious."

"I'll talk to him first thing tomorrow. On his normal schedule, that's around ten or so."

"Talk about what?"

"Report in after my break away from everything. My *vacation*."

A soft, toneless laugh. "Sorry for fucking that one up for you."

"Yeah, well." Weirdly, he felt Sal meant it, but Jack still couldn't wait to call the company looking after the house and telling them to scrub the place top to bottom to eliminate all traces of that weekend. They were discreet too—from what Jack gathered, they had a department dealing with sites where people had died, and that included those where a body had been found only after several weeks or months.

"Listen, Jack, I'd prefer it if you don't show your face in this city for two weeks, but ..."

"I can't do that." He couldn't control anything that was going to happen, but if he hid, that was blood in the water. If anything, he had to be as visible as possible now or he'd be done in Port Francis. Maybe it was sheer pride that overrode the fear, maybe he was stupid for not grabbing a suitcase full of money—metaphorically only, because he kept his legal money in various places he could access from anywhere—and run now, while he could.

"Yeah. Just call me if you change your mind."

Again, the temptation to throw everything away and join Sal—despite everything. *Because* of everything. But what he needed even more than reassurances from Sal, more than cashing out the promises that Sal had made with his touches and those kisses, he needed to keep his wits about him and play this exactly right. He couldn't be at the wrong place at the wrong time and vanish behind bars again. He couldn't trip up and lose the standing for which he'd sacrificed so much already. He needed time to think, recover, and figure out what the ground was like that he stood on before he could take a single step forward.

"I'll call." He ended the call to begin the painstaking

work of repairing as much damage as he could. Right now, the best he could do was deny Sal a part of his victory and move the money beyond his reach. Money was leverage, was freedom, and it gave him options. It was also a great reason to meet Andrea tomorrow and give him an update and get the lay of the land.

32

Sal managed to catch a few winks on the way to the airport. Though the moment his mind relaxed somewhat, memories flashed by. As they so often did, many of them featured Catia. Not just the awful memories either, the funeral or seeing her pale and dead, almost blue in that tiled room and feeling his sanity slither away at the sight of the head wound. Innocent memories of her grimacing when she untangled her hair, or staring intently at her laptop reading the news. Sometimes, she'd ask his opinion about a nude photo or a film star's physical attributes, watching him with her wide-set eyes. Those latter memories were well-worn favorites, soft with use and nostalgia.

But there were also very new memories playing in his mind, memories that felt a whole lot more novel and fresh. Jack tied to the chair, tense and defiant. Jack asleep, hands tied. Jack running hard on the treadmill. Jack pushing his head back against the wall, eyes closed just before he finished himself off.

Sal still managed to fall asleep, arms crossed, legs crossed, while Enzo next to him drove the truck. It was several hours before what counted as "morning rush hour" in Port Francis, but that hour-long trip helped to catch up his sleep after a restless night. He felt sharper and more awake as Enzo pulled into the parking space.

The local airport's domestic connections to all the major hubs were good, which made Port Francis quite attractive for some IT and consultancy companies whose staff had to travel a lot. Consequently, most of the travelers Sal noticed seemed to be young and middle-aged professionals, with only a few families coming back from visits or vacations. He checked the text he'd received against the Arrivals board and motioned for Enzo to follow him to the gate.

With no more baggage than a backpack, their man was one of the first out of the gates. Sal remembered Silvio Spadaro from a short event years back when one of the other East Coast bosses had croaked his last, and Spadaro had been sent to transmit Gianbattista Falchi's regards. Sal had just moved from capo to underboss, and on that night he'd been otherwise distracted, but he'd still noticed the ripple that went through the assembled old boys when Spadaro made his entrance.

Spadaro was just as eye-catching now in the slim-fitting black suit which he wore more like a model and less like an enforcer. In fact, Spadaro was smaller and slenderer than Sal remembered him—more the frame of a teenager than a man, and he played that up to full effect. That was what disconcerted many; Spadaro didn't look like a leg-breaker, didn't even look like he could fight and kill, and yet those who recognized him knew he did both well.

He pulled off sunglasses and there it was, that black stare that Sal remembered. Along with those strangely sexless features and slender build, the unblinking black eyes made him seem a creature all his own. And that was probably how he liked it. Sal nodded toward him and saw Spadaro change direction to walk to him. "Mr. Rausa." No smile, not much in terms of movement in his face.

"Welcome to Port Francis, and thanks for coming. This is Enzo, my right-hand man. He'll get you set up."

"Battista sends his regards." He reached inside his jacket and took a second to switch on his mobile phone. "Shall we?"

"The car is this way." Sal turned and led the way, noticing Spadaro like a black shadow walking barely inside his peripheral vision. With that suit, and Sal's and Enzo's much more practical clothing, they looked like a couple of mercs or security guards picking up a young investor or internet millionaire. If Spadaro learned to smile, he could make a killing on Instagram as an influencer.

Back at the car, Sal took the wheel, Spadaro settled in on the passenger side, and Enzo went in the back. "Figured we'll hit my place and order food in. We have a lot of intel."

"Guns first." Spadaro half-turned to look at him. "I'll need a bike too, if we're hitting that many targets so quickly. I've been looking at a map of the city. I'll have to scout, get my bearings."

"What are you using?"

"Beretta."

"Great, we'll stop at our main supplier. What's your type of bike?"

"Fast." Now Spadaro grinned.

"No problem. There's a dealership in town, we'll get a bike today. Enzo here will look after you and make sure you're set. We'll have to act quickly because I don't know how long the intel will be good." Enzo's silence was very pointed, but Sal was glad his capo didn't comment otherwise on why the half-life of the information was a lot shorter than ideal. Still, Sal doubted that Jack would be rallying the troops.

It was interesting to see Spadaro pick out his weapons— he didn't have any exotic requirements, just grabbed two Berettas and a hunting rifle of the same brand, and a couple cases of bullets. Sal noticed that he wasn't a man for small talk. If anything, he was slightly awkward dealing with the supplier, seemingly frustrated that the man asked any questions at all, as if he'd wanted to just walk in and the supplier should have been able to read his mind. Maybe it was because he was already so focused on the work he was here to do, but there was a lack of visible affect on his features. The black stare never lessened, hadn't even softened when he'd grinned that once.

After Spadaro had picked up his motorbike, he joined them at Sal's place. Sal had bought a generous condo in one of the luxury complexes after he'd sold the grander house on the outskirts because everything there had reminded him of Catia. Without her, the place was too large and too quiet, and sometimes he'd woken in their bed, heart thundering in his chest, believing for a hot-cold minute that she'd slipped out to go to the bathroom or grab a glass of water, and he'd hear the whisper of her bare feet on the carpet when she returned to bed, warm and alive. He'd simply been too fragile to live married to a ghost for long without losing the rest of his mind.

The complex had decent security, and neighbors included future tech tycoons, affluent couples, and scions of wealthy families who went to college in style here. Above all, though, there wasn't any Lo Cascio or Dommarco money tied into the development—his uncle had carved this piece of the city out for himself and reserved a few floors for his use and that of his family. All Sal had to do was pay for the interior design and the configuration he wanted. He'd installed some very secure doors whose specs vastly exceeded the kind of thing that was normal for these places.

The security guy didn't even blink when Sal, Enzo and Spadaro stepped into the elevator—Enzo was a frequent visitor, and Spadaro moved with a confidence that said he had every right to be here too.

Upstairs, Sal showed Spadaro the guest room, and the hitman dropped his backpack at the foot of the bed.

"Come out when you're ready." Sal gestured around. "There are a few locked doors. Those rooms are not in use."

"Keep your dungeon in there?" Spadaro asked without even looking at him.

Sal laughed, surprised. "You think I have a dungeon?"

"Just a vibe." Spadaro shed his jacket and hung it up in the empty wardrobe. He quickly slipped into the shoulder holster and pushed one of the Berettas inside.

"Takes one to know one, in my experience." Sal leaned in the door frame, watching Spadaro stash away his purchases.

Spadaro gave him another one of those uncanny stares. "Battista said your wife was a 'liberated human being' and considering I'm here to help you place the heads of the whole Lo Cascio clan on her grave, you are too. Liberated. Means kinky."

"I gathered that." So Gianbattista Falchi knew a hell of a lot more about Catia than expected. And that, too, placed Falchi into a different light. To his credit, he hadn't even hinted at it, but it seemed his right-hand man and executioner had less delicate sensibilities. "What about you?"

Spadaro bared his teeth. "Plenty liberated myself."

Oh. Sal couldn't sort Spadaro into any preference. Considering how little he gave away, a session with him would be unnerving as fuck. It didn't make him want to compare notes with Spadaro, that was certain. Not that anything was wrong with him—he was more striking than attractive, but Sal liked to have more of a working idea how to approach the other person and decide together what they liked. Spadaro's only preference, as far as he could tell, were Beretta weapons.

"While we're at it, we're going to kill all members of the Lo Cascio except for one. Jack Barsanti, the consigliere."

"Any reason why?"

"He's my guy on the inside."

"You turned Andrea Lo Cascio's consigliere?"

"Took some effort, but yeah. I'll need him alive to complete the takeover." Wishful thinking, maybe, but if Jack had recovered and was now debriefing Andrea, he'd still want to deal with him in person; he wasn't going to outsource that part. "Turns out, he wanted to live."

Spadaro nodded. "I'm ready. Let's see what you have."

33

*Y*our *password has been changed. Please notify us immediately if that wasn't you.*

Sal saw the alert pop on up the laptop screen. He'd been restless after briefing Spadaro with Enzo until deep into the night. It was somewhat pathetic that he'd kept Jack's laptop close, telling himself that if the man got any important emails, he should be aware of it. But apparently one of the first things Jack did to reestablish his life was to log into his favorite porn site and change his password.

Sal pulled the laptop closer. Yep, he'd been logged out. Same with email. That meant Jack was online, and Sal had a good idea where he was right that minute. He closed the laptop, pulled up the site on his tablet and logged into the business end of the site. He'd flagged Jack's account immediately, and yes, there he was, browsing new recommendations to help him relax after the weekend he'd had.

Torn between just glancing over Jack's shoulder and telling him he was watching, a third option won out. The "social" features of the website were strictly opt-in and limited, enough to have people recommend videos to each other and allow them to take part in bidding on and buying the special content.

As "admin", Sal could do whatever the fuck he pleased—including manipulate what videos Jack got to see. So he uploaded one of his private videos for Jack alone. Nobody else would get to see it, and it would be deleted off the site after playing. He pushed the video into Jack's "recommended for you" sidebar and sent him an alert. There was always a small chance the site might be hacked at that very instant (though Sal could almost rule out that Jack knew how to do it), and the download function was blocked. He sat up in bed, grinning to himself while he waited for his favorite subscriber to take the lovingly prepared bait.

And he did. He'd been sampling a few short videos, but apparently nothing had quite appealed to him, because he went to the top-rated recommendation. And watched all fifteen minutes of it, which pleased Sal enormously. He'd gotten a lot better at blowjobs since then. Despite the tagging, it hadn't been the first one he'd ever given. But a bit of play-acting had spiced things up, and the man he'd blown had been happy to play along.

The video and the making of it were perfectly consensual in every way. He'd moved from pretending to be hesitant, to truly enjoying it, to downright greedy over those fifteen minutes, and the fact that the man's cock was absolutely beautiful certainly hadn't hurt. Sal looked a little younger in it—he'd been clean-shaven because Catia had complained about beard burn—but he hadn't changed that much.

As far as online flirting went, it wasn't quite "dick pic" level, except it totally felt like it. Sal reached for Jack's phone and used it to text Jack's new number: *Glad you liked the show. I have a lot more, and plenty of fresh ideas.*

A text buzzed: *How?*

I know my way around computers. Also, I have a backstage pass to that site.

Nothing. Jack was still logged in, but marked inactive. Probably getting his head around the new situation, and Sal couldn't help laughing. He shouldn't be so gleeful about these games, but he was, and he did have plenty of ideas, and Jack hadn't told him to stop.

Then: *But I changed my password.*

No point. And no, nobody else can see this and connect it to you. No need to freak out and run away. Keep enjoying the site.

You shot amateur porn?

I'll tell you the story someday. This video is going away now, but I have more. If he told Jack how many more, he might be shocked. It was one of those things that people should be eased into slowly, if at all. Though his guess was that, since Jack's whole sexuality had focused only on porn, he appreciated it for what it was.

Not sure I can take more.

Sal laughed. With anybody else, he'd have called and ramped up the teasing, but he didn't want to steamroll Jack, and yet, he did want to drive him out of his mind and then show him that watching wasn't nearly as intense as actually involving another person in his orgasm. At least now Jack had a pretty good idea how Sal gave head.

He shared another one the same way.

Feel free to go at your own pace.

No response, and Jack remained "inactive" on the site, but when Sal checked the next morning, that video had been watched and then deleted itself.

No text messages, of course, and considering Jack's online habits, all texts had been deleted and erased. He wasn't the kind of person to send an explicit photo back to prove how much he'd *enjoyed* the clips, unlike other guys Sal had hooked up with. But how circumspect Jack was about the whole thing, while clearly being more inexperienced than prudish, was terribly endearing. It made Sal smile as he stood in the bathroom, getting ready to—finally—kill some people.

34

If it was weird to begin the day watching the man who was now at war with his family have sex with another man, and relive the best bits under the shower, Jack didn't care to be normal anymore. He'd never have imagined watching a "performer" he knew outside of the videos could be hot, but Sal Rausa fucked pretty much the same way he fought—whole-heartedly, passionately, and fiercely.

"Feel free to go at your own pace."

The video was shot with the same man. Though, arguably, determining whether the owner of that cock from the first video was the same guy who held Sal Rausa down on the bed while piledriving into his body in the second was impossible—angle and all. Whoever he was, he was very nice to look at, but Jack found that 95% of his attention was on Sal—every breath, sound, twitch, groan or thrust.

What made Jack even more breathless was that the video featured kissing. It was impossible to tell whether the man was a boyfriend or lover or one-night stand, because if he could tell one thing, both from experience and after watching Sal, it was that he seemed to consider kissing simply part of sex. Even in the middle of a brutal onslaught, he slowed down to grab his partner's head and devour his mouth.

His partner was into it, and if anything, Sal's sole focus seemed to be on blowing the man's mind. That was what surprised him about the video—if pressed, Jack would have assumed that a guy like Sal Rausa would seize and keep control, but the blowjob video and the one where he got fucked showed Sal in a very different light, and he seemed to enjoy that too. A lot.

Jack had questions.

He shook his head, then checked his phone for the *other* text message. This one from Andrea.

Breakfast, my place, @10

He didn't have to confirm that he'd be there. Andrea assumed he would be, and in all those past years, Jack had never disappointed. Turning it over in his head, the text message was no different from hundreds of others. On the surface, there was no need to be anxious, and yet ...

Getting a solid eight hours of sleep had recharged Jack's batteries, and so had Sal Rausa's teasing and flirting. He had to force himself to hold back—the next few days would be dangerous for everybody—but Sal made him believe that there would be a future, and Jack couldn't figure out how he did it. For the first time, there seemed to be something to look forward to, instead of constantly re-evaluating the past and, clinging to the moment because the endless now had to be endured for as long as possible.

The possibilities were dizzying.

He arrived at Andrea's house at ten o'clock sharp, and for what felt like the first time took conscious note of the security personnel in the outsized grounds. The house had already been too large for Andrea's father, and that was before Andrea had torn down part of it and then added two wings, filled in the original pool, and added a heated pool that was three times the size of the previous one.

Ironically, considering Andrea's house was large enough for a televangelist's ego and a harem of toys, it remained largely empty. Of the thirty or so bedrooms, only three were used regularly. Once upon a time, Andrea had imagined that some rooms could serve live-in nannies or live-in security, but all personnel left at the end of their work day. Security wasn't so tight that the men couldn't go home when the night shift or the day shift had arrived. Jack lived so close that he didn't have to stay overnight when Andrea and he worked late—in all those years, he'd stayed four times in total, and every time he'd woken up, gotten dressed, and headed home before Andrea stirred.

Security was light because nobody in their right mind would consider touching Andrea's property, so while the security firm was qualified, they'd never had to deal with a real, live threat. Jack usually checked in with the current team head and asked for an update. Very rarely was there anything of note, but Jack made a point of showing interest.

He continued on toward the house proper, where a maid informed him that Mr. Lo Cascio was taking breakfast on the terrace on the first floor. He gave her his own breakfast order and went up the stairs to one of the tastefully decorated sitting rooms that were never used for anything but as space to walk through on the way to the terrace. The double doors were open.

Andrea lounged at a formally set round table, along with a tablecloth and silverware, and acknowledged him with a startled frown. "What the fuck happened to your face?"

Jack grimaced. "Slipped getting out of the Jacuzzi. Banged my head, and was damned lucky I didn't knock out a tooth or two."

"The fuck. You look like you've been in a car wreck."

"No, the car is fine. So's the Jacuzzi." Jack shrugged and sat down where the second plate was laid. "I don't know, I could pass it off as a battle wound?"

"Doesn't suit you," Andrea stated bluntly. "Good that the kids aren't around with you looking like that."

"Believe me, I feel stupid enough." He angled his body to present the better side to Andrea as if he had something to hide. "What's up?"

"Well, good you're back. Did you deal with whatever you had to deal with?"

"Yes, all done." He leaned back when the maid showed up with a warm croissant and coffee. He waited until she was gone, then took a sip. Andrea, being at home, rarely bothered to get dressed. He'd thrown on a track suit, though he didn't work out until later in the afternoon. Petra dressed him, but left to his own devices, Andrea reverted to bachelor comfort. That alone told Jack that Petra wasn't around, or she'd have pressured Andrea at least into some kind of designer jeans and a T-shirt.

"Does that include sorting out your situation?"

"My ..." Of course, he'd barely thought of anything else,

but he had to make it look casual. "Oh, you mean getting married. Yes, I've brought it up with my girlfriend."

Andrea regarded him with raised eyebrows. "You never mentioned her."

"She's an outsider," Jack murmured. "She thinks I'm consulting for your companies, and for the foreseeable future, that's exactly as it should be. I'm not quite as lucky as you are."

Oh, Andrea liked that, based on how he leaned back smugly. "Yeah, my wife's special. So, what's the timing on the wedding?"

"First, we're engaged. Wedding next May."

Andrea's gaze went to the coffee cup that Jack was lifting. "She happy with the ring?"

"Thrilled. Two-carat solitaire in platinum."

"Good work. Petra will be happy. You have to bring her around so we can get to know her. It'll be important to Petra."

"I appreciate that."

"What's her name? Tell me about her?"

"Ah, she's a good girl. Popping the question came as a surprise. For some reason, Beth thought I had commitment issues." Using Beth's name felt much more natural than any other name he'd rolled around on his tongue. It was also the only women's name that he knew he'd respond to if Andrea or anybody else spoke it around him, and quick, natural responses would be important, especially if he was otherwise distracted.

"Trust me, wives like a husband who is married to his job. Petra likes a lot of time to herself, at least."

Jack didn't detect any emotional disturbance, so Petra's absence wasn't anything special. "Where is she, anyway?"

"Off to some yoga retreat out of state. I couldn't give less of a fuck about all the chakra shit, but at least the yoga makes her so I can bend her whichever way I want." Andrea took a bite from his croissant. "Here's an idea for you: your Betty and her can go do that stuff together. Bond some, you know."

"I think Beth would love that." He wasn't going to rise to that wrong name—he didn't think Andrea was testing him, just that he literally didn't give enough of a fuck about any future wife's name or personality, as long as her presence meant that Jack was no longer suspicious.

He took his time eating the croissant while Andrea seemed to consider several things. But the fact that he seemed extremely comfortable in his skin and relaxed was reassuring. It didn't mean that Andrea's next words wouldn't be stupid or rash, but whatever he said next wouldn't come from a place of rage at least. In some ways Jack could never relax. Especially not now, knowing either Sal Rausa or Andrea wouldn't live to see next month. Or even next week.

"There's going to be a party in the club tonight. Upstairs. Might be a good idea for you to show up. Also ..." Andrea cast him a sly smile. "It's not exactly stuff for fiancées or wives. A couple business friends, and plenty of girls."

Jack's stomach dropped. "Business friends?"

"Entertaining some guys who'll invest in that venture I'm working on."

Ah, yes, Andrea had mentioned he was going to "befriend" some legit businessmen and convince them to put up some cash for the modernization of the Lo Cascio controlled docks. Andrea had always hemmed and hawed about putting up all the money himself; he preferred to have others pay for these things and then take a disproportionate slice of the cake. All business as usual.

"I could use your head there," Andrea said.

Which meant he had to attend—to rein Andrea back in if necessary, but also to show his face so he could manage the business relationship. Speaking of which. "You sure I should show up looking like this?"

Andrea waved his concern away and laughed. "Oh sure. Tell them a pro boxer caught you wrong in sparring. Say you told him not to go easy on you. You're good at serving up the bullshit."

Now that he was married and settled, Andrea's parties rarely happened at his estate; he usually used one of their clubs and kept the alcohol flowing for everybody.

"Sure, I'll be there."

"It's at The Matador. Starts at ten. Entertainment is arranged."

"Understood."

Then Andrea gave him an update about business—a few phone calls he'd had, and his future plans for the redevelopment. Jack forced himself to pay attention, just in case Andrea lived to see it happen. Jack, for his part, informed Andrea that he'd changed passwords and money around purely out of an abundance of caution. He shared the passwords with Andrea and was prepared to show his boss the accounts and changes in case he flipped out about them. He waited for Andrea to call him a "dumbass", but it seemed

Andrea was too preoccupied with the party tonight and what he planned to achieve there to care about much else.

Despite everything, Jack didn't hate Andrea. He'd worked hard to respect him even in his worst moments, of which there had been many. Andrea could be generous and energetic instead of petty and raging, and the good times had been good. He was willing to make tough decisions and live with the consequences, which was the trait that Jack respected most, and also the one that had made him believe Andrea would definitely have him removed if he didn't fall in line.

Now, the only decision left to make was when to kill Andrea instead. Without Sal, Jack stood no real chance—he'd still be forced to run or fight a battle against Andrea loyalists.

And how completely the tables had turned. Here he sat, listening to his enemy over breakfast while Sal Rausa was his one remaining ally. More than two decades of his life turned inside out.

A few times, he considered bringing up Sal—but the moment never seemed quite right. Maybe superstitiously, any question in that direction could alert Andrea that Sal Rausa still existed, and why would his consigliere mention him now? And when Sal made his move, wouldn't Andrea realize that Jack had something to do with it? No, Andrea needed to be more relaxed, less sharp, and ideally distracted. He'd try digging for answers about Catia's death at the party.

He excused himself a little later, and, at the wheel of the car, texted Sal: *Need to meet*. It was a crazy thing to do. He could have used the burner phone to convey the information he had, but with everything now on the knife's edge, he wanted to look into Sal Rausa's eyes when he talked to him. But really it was just an excuse to meet him again, without being drugged, exhausted, scared and in pain. That would be a very different experience.

35

Spadaro hadn't even taken off the biker suit, but at least the helmet rested on the table in the living room. A little arsenal of weaponry and ammo covered the rest.

Sal especially liked the part of Enzo's and Spadaro's plan where the targets would receive delivery messages from a courier with a link to a spoofed website that confirmed the delivery, and was also loaded with some handy malware that would allow them to track or access the phone in case things went wrong. Spadaro or somebody else posed as the courier requiring a signature, which got him close enough to strike either right then or later if the situation required it.

Spadaro had eventually settled on taking out the capos in a specific order, while Enzo and the other boys were going to focus on the soldiers. Sal wasn't worried about the associates—those might report to soldiers and capos, but from the way Jack had told it, none of them had a specific investment in Andrea as boss, or even the Lo Cascio. If they received the same back-up, support, or simple pressure from any other family, they'd fall into whatever hand was open to receive them. They'd be approached and taken in when the time was right.

His phone buzzed.

Need to meet.

Spadaro remained laser focused on the map of Port Francis they'd pinned to the wall. They still had to decide when to deal with Andrea—though Spadaro had checked out his estate that morning and noted it offered several usable approaches to take him out in his own home.

Sal texted Jack the address and added: *I'll pick you up in the garage downstairs.*

The response came immediately: *En route. Twenty minutes.*

"Jack's coming."

Enzo tilted his head. "Asking for protection?"

Now Spadaro also turned away from his map and regarded Sal. "The consigliere?"

"I don't know. And yes." Sal slipped the phone back into his pocket. "In any case, he's under my protection. He might have an idea how to finish Andrea. Or additional targets who were involved with the murder of my wife."

That last bit was more directed at Spadaro, whose dark eyes didn't betray what he thought; he soaked up information without displaying any emotion. Still, Sal gathered that Spadaro loved his job the same way he loved fast bikes and Berettas. He didn't tell war stories, but the kind of questions he asked, the way he approached everything here betrayed a ruthless intelligence that never rested, never paused, and had no ability to compute either hesitation or mercy. As a human being, Spadaro was clearly seriously damaged. As an executioner, he was perfect.

"Who's going to kill Lo Cascio?" Spadaro turned his dark gaze on Sal. "Any specific thoughts about it?"

Over the years, Sal had entertained a lot of revenge fantasies. At first, they'd focused on Andrea, but they'd widened—not only was Andrea going to die, but everything he'd built, and his family had built, his very legacy would be scrubbed off the map. Ten years from now, people would barely remember his name. Whether he'd do it with his own hands, though, was a different matter. Spadaro was likely better equipped, considering he wouldn't be blinded by rage.

"No, but if you end up doing it, send me a photo of the body."

Spadaro flashed one of his cold, bright smiles, all teeth, and none of it reached his eyes. "Will do."

"Why do they call you the Barracuda?" Enzo suddenly asked. "That's an ugly fucking fish."

Spadaro gave a small nod. "Because they only attack *once*."

Enzo pursed his lips in an "okay, I'm impressed" expression.

"And they're fast." Spadaro shrugged. "Battista's idea."

That made sense. Plus, the man's coldness and expressionless face made that nickname even more fitting. As far as Cosa Nostra nicknames went, this one was both flattering and accurate.

Spadaro cast another glance at his map. "When do you want me to start?"

"You could take today to familiarize yourself some more if you need."

Spadaro shrugged. "I'm all set."

"Enzo?"

"I'll start tonight. Late enough so most civilians are off the streets. Some guys might be off to clubs, but we've given them the opportunity to schedule a one-hour same-day delivery slot, so hopefully they'll use that." Enzo laughed, shaking his head, so clearly in love with his idea and contribution that it made Sal smile. "So we can be sure our courier will catch them."

Spadaro smirked. "We are ambush hunters. Always good to know where the prey will be."

"I'm glad you both are having fun," Sal muttered, but found himself enjoying this part of plotting the mass-murder of the whole Lo Cascio clan. His phone buzzed again. "I'll go pick up Jack."

He checked the screen on the way down, but it was just Jack telling him he'd arrived outside the garage, so Sal phoned security and told them to let the silver Porsche inside. He headed toward the parking spaces marked "Guests", and there Jack was, closing the car door behind himself with a satisfying thud. Sal's heart skipped a painful beat, and his fingers tingled with the urge to touch him. He could lust over lovers, enjoy the anticipation of meeting a hook-up, wholly feast on an attractive couple hosting him at their house, but this was unlike him.

Instead of walking up to Jack and grabbing him in a tight hug, he let him come toward him. Despite the tension around Jack's lips, he couldn't help but smile. The harsh neon lights of the car park were decidedly unkind to Jack— they made him look pale, and the bruises looked more serious. It would take weeks for the discoloration to vanish, though the swelling was definitely down. But despite all that, Jack still looked amazing in his classic suit and shirt. "Let's go to the elevator." *Because I don't know what I'll do if we don't get away from any potentially curious eyes.*

"Yeah, good idea." Jack sounded a little breathless himself.

Sal stepped into the elevator first and hit the button once Jack had joined him. The moment the doors closed, Jack shifted his weight uneasily and then hit the "stop" button. He turned around and the last thing Sal saw before Jack was right up in his space and kissed him was an expression somewhere between despair and pure need.

"Fuck," he muttered before he kissed him back. This kind of kiss—both of them clear-headed, or as clear-headed as they could possibly be, given the circumstances—made his soul feel raw.

Emboldened, Jack grabbed him by the shoulders and pushed him back against the wall of the cabin, and Sal loved that urgency. He didn't fight him, but grabbed Jack's belt and pulled him even closer, until their bodies were grinding together. Jack gasped, broke the kiss and pressed his forehead against Sal's. "You're trying to destroy my sanity, aren't you?"

"Why, is it working?" Sal grinned and grabbed Jack by the neck. "And are you enjoying it?"

"It scares me to death."

"That makes two of us, but we got this."

"You think?"

"I do." Sal pushed Jack back enough so he could look him in the eyes. "Why are you here? What's wrong?"

"Nothing's wrong. I needed to see you. And Andrea's

going to have a party tonight, and I have to be there. And maybe you can do something with that." Jack closed his eyes. "But mostly I needed to see you. After last night ..."

"Liked the videos?"

Jack nodded. "I want ..."

Sal almost didn't expect Jack to say the words. What the man needed was plenty clear from the way he sought every bit of contact he could get, that shine in his eyes, and a slight flush that spoke of a need so strong it was melting his barriers from the inside. Getting somebody like Jack—who'd denied himself for so long—to such a state took some doing, but Sal didn't gloat. He found it both terribly endearing and hot as hell that Jack had come to him not just willingly, but clearly craving him, and this moment was the payoff he'd been after ever since he'd decided he'd try to seduce the man, mind and body and soul.

Jack tried to collect himself, swallowed. "I want you. Like that. If I can."

"Anything specific?"

"No. All of it. I need to know what it feels like, what you feel like." He looked almost sheepish then, as if he seriously thought Sal might be toying with him. "If I'm going to die, worst-case scenario, if everything goes sideways and I catch a bullet, I want to know what it's like to ... have sex with a man." Another hard swallow. "With you."

This wasn't the first time that Sal had been propositioned in an elevator, but definitely the sweetest and most heart-felt one. "Same. With you. I know what it's like, but I'm definitely up to fuck you specifically."

"Oh, thank God," Jack muttered, and Sal chuckled.

"I'm not playing. You need to know that before we get out

of this elevator and into my bedroom." He reached past Jack and hit the stop button again, and with a small jerk, the cabin resumed its smooth movement. "They check on elevators quickly here, and the technicians can have the door open in less than a minute, so we should have this conversation upstairs."

"All right." Jack straightened his suit but looked very flustered. "I still feel … stupid. Insecure. Worried. You're right, how can I get this old and …"

"It's hot." Sal winked at him. "You won't have any bad sexual habits to unlearn, for one. It gets tiring really fucking quickly if a partner has a script in their head about how sex is supposed to go. You don't have that. And that's hot."

"I know porn isn't actual sex …"

"I noticed that you prefer the amateur stuff anyway."

"How …"

"I own that site, and a few others. Compared to some other business interests, it's good, clean fun." Sal kept his hand on Jack's shoulder even when the door opened, guided him along the corridor, and then opened the door to the penthouse. "Enzo and another guy are in the apartment making plans. They both know who you are."

"You own that site? Wow."

"I'll tell you that story some other time, but yeah. I like this kind of stuff because it can't be disrupted easily." A lot of classic Cosa Nostra activities had translated pretty well— gambling, loan sharking, prostitution, and any number of frauds and scams. Of course, Sal wasn't the only one in that space by far, but he'd moved into it the most aggressively.

Both Spadaro and Enzo looked up when Sal came back to the living room. "Guys, Jack Barsanti."

Enzo gave a lopsided grin. "I think we should go grab that Thai you wanted, eh, Barracuda?"

Spadaro glanced quizzically at him.

Thanks for making this awkward, Enzo. "Let's hear first what Jack has to say. Or maybe we should do that when you come back." Arguably torturing Jack even more was completely unnecessary at this point, but he might be less distracted after Sal was done with him.

"It's okay, boss." Enzo stood and grabbed his wallet and jacket. "Silvio here claims the Thai in London is better than anything we have."

"I hope you're taking him to the Ayutthaya?" Jack asked.

"You bet your ass I am." Enzo sized up Spadaro, who was slowly rising from his seat. "Port Francis is small but mighty."

"Challenge accepted," Spadaro stated bluntly.

"Full tasting menu, then," Jack added.

"Definitely." Enzo nodded to Jack with a co-conspirator's smirk, and then looked at Sal. "Two hours."

"Noted." Sal waited for the door to close behind the unlikely late lunch companions, then smiled at Jack, who seemed both amused and embarrassed. "Good old reliable Enzo. Bedroom?"

"He's okay with this?"

"More than okay. Enzo and I are ... not boyfriends, or partners, or even really lovers. It's complex, but jealousy doesn't play a part in it."

"I want to know everything." Jack's tone suggested a dozen meanings. Sal all but pushed him toward the bedroom, and for some added privacy—Enzo had keys to the penthouse—locked the door behind them.

36

The large bed was unmade, and Jack imagined that Sal had risen from it naked, and that the sheets would smell of him. Whatever his relationship with Enzo or that hard-eyed stranger was, there was only one pillow on the bed, and maybe Sal had lain there and stroked himself when he'd sent Jack those videos. The shutters were nearly closed, allowing in no more than an intimate gloom that was a whole lot less unnerving for these things than all the light in Jack's house. Jack also noticed how the gloom softened the cast of Sal's face, and imagined that his own bruising didn't look so bad right now.

Sal stood close and placed a hand on Jack's chest. "No false bravado, okay? If something doesn't feel good, tell me. I want to do this right."

That was the most considerate anybody had ever been to him. Jack couldn't even remember when somebody had last cared what he liked or what he felt. Finding it with a man who posed the greatest risk to his life, and who should be an enemy was mind-twistingly bizarre. Jack touched Sal's chest in return and felt the man's steady breath anchoring him. He wore a light woolen sweater, cashmere most likely, and when Jack slid his hands underneath, all he encountered was warm, naked skin. He pushed higher, and Sal helped by pulling the sweater up and finally over his head, to toss it into one corner of the room without looking.

"That's right. This happens at your pace." Sal spoke in a low rumble that made Jack want to push him to the bed and do all the things he only knew from watching. What he'd never taken into account when it came to imagining sex was how hard his heart would be beating.

He moved closer to kiss the place between Sal's collar bones. Sal's hands on his waist and his smell in Jack's nose steadied and weakened him at the same time. He kissed Sal's throat, sandpapery with stubble, then dropped one hand to cup Sal's groin, feeling his hard cock through the cloth. That gave him more confidence, the fact that while Sal seemed in no rush, he clearly wouldn't mind if he did push for more.

"Same goes for you," Jack whispered. "Is there anything you want, or don't want?"

"I'm kind of into everything to a ridiculous degree." Sal chuckled. "If you just want to kiss and touch, I'm game. If you want a sixty-nine, I'm game. If you're heading straight for anal, God, yeah, game. Taking and giving. But don't let that influence your choices."

"What are you doing with Enzo?"

"It's bad form to ask that." Sal's eyes sparkled. "But he's into bottoming."

"Huh. Wouldn't have guessed."

"Neither had he, but that's how that goes." Sal shrugged. "I like it either way. I don't judge."

"No, you don't." Jack shed his jacket and opened the buttons of his shirts. Together, they got rid of his shirt and undershirt, and the next brush of skin against skin was as intoxicating as that full-body contact under the shower. Jack managed to kick off his shoes and pushed them to the side while they shared another, more heated kiss, hands grasping and pulling, bodies flush against each other. Jack managed to gather enough thoughts to open the button of his own trousers and pull down the zipper, and then Sal's hands were at his boxers, shoving them halfway down his thighs. He looked down when he took hold of Jack's cock, making Jack shake. "Your turn."

Trying hard to focus, Jack managed to unbutton Sal's pants and groaned with frustration when he encountered three further buttons that put up significant resistance before he'd freed Sal's cock. It felt amazing in his hand, thick and long and beautiful, and his touch made Sal gasp softly. Jack stroked it, but then nudged Sal toward the bed.

Sal sat down, resting back on his elbows while Jack removed the sturdy boots and his pants. He straightened but didn't quite have it in him to join Sal on the bed.

All of this was completely new territory. He pushed between Sal's legs, placed a hand around his cock and moved even closer. When his breath hit Sal's naked skin, the man tensed slightly, but that was nothing compared to when Jack opened his lips and took the tip into his mouth. The heat and taste and the sheer feeling of taboo, of doing the unimaginable, tore through his mind and made him take a little more, and then explore that silky skin with his tongue.

Sal drew a shuddering breath and opened his legs
further, so he was definitely doing the right thing. Jack
couldn't imagine how some guys and women got something
that size down their throats, but even so, it was shockingly
intimate and hot. Based on how Sal's breathing shifted and
the muscles of his thighs tensed, he got plenty of enjoyment
out of it.

"If you use that hand to stroke and squeeze my balls, you
could make me come," Sal whispered. "I also like a couple
fingers up my ass, but feel free to develop your own style."

Jack decided that talking was overrated in this case, but
glanced up at Sal, and was pleasantly shocked by the heat in
the man's eyes. He pulled back a little and flicked his tongue
over the tip, grinning when Sal hissed. "It's the visuals,
right?"

"It's everything. First, it's sexy as fuck that you're trying
things out, and I definitely get off on communication,
because I don't know you that well yet."

Yet. That last word zinged through Jack's chest like a little
electric spark. "I'm getting used to talking about it."

"I know. You're doing good. Now do me a favor and put
my cock back in your mouth because it feels great, and I
think you like it too."

Do me a favor. Jack grinned and made a point of sucking
the tip again, this time speeding up his movements and
increasing the suction, noting from the corners of his eyes
how Sal's fingers tightened in the bedsheets. That spurred
him on. He moved his hand up and down the thick shaft,
and eventually managed to time the strokes of his hand with
the movements of his head and tongue.

"That I'm the first person in this fucked-up world to see

you like this." Sal's voice barely carried, but Jack still noticed the small tremble in it, and he glanced up again as Sal was wetting his lips.

Jack stopped to swallow and relax his jaw, but licked along the shaft, tracing a pulsing vein and following it to Sal's shaved balls—interesting—and toyed with them, but remembered to continue the stroking. "Andrea would have a fucking heart attack, that's for sure."

The vibrations from Sal's laughter travelled down to his whole body. "Yeah, I was thinking that. But 'If Andrea could see you like that' didn't have the vibe I was going for."

"Why not?"

"I'm not sure you're into humiliation."

The words didn't hold a sting. The only thing that was objectionable about them was the mention of Andrea. In a remote, purely abstract way, he knew Andrea was attractive —his boss definitely liked to preen and show off—but even in their best, most comradely moments, there had never been any kind of attraction. He'd definitely never pined for, or ever considered Andrea in that way.

"I don't feel humiliated." He gently nipped the inside of Sal's thigh, allowing balls and cock to brush along his cheek. Sal fell back onto the bed and lifted his knees somewhat.

"Fuck, come here."

Jack shed the last of his clothes before he joined Sal on the bed; he was going to continue with the blowjob, but it seemed he'd done very well, because Sal pulled him closer and into a heated kiss. Sal's legs closed around his hips, and before Jack figured out angles and how to move, his own cock was grinding against Sal's slightly sweat-damp belly, feeling the flexing muscles underneath, and running along-side Sal's cock that was trapped between them.

He only broke the kiss to focus on Sal's nipples—the bars through them fascinated him and he assumed Sal liked having them played with. He tried twisting them with his tongue and teeth, and sure enough, the man groaned and breathed heavier as he did. That was hot, so Jack alternated between nipples while also sliding his cock against Sal's body.

Having this man underneath him still felt inconceivable. But Sal was visibly enjoying this—the way he closed his eyes or pressed his lips together. He wasn't quiet, either—moans and groans and pants taught Jack even more what Sal liked. Still, Sal was holding back, moving both of them further up the bed, and at some point he stuffed the pillow under his neck for support.

"Suggestion?" Sal said between kisses.

"I'm listening."

"Condom and lube?"

Jack nodded, struggling with what to say. It wasn't "are you sure?" because Sal was clearly up for it, but still, nerves hit him. He was too aware that he'd never done this before, and while he was eager to learn, it seemed like a huge thing. He'd only get one chance to make a first impression, so to speak.

Sal reached over to the nightstand, and somehow managed to kiss Jack, open the condom wrapper, and slide the slick latex down Jack's length. "I'd fuck you without one, but it's good manners with a new partner ..."

"Nice. Getting an education with my orgasm."

Sal glanced at him quizzically, but broke into a grin. "Singular? We have two hours." He opened the lube and covered the condom with it, then pushed the slippery fingers between his own cheeks. He curved his back more and pulled Jack closer. "See if you like this."

Jack adjusted his position, and Sal guided him, encouraging him with his legs and nods, until he seemed to be in the right place. Jack laughed with exasperation at his own first attempt. Guys in porn made it look so easy and hot, and no doubt Sal was fantastic at it, but here they were with him fumbling around and self-conscious.

"Relax. Take a breath. Slowly," Sal said. "No pressure. Except of course I want to feel you."

"Same," Jack gritted and pushed, finding that Sal's body was suddenly yielding to him. But even more astonishing and sexy was how he pushed his head back against the pillow when Jack entered him. "This is the part ... where you tell me how big I am," Jack chuckled, because this was weird and incredible, and it took everything he had to move slowly and savor it.

Sal laughed. "So praise gets you off."

"Worth trying."

Sal laughed harder. "Should have done that, rather than tie you to a chair. Fuck. It could have been so easy."

Jack had never have imagined sex could be like this; intense, but also playful and funny. It wasn't common in porn, though he loved the rare couple that laughed or grinned while fucking. Banter was also pretty rare, and he loved that Sal's sense of humor didn't even fail when he had his legs in the air. Maybe it was the pure confidence, the way he clearly loved inhabiting his own skin that made him so sexy, and that confidence withstood minor indignities such as an inexperienced lover.

Jack pushed deeper against the slick resistance of that powerful body, and, with Sal's legs pulling him closer, found himself lodged inside Sal's body as far as he could go. Sal's breathing was noticeably faster, muscles tensing with every breath. Despite the condom, he felt every movement inside Sal. Everything was totally new and intense and yet so good.

He shifted his weight and kissed Sal, covering him with his body, then tried thrusting, well, really more rocking into Sal. Careful to keep part of his weight on a hand next to Sal's head, he grabbed his neck with the other and pulled him up into the kiss while he pushed harder. The way Sal grew more and more breathless, and moved against him as much as he could, winding up tenser and tighter, encouraged Jack. "Like that?"

"Fucking love it," Sal whispered.

That hadn't been the question, but Jack didn't doubt the answer. He focused on his movements, realizing that short, measured thrusts worked best in this position, because they also enabled him to rub alongside Sal's cock. While sweat and precum gathered between their bodies, Sal flexed around him, and between the kisses and their increasingly harsh movements, Jack could almost feel Sal yield to him. Chasing his own orgasm as he gripped his cock hard and spurred Jack on with bared teeth, Sal panted and moaned. Unlike in porn, where everything was done for effect, none of this was faked. Not Sal's tension that wound tighter and tighter, and not Jack's breathless wonder as he got closer and closer.

It was Jack who came first. Coming inside Sal felt incredible—he'd never imagined he'd get to feel so viscerally close to another person, that he could have the chance to experience this at all. Coming had always been the end result, the goal he'd chased, but with Sal devouring his mouth, it was more than a goal now—it was total bliss. He kept moving while Sal chased his own orgasm, because feeling that vice-like squeeze around him wrung a few more spurts out of him, and then Sal collapsed onto the mattress, letting his legs fall open.

He was panting, but the lightness returned almost immediately. Jack rolled off Sal and collapsed by him on the mattress, overwhelmed with the sensation, and definitely the aftermath.

"For the record, it's not just the size, but also technique," Sal said.

Jack laughed softly. "Worked for you?"

"Oh yeah. Much bigger, and I'd struggle. Your cock is just right." Sal flashed him a grin. "Sorry, too breathless to come up with more effusive praise. Gimme a minute."

"No need for more compliments. You already got me off."

They laughed together, and Jack stretched out an arm and pulled Sal closer when he took the offer. There was a strange kind of buzzing peace while they both relaxed, but the presence of another person in the same bed kept Jack awake. He'd never imagined how beautiful it was to have another person's head rest on his shoulder. Sal placed a hand on Jack's stomach and very lightly stroked the skin there with the backs of his fingers.

"Praise, huh? What's the story?"

"Really, are we going to talk about that?" Jack shook his head. "I don't know. I guess I don't get a lot of it? I didn't think I needed or wanted it, either. But it felt good when it came from you."

"Ah, understood." Sal kissed Jack's chest. "One sec." He reached down and plucked the condom from Jack's cock, then left the bed in one fluid motion and vanished into the bathroom. When he came back, he was barely more than a dark silhouette against the sparse light creeping through the shutters. Now Jack wished the room were lit like an NFL stadium during a game. He didn't want to miss a thing, and watching Sal move around naked was something he could get used to.

Sal returned to his place against Jack's shoulder. "I want to apologize again for what I did to you."

"It's okay. We're already joking about it."

"Yes. Though it's hilarious that I first put you in your own closet, and then dragged you out of it."

Jack smiled. "Jacuzzi sex is definitely never going to happen."

"I don't know. Could be therapeutic." Sal's tone was light enough to suggest he was joking too.

"Tell me about Enzo and you?"

"It's good friends with occasional benefits. He's very good at spotting when I need to release some steam with somebody I trust and who knows me. He isn't even into men, but he's into getting bossed around, and he'll let a man fuck him when he's in the right headspace, which is submissive. His ideal partner is a woman who loves to put a man in his place and peg him until he comes, at least every now and then. I'm sure he could find somebody, but I don't think he's even currently looking."

"Why not?"

Sal drew a long breath and released it. "He's been too focused on keeping me sane. With everything going on, I don't think he had the spare capacity."

"But if he's straight ..."

"Straight-ish. Quasi-straight. Plenty of men who have sex with men would call themselves straight. More common than you'd think. I never pushed him into anything he didn't enjoy."

Jack turned his head to look at Sal. "I didn't think you did. Doesn't it feel strange to sleep with somebody who's straight?"

"Just means he's not romantically available. Neither was I, but once all of this is over ..." Sal rubbed over his face. "Once I can allow myself to let it all go, the fucking pain, that rage ... once that's done, I could be open to feeling something more. Something deep. Fuck, I want to."

Jack's heart clenched. He was almost sure Sal was signaling that *they* could have something more, something deep and meaningful. It scared him witless because his own feelings were all over the place, and he wasn't used to feeling anything so intensely. He'd thought he had his life and job under control and that both pretty much overlapped completely. But ever since Sal had confronted him, the spaces in his mind that had been tidy and well-ordered didn't feel like that at all anymore. And it all could still go wrong. It was bound to, wasn't it?

"I don't think I'm a very emotional person," Jack said carefully. "Not sure I ever was. I couldn't allow it. I had to be too careful."

"Getting past that takes work." Sal traced the line of

Jack's ribcage with a thumb. "I know just the thing for you. It helped me."

"What's that? Getting fucked senseless?" Sex worked. Sex allowed him to stay in the moment, focus on somebody else, and enjoy the sensation.

"Ropes. Specifically shibari. And yeah, it can lead to sex, but it's also its own thing. It's hard to describe what it does, but if you ever want to get tied up again, I have plenty of rope."

Strangely, the thought of Sal tying him up triggered zero horror, even though the skin around his wrists was still somewhat tender from the zip ties and his automatic struggles and movements and jerks. He hadn't even fought the ties, which was why he wasn't bruised or chafed, but it had still been enough to make him very aware of his wrists. "You like getting tied up?"

"With the right rigger, yes." Sal chuckled. "With the right person, I like pretty much anything. Though shibari isn't something I do casually, or at least not often. It's too tied up with other things, pun intended."

All Jack knew about shibari were some artsy black and white photos of rope patterns on skin, and while they'd been attractive in a remote way, they hadn't hit him deep down. But Sal bringing it up shifted his perspective, and he could imagine Sal's powerful body trussed up like that, all his energy carefully restricted and contained, and all of that became a tantalizing possibility. And if Sal felt similarly about him, then ... "I'd try it."

"Now?"

Shit. One step forward and he felt like rushing two steps back, but hadn't he said he wanted to feel everything? And if that was what Sal wanted to do, and he clearly did, then Jack was game.

"Shibari isn't something I do casually, or at least not often."

Weren't they both in totally unchartered waters here, unable to see coasts or lighthouses? Though it all still felt strangely safer and saner than anything else in Jack's life. "Yes. Let's try that."

Sal kissed him and stood. "How are your wrists?"

"Tender."

"Yeah, I should have used rope instead. But I figured I wasn't going to waste a good rope on a piece of shit. Obviously, I was totally wrong."

"If we'd known how that whole weekend would go, none of us would have made those decisions." Jack sat up and placed his arms around his knees. "But I don't regret a thing."

"I do, a little." Sal opened his wardrobe and tossed a length of white rope onto the bed near Jack's thigh. "Touch it."

It was surprisingly soft, almost silky and the thickness of a finger, but no doubt sturdy, solid rope. Sal also placed bandage scissors on the nightstand. "I wouldn't do this if you hadn't already proven that you can talk to me, Jack. With this, it's even more important, because you will quite literally be helpless."

"Nothing new there."

"Probably not, but also totally different." Sal grinned. "Also, this doesn't have to lead to sex, you can just enjoy the tying. Similarly, if it turns you on, we don't have to do anything about it, or I can untie you before anything sexual happens. There's huge variation in how people respond.

Some want the tightness and helplessness, others get so horny they'd fuck an army if one were around."

"What about you?"

"It depends on what I'm bringing to the session and who does it, but yeah, it turns me on."

"So I could do that to you?"

Sal's eyes narrowed with speculation, and then darted to Jack's hands. His lips parted slightly, and he wetted them. "You could be pretty good at it too, considering how smart and methodical you are about everything. I could teach you. Would you like that?"

"Tying you up? Yes."

A deep, harsh exhale, almost a hiss. "Perfect."

That was what tipped the balance, and anticipation rippled through Jack, part nerves, part attraction, and he watched, slightly breathless, as Sal returned to the bed, one leg underneath him, and loosened the coil of rope, playfully letting it touch Jack's skin, but there was no fixed purpose to it. The gentle, conscious way he did this indicated that the rope was harmless, no more than a toy, and Jack was willing to believe it.

"So what's going to happen? If I get turned on?"

"What do you want to happen?"

"I'm ... expecting you'll fuck me while we still have time."

Sal smiled. "I'd like that a lot, but there's something I want to show you before we take that step. Don't get me wrong, I want to take more time to teach your body how much fun it'll be, rather than thrust in and hope you'll eventually relax enough that it's not painful. I'm not that much of a bastard."

You're not a bastard at all. Jack nodded, feeling some of the tension dissipate. "Did it ... did it hurt for you? I feel so fucking weird to even ask that."

Sal placed an arm around Jack's shoulders and pulled him into a kiss. "No. Pretty sure Catia understood that it would be the first and only time if she'd have hurt me."

All right, so more puzzle pieces dropped in place, and Jack wasn't surprised that it had been his wife, considering what he'd told Jack about her, and how openly he talked about pegging, though he talked openly about everything. "Were you tied up?"

"Like a Thanksgiving turkey." Sal laughed. He took a length of the rope and scooted closer to Jack, and deliberately let it trail over Jack's leg. Warm, smooth, light enough to be almost a tickle. Jack shifted his weight, mimicking Sal's position, one leg up and one down, while Sal almost bracketed his body with his legs from behind.

Jack watched with some apprehension as Sal formed a loop and placed it around Jack's wrist, and tugged at it, just demonstrating that the rope would and could hold him. Jack nodded, and watched, captivated, how Sal looped the rope around both of his hands—unlike ratcheting the zip ties tight, this felt more like a wrapping, a firm kind of shell that restricted his movement, but felt as soothing as putting on a heavy coat.

While Sal worked quickly with deft hands, nothing felt rushed or forced. If anything, Jack was surprised at how focused Sal was—all his attention was on the rope touching Jack's skin. From behind, Sal pulled on the rope and took Jack's bound wrists and lifted his arms until his elbows pointed upward and his hands were behind his neck. Jack felt the stretch in his shoulders and chest, and his focus shifted to his chest and belly that were both exposed and helpless. A tugging on the rope, and one of Sal's hands came around to rest between Jack's pecs, more rope tugged into his thumb and a loop dangled down to his belly and brushing his groin.

A slow, deliberate movement looped the rope across his pecs, above his nipples and under his arms, and then a forceful tightening and whisper of rope, and another movement. A knot? Some kind of fastening? What was strange about this was that now every breath made Jack aware of the rope around his chest, and Sal's strong grip told him that Jack himself was now totally out of his depth, and, yes, helpless. Half kneeling, half sitting on the bed, arms tied back like that, he couldn't have reached the cutting tool if he'd set his mind to it.

"Woah."

"It's basic, but even this gets the job done," Sal murmured close to his ear, hand on the knot or connection in his back, while his other hand lay flat on Jack's stomach. "You're doing really well. How do you feel?"

"Safe. Held. It's like ... some kind of embrace. I know you're doing this." Did that make sense? Words were much harder to find and chain together to form sentences. It seemed like too much effort, and he didn't want to chase away that floaty feeling just to make more of an effort.

"Perfect."

Another loop across his chest, this time below his nipples, and the tightening now shifted all of Jack's awareness to his pecs and specifically his nipples. There was no way Sal brushed them by accident—not to turn him on, but to direct his awareness.

"I'd give everything to put you in a harness," Sal murmured near his ear. "I could show you off like that and everybody would see how beautiful you are."

"I know exactly what you're doing with the praise," Jack shot back.

"It's not about that at all." Sal placed a hand on Jack's throat and bent it back in a gentle movement. Jack suddenly struggled to keep his eyes open, so he closed them and barely noticed the drawn-out sigh that came from his lips. Sal did something else—moved Jack's leg by pushing gently against the inside of his knee, and then the touch of the rope, slow, gentle, around his ankle, similarly safe and secure as around his hands.

Another tugging and tightening and Jack realized that his leg was now somehow connected to the knot in the back. A different coil of rope slid under the tied leg, and Sal slowly connected thigh and lower leg to each other. Each movement of rope a caress, every knot a tightening and release that began to mirror the tension and then the much deeper relaxation in Jack's body. Nothing hurt or was unpleasant— even the position of his hands began to feel natural and comfortable, and Sal's support in his back remained steadfast and dependable.

A loop of rope trailed up from his chest and across his throat, but no tightening followed, instead the rope came up to his face and slid between his teeth, and Jack was almost glad to have something so tangible, so intrusive, that focused him again. The rope in his mouth tightened, and that little jerk travelled all the way through his body, a hot-cold moment of near shock, if shock could be both languid and intense. He felt like he was losing his balance, as his body-weight shifted, but it was Sal pulling the ropes and holding Jack a little bit off balance.

It washed over him as a tremendous, sensual, full-body release when he came to rest against Sal's naked skin, so grateful for the man's presence and strength. Still, Sal kept working on the ropes, adjusting here and there, loosening one loop, while building another one—the one in his mouth vanished and a feather light touch of fingers followed. Sal adjusted the position of his arms and lowered them in front of Jack's chest, which felt like a bit of a rest, but a loop then appeared around Jack's belly and around his hips, connected to the ones across his torso.

"How are you feeling?"

"Hard ... to say. Turned on, relaxed, and I feel everything, but I'm not sure about time and place."

"Good. Do you want me to do something about your erection?"

"That question is harder to answer than it should be, right?"

Sal chuckled. "Right."

What Jack then realized was that the inner voice, the one with which he talked to himself, was completely silent. It was both disorienting and a relief. There was complete silence inside—he felt both empty and hollow, but not in a bad way. As if all weight had been removed, and he couldn't even be bothered to reach for it and try to reclaim it. The ropes held him as surely as his own muscles and bones held his own soul, his breath and pulse.

"Yes, please."

"What do you want? I could show you something new, but it's intense."

"Yes."

Again, Sal adjusted Jack's position so Jack was lying over Sal's bent leg on the bed, with Sal curled over and around him, but still sitting. He then pushed Jack's legs apart. Sal's hand felt white hot when it settled on Jack's ass, and Jack assumed working the ropes like that was responsible for the heat in his palms. He shuddered when Sal's fingers slid between his ass cheeks.

A small clicking sound, and something slick and cold dribbled on his ass, with Sal's hand massaging his glutes and then returning to the place in between, sliding up and down, with enough pressure that Jack tensed a little in anticipation. And sure enough, two fingers rubbed against his opening. Jack gasped when they pushed in a little, to test him, and withdrew, testing and then pulling back.

"Please ... do it, Sal. I'm good. I'm really good."

"I believe you." Sal shifted his weight, and his next words were barely louder than a breath. "There will be times when I fuck you like this, if you want me to. I'll fuck you with the rope first, like this, all over, and with my eyes, watching you struggle to hold your balance, and maybe I'll add some pain so the release will be even better. You'll become even calmer and sink even deeper into that place where you're all mine. I'll make you feel how strong you are and how beautiful, and I'll keep your need simmering all night. We'll have all the time in the world, because it's just us."

"Just us," Jack echoed, unable to fathom the depth behind those words, but it was what he needed to hear.

And then something pushed against his opening, something harder and colder than a finger, and slid easily a small way inside, where it touched something tender and sensitive in a shock of pleasure. It also seemed to push against the outside of his body behind his balls, and rapidly warmed to body temperature.

Sal took the ropes and rolled Jack onto his side. The thing moved with him and stayed inside his body, and just this movement felt strange and almost disturbingly intense. Sal moved on the bed, but didn't break the contact, and that thing inside Jack began to vibrate. It was no more than a very low hum, but the place it touched was so sensitive Jack's whole body tensed. Then it stopped.

Jack managed to blink his eyes open. "What ...?"

"Feel good?" Sal grinned at him.

Jack couldn't even describe the feeling—it was too strange, too intense to feel good, but his balls tightened when it started up again, and he saw Sal holding his phone. A tap of his finger on the screen stopped the vibration. "Fuck. You control it with ..."

"Yep." Sal put the phone down, then seemed to reconsider. "I'd untie you so you can play with the programs, but this one's pretty good, so you can relax if you want."

Making it sound totally optional. The next time, the vibration was a little stronger, and came with noticeable pulses that felt amazing both on the outside and inside. Jack fell back onto his side. He was aware of Sal's hand on his bound wrists, holding them against Jack's chest, while the toy vibrated on and off, a little stronger with every cycle, until it grew so intense that Jack could do nothing but pant and writhe in the ropes, surrendering to the feeling until he heard himself begging for release. Sal held him, and then, when Jack didn't feel he could take even a second more, closed his hand around Jack's cock and stroked over the tip one, twice, and Jack nearly screamed.

Or actually screamed. He wasn't quite sure. Sal kept stroking his cock through an orgasm so intense he wouldn't have been surprised if he'd passed out. Then, calmly, Sal switched the toy off, but kept it inside. He untied Jack's leg and lengthened it, which was a huge relief, then he shifted his weight and lay down next to Jack. He pushed his cock between Jack's legs and thrust between them a few times until he, too, came, and then he kissed Jack with one of those devouring kisses.

It was a good thing that the ropes still anchored him. Without them, he might have floated off or turned into vapor, or nothing but light. His mind held no more sharp edges, no guilt, no stress, just an endless floating feeling, and the best thing was that he could just simply bask in it.

37

J ack was still shuddering long after Sal had taken off the ropes and removed the massager. Sal had quickly checked Jack's skin for rope marks, but while bruises and rope burns could happen when things got too heated, there wasn't a trace on his body, at least nothing that wouldn't vanish over the next few minutes. Now Jack was lying on his side, legs pulled up, hands still in front of his body, gaze completely turned inward.

Clearly, he was crashing hard, if those shudders were anything to go by. Sal stretched out and ran a hand over the side of Jack's neck, to his shoulders, down to his elbow. He kept the touch light, but noticeable, and remained so close that Jack would be able to feel his body even if he didn't currently want to communicate. Some people needed to stay in that place a while longer, others dropped right off to sleep, others shrugged it off under a shower. Catia had dozed a little and then awoken with such a boundless appetite that Sal had taken to checking the contents of the fridge *before* they played, though he didn't have to worry—Catia usually kept bites and snacks on hand for both of them when it was clear neither of them would be terribly interested in food preparation that day or night or weekend.

After a while, Sal moved closer and placed a kiss on Jack's forehead. "Need anything?"

No response, but when he pulled back, Jack's hand closed around his wrist. "Just you."

Sal let him have the hand and relaxed, though he pulled Jack onto his shoulder. The shivers became less noticeable and then stopped.

"You weren't joking," Jack eventually said.

"About it being intense? I don't joke about that kind of stuff. You all right?"

"A bit light-headed, I think."

"Yeah, I should have asked whether you'd eaten anything. Wait here." He slid out from under Jack, then slipped into his pants and left the bedroom, but kept the door open a crack, and then processed that there were voices coming from the living room—Enzo and Spadaro. Shit. He must have lost track of time. He walked to the kitchen, poured some juice and found sliced ham and cheese as well as a handful of chilled grapes. He wasn't familiar enough with Jack to know what he considered a snack (aside from his stack of protein drinks in his fridge at home), but the salt and sugar might be just the thing. At least, they appealed a lot to Sal.

He did check in the living room, to find Enzo and Spadaro apparently going over the plans again.

"When did you come back?"

"After two hours." Enzo's grin was a marked contrast to Spadaro's total blank.

"Ah. You hear anything?"

"Sounded like 'Sal at work'." Enzo chuckled.

"He actually said that," Spadaro assisted, still with a completely straight face. Remarkably, Spadaro didn't mind —not that he seemed to mind much in general, as if shooting several men represented nothing but a fun challenge for him—but that was an impressive poker face. He couldn't be that ignorant, which left politeness—after all, it wasn't his business to comment on the sexuality of a boss, especially if it was out of the norm. Another option was that Falchi had briefed him, though again Sal wondered how much insight *Il Gentiluomo* had into Sal's preferences.

Sal shook his head. "So, the London/Port Francis face-off —who wins?"

Enzo's grin broadened.

Spadaro's façade cracked. "That was a good meal. You'll have to come to London—the Indian place there will equalize in the second round."

"I'll leave the discussions about the re-match to you," Sal said. "Let me check on Jack and we'll finalize plans."

Neither protested, so he walked back into the kitchen, loaded up on the snacks and juice and returned to the bedroom. Jack stirred and sat up, still bleary-eyed, but he was getting sharper around the edges, and reached eagerly for the juice when Sal offered it. Sal also adjusted the shutters to let in some more light. Then he sat down and put the plate on the bed. Relief flooded him when Jack recovered so quickly, eating and drinking.

"Better?"

"Worried?"

"A little, yeah."

"It was ... emotionally overwhelming." Jack smiled and cast down his eyes as if shy about talking feelings. "But I think I know what you meant, that it's better to experience it. It's ... unlike anything else."

"But you liked it?"

"Oh, absolutely." Jack looked up and grinned. "We could do that again." A hint of caution in that sentence, as if he expected rejection or qualification, but Sal didn't have either for him. He normally let these kinds of connections develop on their own, took it one day at a time, happy to commit for another day or night, and also to walk away if things no longer worked, no hard feelings. But Jack ... Jack had no experience with relationships, didn't do serious *or* casual, barely even *did*.

"Yes, we can." Sal helped him polish off the plate of ham and cheese and grapes, then stood. "Grab a shower and get dressed. I think Enzo and the Barracuda might have some questions."

"That's Silvio Spadaro? Gianbattista Falchi's hitman?"

"Yeah, we needed another capable pair of hands. Falchi was apparently fond of my wife, so ..."

"I see." Jack got off the bed. "Back to work."

Sal grabbed and kissed him. "Appreciate it." He let Jack have the en suite, and used the guest shower, because he knew that showering together meant they'd let Enzo and Spadaro wait even longer. Sal would definitely get side-tracked and distracted trying to be close to Jack and learn everything there was to be learned about him. He'd pulled so many people into his plans and would expose them to danger. The least he could do was refocus his attention on the war.

And what strange luck that his quest to avenge his wife had brought him close to a man he could easily fall for.

If he hadn't already.

None of his casual encounters or hook-ups had got so close so quickly, but of course with Jack there was much less of the usual subterfuge. Jack had already seen him at his worst, knew the truth about him and none of the usual barriers applied. They were both men forged in similar fires, raised with similar codes and delusions, and both of them had reached the very limits of what they could bear. Andrea had no idea how valuable an asset Jack was.

When he dressed and combed back his hair, some water drops were still running into his neck, but he was impatient to get back, so he joined the others around the table. About five minutes later, Jack appeared, flushed from the shower, but awake and energized. He walked in, fully suited, cast a glance across the map, then seemingly forced himself to not look too closely.

Leaned back, one arm on the back of the couch, Spadaro watched him, then looked at Sal. "Who's going to kill Lo Cascio and when?"

Jack cleared his throat. "He's going to have a party tonight at his club starting at ten. There will be businessmen, girls, lots of alcohol. He insisted I join him." Tension around his lips signaled disgust.

Spadaro placed his flat hands together as if in prayer and tapped his thin lips a few times. "Girls, you say?"

Jack drew a deep breath and nodded. "His wife's out of town, so he'll take one or two, and the others are for his business contacts. I'm hoping I can pretend I'm too drunk." He was clearly aiming for a neutral tone, but Sal heard the loathing underneath. "Unless you manage to kill him before the party."

"What about you? Did you never want to pull the trigger?" Spadaro asked.

Jack blinked a few times. "If there is no other way."

Spadaro looked back at Sal. "I'll handle it."

Sal nodded. "I think that's the best approach." Jack was capable of it, but Sal didn't feel he killed as easily as Spadaro did, and considering Andrea was his boss, he might hesitate or have second thoughts. Always easier to kill a stranger, though in their circles, Jack had very likely been involved in the killing of people he'd known well.

"How are you going to do it?" Jack remained tense around the shoulders.

Spadaro stood. "You'll help me get me in there. Call Andrea, say you're bringing a girl to the party. Tell him whatever you need to get past security."

"Hold on, what girl?"

"The girl's me." Spadaro gave one of those unsettling, all-teeth barracuda grins. "Done it before, killed half a dozen Russians. Stupid men don't feel threatened by a girl."

Jack frowned but didn't seem to have an immediate response.

Even Sal needed a moment to compute what Spadaro had said, but unlike Jack, he assumed, he could see it. Spadaro's slim build with his long legs, smooth skin and androgynous features already took him halfway there, so who knew what Spadaro could do with some makeup and a wig? "I like it. Can you demonstrate the look?"

"Sure can." Spadaro picked up his helmet. "I'll need to get a few things. Does he have any preference? Is there a dress code?"

"Uhm. Blonde. No dress code. Sexy, I guess."

Spadaro acknowledged that with a nod and was out of the door. They all looked at each other for a few seconds. "I can't show up with a drag act," Jack finally said. "If Andrea has even the slightest suspicion, I'm dead. And so's he."

"If it's not good enough to fool Andrea long enough to get close to him, we'll come up with a different idea." Sal leaned back in his chair. "Though I'll say I like the idea that Andrea will get killed by a guy in dress."

"I hope he blows Andrea's head off while he's groping him." Enzo laughed.

Sal grinned, though based on the caution in Jack's eyes, Jack didn't find it funny. Hopefully he would in time.

38

*"*A *guy in dress.*"

Jack wasn't sure that was what he was seeing when Spadaro returned. He was the least one here qualified to make a judgment, but Spadaro wore the heels and small black dress with the same ease as he'd worn the tailored suit or the motorcycle gear. For all his striking appearance, he possessed that intangible quality of models or actors whose personality shifted depending on their roles or clothes and make-up. And while those black eyes hadn't changed in the slightest and were places without light or much in the way of emotion, Spadaro flicked open candy-colored sunglasses that perfectly matched the lipstick and hid them away, leaving a leggy, somewhat angular girl with jaw-length platinum-blonde hair holding a rhinestone- encrusted silver clutch in front of her.

"I guess what shocks me most is that you can walk in those," Sal said.

Spadaro kept his focus on Jack. "Your decision. You okay to risk it?"

"If you're trying to get ... close to Andrea, his type is more curvy."

"I'll handle that part." Spadaro kept looking at him. "I need you to not get jittery. Can you act as if we know each other well?"

Can you? Well, yes. "You mean, get familiar?"

"If necessary. Wouldn't send the right message if I sit on your lap and you freak out."

Oh Jesus. Jack swallowed and nodded. "Sure, okay." Anything that helped to get this over with. If it helped Spadaro to kill Andrea, and if that was how he wanted to play it, Jack could assist. Hell, a few days ago he'd seriously considered marrying a woman and playing a straight man for the rest of his life. He could play that role for a few hours —no marriage necessary, and even better because it didn't involve a friend who had no idea what she was getting herself into.

That seemed to be enough for Spadaro, who vanished again to "refine the look". Jack caught a grin from Enzo and shrugged.

"Did your visit to the Ayutthaya go well?" Jack asked, mostly to say something.

"He didn't talk much, which was cool with me, but I bet he's got some interesting stories." Enzo leaned forward. "I'm going to handle the capos and some of the soldiers with the boys and Spadaro can join us when he's done. We'll hunt down the others over the next twenty-four hours. Jack, is there anybody else who'd flip too?"

Jack had pondered that question distantly a few times.

Was there a man whose life he should be saving? A few had grumbled about Andrea's leadership style, but there were no outright rebels—the takings had been too good, and the troops had been happy with the money they'd been making, so morale was solid. If anything, a level of sated complacency had settled in, which wasn't in and of itself a bad thing. After the War, not living tooth and claw had been welcome.

The truth was, while he liked a few made men more than others, he wasn't close with anybody these days. Tony hadn't survived the last War, and Jack had kept his distance emotionally, also because he had to be seen as impartial. He was considered efficient, disinterested when it came to business conflicts, and smart, and none of those made him top of the list when it came to hanging out, having fun, or even becoming the godfather of children.

"No, I don't think so." And like that, a weight dropped off his shoulders—he'd served their interests so long, had judged fairly, had punished and reined in where necessary and possible, but aside from Tony, or moments of comradery, he'd simply gotten used to these men the same way he'd gotten used to fellow prisoners. Over the years, there were a few he'd considered friends, but he'd seen too much betrayal and self-interest to ever turn his back. Strange to now condemn all of them to death, though.

"Not your call," Sal reminded him, and placed a hand on Jack's shoulder. "But that keeps it simple. Also, once Andrea's down, we'll access the accounts and the rest. Who else has access to the finances?"

Yes. That. Jack had expected Sal to confront him about the money and passwords, but he hadn't. He'd secured everything again as leverage, expecting to have to prove or negotiate his value in the days after Andrea had fallen, because he was still the man who held the purse strings. Sal's tone indicated he assumed Jack would cooperate when it came to the money, as if they were real allies, co-conspirators, and after what had happened in the bedroom, Jack felt he could trust him. Silly. Naïve. But he had no emotional reserves left to fight. Maybe he could trust one man in his life.

"Andrea and me, that's it. There's an accountant if we need him, but I'm handling all that. Andrea never let anybody else get near the money."

"He should have respected you more, then," Sal said. "Right?"

"Right." Andrea and Jack had both held the power to destroy each other, and really, Jack was just acting before Andrea could. "I think I should leave you to it—I could use a workout to calm down. Can you give Spadaro my phone number so we can arrange to meet?"

"You sure you want to leave?" Sal asked.

"I don't, but I'll be useless for the planning, and I'd rather not know. If there's anything, Spadaro can tell me. I should keep up my normal routine, which at this point is to have a workout and make a few calls." The building tension was settling in his bones and muscles, though thankfully there was no guilt. The most he felt was a kind of hollow regret, maybe a sense of failure, but a part of him was already moving the puzzle pieces to understand a world without the Lo Cascio.

With Andrea gone, the remaining reins all gathered in Jack's hands, and he'd have to play everything in the right order, with the right touch, to not be compromised himself in case somebody realized he was the traitor. Another thing he needed to get ready was his escape. If it all went south, if Sal did turn against him, he'd still make it out in one piece, and with enough money to hide for the rest of his life.

"Okay. I'll see you out."

Jack nodded, then paused and turned toward Enzo. "Good luck."

Enzo looked up and gave him a grin. "See you at the victory party, Jack. Stay safe."

"You too."

Sal took his hand off Jack's shoulder blades once they were in the elevator, but he remained very close. After a little while, he cleared his throat. "I'll let Spadaro know it's more important to protect you than kill Andrea."

Jack found himself smiling. "I can protect myself."

"Still." Sal looked up to the ceiling of the cabin, and then back down. "You're really quite special. I hate sending you into danger."

"And that's not *your* call, Sal."

"Yeah, but still ..."

"There's no viable alternative. You do your part, I'm doing my part, Spadaro and Enzo do theirs, and we'll see how the chips fall." He pulled Sal into a kiss, enjoyed his smell, and taste, and the strong body against him, then separated too quickly and strode out of the elevator as the doors chimed open.

Head in the game.

And he managed it, mostly. The drive grounded him, the need to focus on the traffic, then to pick up his workout clothes, and another short drive to the local high-end gym. He could have driven to Andrea's estate and used the gym there, like he'd often done in the past, but that ran the risk of having Andrea attempt to compete against him—"friendly", of course, and the quandary whether he should let him "win". Andrea seemed to believe that the few years of age difference entitled him to victory in all disciplines. He did have more energy and he was strong, but he'd never learned to pace himself.

What Jack didn't want right now was to have Andrea spot him or ask him to do it. He'd drop the weight on Andrea's throat himself if given half a chance, or beat him to death with a barbell, just to be done with it. Not because he hated him, but it would release the stress trapped in his muscles that was screaming to get out.

In the gym, he picked up one of the resident personal trainers along with his day pass, but she quickly realized he knew what he was doing and mostly held a towel and a water bottle for him. She caught on that he wasn't feeling chatty. He was grateful for her help though when it came to stretching.

He changed into his "party" clothes after the shower, massage, and haircut all under the same roof, forcing himself to not check the phone. Nobody called or messaged him during his "wellness break", which was a relief.

To start off the evening, he settled in one of his favorite restaurants and ordered a small flock of tapas. He ate slowly, enjoying the post-workout and post-massage buzz, but nothing quite touched the delicious memory of ropes holding him while Sal Rausa teased wholly new and unimagined sensations from his body. He had to turn away and look out of the window so no one thought he was smiling that way at *them*.

His phone buzzed—unknown caller ID—and he answered. "Yes?"

"I'm outside the coffee shop on Admiral Drive." The voice was husky but sounded enough like Silvio Spadaro that Jack didn't have to ask stupid questions. "Same dress."

"I'll be there in ten. Silver Porsche."

"They'll think you're picking up a hooker." A small, throaty laugh.

"That works." A guy in his forties, a car with power under the hood, and a leggy girl in a short dress. He'd look like one of an estimated hundred thousand well-to-do middle managers in this town grabbing some extra-marital action.

When he paid for his meal, he tipped even more generously than usual for good luck, and returned to the car. Admiral Drive was one of the main shopping areas of Port Francis, and the road and parking spaces were designed to drop off people or pick them up, and the best area for that was the coffee shop.

He spotted the Barracuda outside, standing easily and gracefully in Louboutin heels. The area should have been too busy and crowded for Spadaro to attract too much attention, but a couple of young men—young professionals by the look of them—were clearly on the way to the watering holes downtown, and had paused to leer at her. At this point, even attempting to think of Spadaro as "him" seemed like an extra effort, and making the switch would help with pulling off the plan.

"Seriously?" Jack muttered to himself, halted the car in the middle of the road without bothering to park, and pushed open the door. Spadaro didn't seem to spot him, instead watching the boys who stalked around her, unaware that they were literally flirting with death. Jack left the car and strode toward Spadaro.

"Oh, there you are," he said louder than strictly necessary.

Spadaro cast him a glance, then gave a big smile. "Oh, hi *Daddy*."

What the everloving ...?

Jack glanced at the two young men. "There a problem here?"

They muttered something, didn't meet his gaze, and slunk off into the nearest bar.

Jack offered his arm to Spadaro, opened the door, and helped her into the car, though Spadaro's balance was perfect and she only took Jack's arm for appearance's sake.

Jack closed the door after her and returned to the driver's seat. "What was that?"

"Harmless fun and a way to get into the role." Spadaro pulled out a small mirror to check her make-up. A whiff of a perfume hit Jack. It wasn't unpleasant so much as unbelievably sweet, reminding him of bubblegum and spun sugar.

"'Daddy?'" Jack asked.

"Guys your age are Daddies. It's a term of appreciation."

"Appreciation?" This was getting weirder by the second.

Spadaro rolled her eyes. "They probably thought you're my pimp. That's a story we can go with. Except I don't think we could sell Andrea on you being suddenly in the sex trade."

Jack started the car again and joined the light stream of traffic. "He knows I'm not."

"That's what I'm saying." Spadaro clicked the mirror

shut and dropped it into the clutch. "Park near the emergency exit. Where do you think Andrea will take a girl or two?" The tone told Jack that Spadaro had no doubt about how things would go down. He envied the killer that confidence.

"There are private booths."

"Cameras?"

"No, Andrea sometimes does business there. There are cameras near the entrance and in the back alley. He relies on club security." Jack stopped at a red light and tapped his fingers against the wheel. "And rolling into the club with a couple submachine guns would kill so many civilians and bring so much heat that nobody even did anything like that even during the War."

"Yeah, not how I'd do it."

"What's your plan?"

"I'll separate him from the herd and take him out. How and when depends on how stupid he is."

"Don't underestimate him." Jack set the car back in motion.

"I'm not. That's why I'm using all these distractions." Spadaro crossed her legs and angled them just so in a movement that struck Jack as one of the most feminine things he'd seen in his life. "Best outcome—totally silent takedown, nobody sees a thing."

"The best outcome will be if he tells me first who killed Sal's wife." That was still a risk, but hopefully alcohol and girls would loosen Andrea's tongue.

"The very best outcome would be he tells you what you need to know, nobody hears him die, and I'm sending Sal Rausa a photo of Andrea Lo Cascio's naked ass with a pink dildo rammed in all the way." Spadaro smiled sweetly while Jack almost choked on a breath.

"Or ..." Spadaro regarded her fake pink fingernails, "We shouldn't give away to the straights how good that feels, which is why I'll kill him first."

"Jesus. You're not taking any prisoners, are you?"

Spadaro gave him one of those dark glances. "Never do."

Jack focused on the road, glad that the pure mechanics of driving a car through semi-busy late evening traffic gave him an excuse to dodge what Spadaro apparently considered small talk. Still, the "we" in that sentence disturbed him—but then, the moment Spadaro had reappeared as one of the most believable crossdressers he'd ever seen, the whole concept of the Barracuda being nothing but a roving killer had disintegrated.

They arrived at the club. Andrea had apparently taken his screaming red Lamborghini out for a spin this evening; it stood in the row marked "VIP parking", where security could keep an eye on it.

He helped Spadaro out of the car, and noticed Spadaro's warm, dry fingers. No hint of nerves.

Even out here they could hear the music beat thumping. "Any signals I should be aware of?"

"I don't do safewords." Spadaro squeezed his hand and straightened up. "Let's play it by ear."

Jack closed the car door and walked Spadaro to the entrance. The bouncers on duty only spared him a brief glance before they waved Jack through. Spadaro got a disinterested look, but nobody asked questions, probably because they'd seen several similar girls brought in. Spadaro regarded the front door and the area around it with

interest, even pulling down her sunglasses for an unob-
structed view.

Once inside, the thumping beat of the music, in combination with the milling crowd, and the red, pink and purple
strobe lights, crashed over Jack like a violent wave. He
paused to steel himself. He remembered standing right here,
in what back then had been a warehouse, as Andrea's father
had laid out his plans for a strip club. Ultimately, it had
become a loud, busy disco that, back that, existed so that
local college kids could deal ecstasy and Ritalin under the
table.

When Andrea took the helm of the Lo Cascio, he'd
closed it for three months, and it had reincarnated as The
Matador. Part bar, part club, it was a place where a virgin
cocktail set you back at least thirty bucks, but some house
specials easily went into the hundreds. The clientele had
then shifted to the kind of people who liked to see and be
seen and appreciated both an extensive cocktail list and a
talented DJ—as well as all the people who stalked them,
from confidence tricksters and drug dealers to sex workers.

Thankfully, Andrea didn't rub shoulders with the locals
down here. Spadaro in tow, Jack crossed the room and
walked up the stairs, past a bald security guy who had his
hands folded in front of his groin and whose job it was to
make sure people who'd gotten lost on the way to the bathrooms didn't stumble into one of Andrea's meetings.
Upstairs, another security guy stood outside the VIP lounge,
and he too let Jack pass.

Jack opened the door and walked through first.

Once the door closed behind him, the infernal noise
from downstairs had lessened to a pervasive vibration in the

pit of his stomach. A less ear-splitting version of the same track was playing here. Andrea's party had already started. The private bar was staffed by two women who wore the usual high-waisted black pants and sequined bolero jackets cut in a way to show more than a hint of their breasts and bare stomachs.

Shirt undone to his solar plexus, Andrea sat in one of the niches with four other guys ranging in age from forties to late fifties, drinking and laughing, and a mirror was out with lines of white powder. His father would never have tolerated that stuff, firmly believing that drugs of any kind were a weakness that brought too much attention from the Feds. He'd had wiseguys vanished whom he suspected of having taken so much as a nose full.

Andrea stilled and blinked slowly when he noticed Jack. "Jack! Great! We were just talking about you." He waved Jack closer. "Guys, that's Jack Barsanti, best fucking right-hand man a guy could want."

Jack listened for a while to the haphazard introductions: real estate developer, a local politician, two rich "sponsors" apparently happy to get fleeced and skinned.

Jack took a step away from Spadaro. "Didn't think wine suited the occasion, so I brought a different gift."

"Thank you, Daddy." Spadaro shifted her weight in a way that displayed her whole body.

Pleased, Andrea laughed. "Get a drink, honey, we gotta do some business first." He wasn't even subtle, eyeing her ass when Spadaro turned around and walked toward the bar. There were other girls, some lounging near the bar, some dancing, and Jack forced himself to study them for a while before he sat down among the guys, heartsick to even pretend he cared in the least.

The music made it hard to concentrate too, and he almost startled when Spadaro returned a while later, hips swaying, and offered him a tumbler with what looked like two fingers of whiskey and ice. When Jack tried to ignore the glass, Spadaro shook it in a long-fingered hand, making the ice cubes sing.

All right, then. Jack took the drink, noticed Spadaro dip a finger into it and, once she'd released the glass, place the finger between her lips to suck off the liquid. All the time, all of Spadaro's attention was on him, and damn, he wasn't even interested in any way in the killer, or the presented façade, but something about that total focus made his heart beat harder.

Andrea was grinning, tip of the tongue against his front teeth, head tilted, and gaze raking Spadaro, who, probably to spite him, didn't grace him with a single look. Jack didn't know how to respond, so he took a big gulp of the alcohol, bracing himself for the burn.

That didn't come.

Fucking iced tea.

Spadaro waited for him to drink down the whole glass, and part of Jack wanted the promised alcohol, but Spadaro had probably decided they'd both stay sober. Then she gathered up the glass and walked back toward the bar as if that were the only thing on her mind.

"You're fucking her?" Andrea asked.

"Used to. Might again. Not currently." Covering every base there was. "As I said, she's a gift. Not exactly wife material, that one."

Thankfully, the four suits weighed in with observations about wives and mistresses, and the desired qualities of each. Jack tried to relax and pretend he cared by repeating whatever people said out loud in his head to himself. When he felt Andrea was starting to get restless, he leaned in to him. "Can I talk to you in private?"

"Something important?"

"'Fraid so. But it's brief."

"Right. Need to piss anyway," Andrea muttered, stood and nodded to his guests. "Gentlemen, the buffet is open. Enjoy. I'll be back in a minute." Since there was no food, the suits caught the meaning, and so did the girls, some of whom now joined the guests with more drinks.

Andrea headed for the private bathrooms down the corridor. Jack entered the bathroom, but faced away. "What's this about? It better be fucking urgent."

"I think Sal Rausa is a problem." He didn't like talking to the wall, but turning his head was out of the question until Andrea had zipped up. Though, would a straight guy do the same, or would he simply not worry?

"Rausa?" Andrea scoffed. "Haven't seen nose or tail of him. He still around?"

"Apparently." He tried to ignore the sound of splashing piss. "I talked to Cassaro at the Prizzi wedding, and he thinks Rausa isn't done."

"Based on what?"

"Maybe he's behind the Dommarco associate going missing. It wasn't us."

"Cassaro is like any old man—jumping at shadows. Rausa hasn't been a problem for years." Andrea zipped up and flushed.

"I know that, but I still checked with some people and ... I don't know, Andrea, but I'm getting uneasy." He half turned and saw Andrea admire himself in the mirror, running a hand through his hair, then baring his teeth as if to check he had nothing stuck in them. "We should deal with him."

"So bloodthirsty all of a sudden." Andrea paused with his grimacing and met Jack's gaze in the mirror. "You figure you'll need Dommarco's okay for that?"

"If I get yours, I'll make the case to Cassaro and Guy Dommarco in person."

"Wouldn't want to disturb the peace too much?" Andrea's sing-song could have been playful, but Jack placed it as mockery.

"If bodies drop, they'll get restless too. And Rausa's still a boss."

"So old-fashioned. If they let you run this city, you'd have a Commission up and running within days, including a fucking board of directors." Andrea took the door handle and slapped Jack on the shoulder.

"Rausa will target you first. I understand there's bad blood between you."

"And that has you spooked?" Andrea had been about to open the door, but then faced Jack again and grabbed both his arms. "Enough that you want to have him killed?"

Slippery son of a bitch. "It's a threat I can't completely assess. I wasn't present while a lot of that history was written."

Andrea frowned as if having to focus to remember, but he couldn't possibly be that drunk, could he? "He had some axes to grind, never wanted a part of the peace talks, then fucked off to sulk. Nothing much there."

"What happened?" *Give me something, Andrea.*

"Eh. He couldn't protect his own fucking wife, that's what happened. So what. If he makes the wrong move, we'll finish him off, but not tonight. I got something better to do, and so do you."

Nobody ever asked who had committed any particular murder, it just wasn't done. The same way, once tonight was finished, Sal, Enzo and Jack would never mention to anyone why Silvio Spadaro had been in town. Even with Andrea, it was rarely necessary to be so blunt. But this was Andrea's club, his party, and not a clueless witness within earshot.

Jack was Andrea's right hand, the one man he *had* to trust. One final push, then.

"Who killed his wife? Did you give the order?"

Andrea placed an arm around Jack's shoulders, and for a long hot-cold moment, Jack couldn't parse the touch. Although he knew Andrea well after all those years, he had no idea whether it was friendly or threatening, and maybe even Andrea didn't know one from the other.

"Ask Vic. He has the story."

Jack was about to protest or plead, but Andrea placed a finger on Jack's lips. He shuddered because the touch was way too intimate—and Andrea still hadn't washed his hands.

"No more business tonight, Jack, come on. Relax."

It couldn't be clearer. As much as Jack hated it, he had to retreat and hope that he could make Vic Decesare talk instead.

"Sorry. I just like having all of the puzzle pieces."

Another pat on the shoulder. "Yeah, good man. Now let's go back or people might get ideas."

Jack remembered the proper response was laughter, not

freeing himself and looking horrified. "I like you, Andrea, but not that much."

When they returned to the guests, the temperature had risen—a couple of the girls were still dancing, others were sitting between the guests, drinking, laughing, and getting quite touchy-feely. Opposite of the men, Spadaro was kissing one of the other girls, a blonde in a short white skirt, whose top had ridden up to reveal her tanned belly. From the way the girls kissed, Jack felt both Spadaro and her were definitely into each other, or at least into this.

Next to him, Andrea stopped and watched the show. Spadaro seemingly had no attention for Andrea, but her fingers moved along the insides of the other girl's thighs as she opened them. The blonde's lids were heavy though she briefly became lucid enough to look at Andrea, and then she moaned.

"I think I'll have both of them. Your girl can lick my balls while I fuck that one."

Knock yourself out, Jack thought. "Go for it."

Andrea swaggered toward Spadaro and leaned against the back of the seat, watching from up close, almost breathing down on the girls while Spadaro had her fingers up the blonde's skirt. Jack felt uneasy—he still recognized the killer in the girl, aware that that sinewy strength wasn't for pleasure, but for snapping back and striking without warning. And while the blonde seemed to enjoy it, based on her breathy moans and squirms, bait was all she was. Chum in the water.

And yet, even to Jack it was hot. Maybe it was because he'd spent a lifetime watching bodies do what bodies did, or because he knew Andrea had finally met more than his match while still thinking he was in control, or maybe it was because Spadaro played both the girl and the audience perfectly. Jack turned to pick up another drink from the bar, and then watched as Andrea used his well-worn pick-up smile.

But Spadaro made it difficult for him, seemingly a whole lot more interested in pleasuring the blonde. Andrea spoke, but Jack didn't pay attention to the words. It didn't matter what he'd said. Andrea knew he was good-looking, and could even be charming, but he displayed his wealth and wore his power with the subtlety of a jackhammer. He had made his expectations of the two women clear.

Dragging her mouth away from the blonde, Spadaro gave Andrea a smoldering black look, licked her open lips and smiled invitingly. Andrea sat down and kissed the blonde too, which, dazed and turned on, she responded to, while Spadaro's fingers remained where they were. Spadaro whispered something into Andrea's ear and then closed her teeth gently around the outer rim of it, pulling noticeably. When Andrea jerked, Spadaro merely laughed.

Jack took a sip from the alcohol and forced himself to look away. There was no reason why he should be too interested in what Andrea got up to sexually, even if his alleged "sometimes lover" was involved. He walked slowly to the one-way mirror wall that offered a great view of the pulsing dancing crowd on the first floor. He gazed down at the writhing bodies, holding his whiskey glass in one hand, and trying to look thoughtful and calm instead of stressed, while the music vibrated up against his feet.

When he turned around again, Andrea was on the move, one arm around each of the girls. The blonde staggered as if extremely drunk and Jack was worried she might fall and the whole plan would go sideways. He caught a quick glance from Spadaro, who seemed to have it all well in hand. She definitely didn't look like she needed support or help.

Jack took a deep breath and forced himself to remain where he was, but watched the reflection as Andrea walked past the upstairs bar and down a rarely used corridor. That way were two private lounges—round rooms that had only enough space to seat six or eight people around a table. Low light and soundproofing made them suitable for a lap dance or other more private business. Good choice, they were close enough that even the very drunk blonde would be able to make it. Also, considering how eager Andrea had looked, he wouldn't give them a tour of the club first.

A week ago, my life still made sense.

Jack didn't pay attention to the girls or the guests. He waited for the time to pass, measured in heartbeats that were hard and fast enough that he could feel them. He measured in breaths, in the beat of the music, and the laughter coming from the sitting area. After about ten minutes, he set down his glass and followed Andrea with all the purpose of a man headed toward the restroom.

Down the corridor, the door of the first private lounge was closed. Jack approached it, heart pounding up into his head and against the base of his skull. He'd never enjoyed betrayal, never relished the twisted power it came with. Even now, he remembered the shocked and hurt expression of the man he'd killed to secure his place among the *men of honor*. Jack wasn't made to turn against people he would have otherwise considered allies. It was a sad fact that not every-body had the same compunctions—he'd spent his life watching his back, wasted it, because he'd never really trusted anybody with any of the things that truly mattered to him.

He couldn't hear anything on the other side of the door, so he leaned closer. After a minute or so, he heard something soft and heavy fall onto the ground. A quick glance down the corridor, and he opened the door.

Inside, he first noticed the blonde stretched out on the seats, heels on the floor, wearing lace panties and nothing else, hands above her head. She was breathing. Passed out. Andrea had fallen between seats and table, shirtless and face first, and Spadaro was kneeling on him, pulling a stiletto from his back. Andrea was still moving, trying to push himself up, fingers trying to find purchase against the fake red leather seats, or maybe reach the gun holster in his back, but while he was strong and fit, Spadaro was working against him and didn't let him come back up. Andrea made a wheezing, wet sound that gave Jack goosebumps.

"Come in and close the door," Spadaro said calmly and stabbed Andrea in the back again. He pulled the knife out and tossed it carelessly on the table.

Andrea was choking—his chest moved but he was unable to breathe. Spadaro must have stabbed him in both lungs. Nasty way to go, but mostly, it kept Andrea from screaming or fighting.

"What about her?"

"She shouldn't have drunk the cocktail I gave her," Spadaro said calmly, still focused on the man dying underneath her. "Anyfuckingthing could have happened to her."

"You drugged her?"

Spadaro shrugged. "Didn't want her to freak out and get in the way."

"That's ... surprisingly nice of you."

"Not like she'll remember enough to tell the cops. Not that there's any reason for her to talk to anybody." Spadaro glanced down to Andrea who'd stopped moving. "Job's done."

"Yeah, looks like it."

Spadaro reached out to place two fingers against Andrea's neck, then straightened, gathered up the knife, wiped it on Andrea's shirt and closed it, then put it back in her clutch. "Don't tell me you were worried?"

"No, I've heard you're ..." Good? Ruthless? Efficient? None of the words did Spadaro justice.

"Scary?" Spadaro volunteered. "I get that a lot."

Spadaro's lipstick was smeared slightly, but while that would have made anybody else look more vulnerable, it looked more like war paint on a surprisingly delicate face. Jack was tempted to offer his jacket and chided himself for the impulsive chivalry.

"I'm glad I didn't have to do it," Jack confessed.

"I know a guy who says I have so much Scorpio in my horoscope, hard to be anything else." Spadaro offered a weird, thin-lipped smile. "Sal wants the body to vanish."

Much of Sal's plan would work better if the rest of the Lo Cascio didn't know what hit them at least for a day or two, and the Dommarco stayed in the dark as well until it was all done. Taking out those Lo Cascio capos who displayed more initiative than the others would be the next move, and Spadaro was unlikely to get any rest until that work was done. But witnessing Spadaro's fierceness and focus at work convinced Jack that those capos would find their match and more in the killer.

"Do you have a plan to stay safe?"

"What?" Jack did his best to ignore the one dead and one unconscious body, as if either of them could hear him or were in any state to care. "You mean during the war?"

"You'll be the last man standing. People will ask questions. And Sal Rausa won't need you once it's over. Do you have anybody in your corner?"

Jack met Spadaro's black gaze, unable to read anything in those eyes except a razor-sharp, honed attention. "I hope Sal lets me leave." *Hope.* But how much did he have to go on? Except for the magnetism, and the attraction, and the mutual respect. He didn't think Sal Rausa had it in him to have Jack hunted down and murdered, after everything. He'd finally retire and vanish. Best case ... hell, it had been so goddamned long since he could even contemplate a best-case scenario. "I'll see what's possible. I now have a chance." He nodded toward Andrea.

A knock on the door.

Spadaro was on her feet and next to the door like a flash, Andrea's gun drawn. Jack raised a hand and stepped to the door. "Yes?"

"Boss, sorry to disturb, there's something you should see."

Jack made sure that whoever was outside wouldn't be able to catch a glimpse of Andrea on the floor. When he cracked open the door, he blocked as much of the other man's vision as he could. He noticed that Spadaro had the gun angled and pointed to execute the guy. It was Mauro, in charge of security tonight.

"Yes, Mauro?"

The soldier blinked, either because he hadn't expected Jack here, or because of the bruises on Jack's face. "There's a couple Rausa capos downstairs."

"What are they doing?"

"Sizing up the place, swaggering around." Mauro gritted his teeth. "Looks like two capos and four others."

Open provocation, especially because they were showing up in force and drawing attention to themselves rather than sitting at the bar with a cocktail in hand. But it would distract club security somewhat. Jack found it mildly disturbing how calm and relaxed Spadaro remained.

Just then, a low groan came from the blonde girl. A scrabbling sound, like fingernails on leather seats. *Shit, she's waking up.*

Spadaro left the position by the door. "Oh you like that, don't you, baby?" she said in her girl voice.

And then in a deeper voice, approximating Andrea's tone, "Mmmm-mmmh."

Jesus. We're all going to die because of badly acted cheap porn dialogue.

Mauro raised his eyebrows and tried to sneak a glance past Jack. Nosy bastard.

Jack shrugged as nonchalantly as he could, while his heart tried to escape his rib cage. "We don't need that kind of shit. Clear the VIP lounge and the upstairs floor. Move the customers to a different bar. No need to draw attention, say there's an electrical fault or something. Drinks on the house. Do it now. And, Mauro?"

Mauro had been about to turn, but then made eye contact again.

"Get some of our guys out front and visible. No violence, unless they start it. Call me if necessary."

"Understood." Mauro set his jaw and turned to leave.

Jack closed the door and suddenly became aware of the metallic tang mixing with stale air and Spadaro's sweet perfume. Hopefully, that blood smell hadn't registered with the soldier.

Spadaro cast a glance at the girl, then refocused on Andrea.

"He can't have bought that," Jack said. "Christ, what were you thinking?"

"You need to calm down. I gave him what he expected to hear. People run on expectations. It's our fucking software."

No point arguing that, not now, not with a killer on a mission, but Jack didn't want to be here when Mauro doubted what he'd heard, or realized what he'd smelled.

"We should leave through the delivery entrance." Andrea often liked to duck in and out of the club discreetly, especially when he had girls with him.

Spadaro searched Andrea's jacket and dropped the Lamborghini's keys in her clutch, along with the card that opened the back entrance. Then she picked up Andrea's gun again, checked it, and shrugged. "You should be nowhere near here."

"I'll help move the body."

"I'm stronger than I look." Spadaro's lips quirked into a small smile. "The new king next to the warm body of the dead king, it's bad optics."

This isn't a coup, Jack was tempted to say, but of course, the others wouldn't think that. "What can I do to help?"

Spadaro gathered up Andrea's discarded clothes. "Go out there and act normal."

"Keep in mind there's a camera at the back."

Spadaro straightened, turned and made Jack feel the full force of that black stare. "I got this. You do your job, let me do mine." She still sounded flat, emotionless, but Jack felt it was the closest Spadaro had come to being irritated or angry so far.

"Okay." Jack took a couple deep breaths and left the private lounge. He resisted pulling at his sleeves or straightening his jacket, but took a moment to gather himself.

Right. Rausa capos. All he had to do was pretend that the distraction was the actual main event and keep the mask in place for just a few more hours.

He sauntered downstairs to join the subtle stand-off with the Rausa men, and was relieved to find Enzo was clearly the ringleader—all the other men took their cues from him. Mauro, along with security from the second floor, had already reinforced the guys downstairs, and after a mutual staredown that was mostly lost on the people of Port Francis eager for overpriced cocktails and a fun night out, Jack stepped up to Enzo.

"I think you and your boys are in the wrong club."

Enzo lifted his eyebrows and tilted his head, then gestured at his own face. "That from the last time you played bouncer? Maybe you should let the big boys handle this?"

Jack was glad when Enzo didn't go all out with his provocation. If he'd called him a "bitch" or worse, in front of everybody, Jack would have had to take the altercation to a whole new level. "If your boss has any issues, he can bring them to me." Jack stepped up to the bar, turning his back on Enzo on purpose, and motioned the barkeeper to hand over a bottle of top-shelf liquor. He offered the bottle to Enzo. "With my compliments."

Enzo stared at him, but accepted the bottle, and weighed it for a tense moment as if considering whether to smash it and glass him. But that was why Jack had chosen that bottle of eighty-year old French cognac that went for five hundred dollars on the open market.

Enzo gave a toothy grin, lifted the bottle in a mock salute and left.

And just when the security guys were beginning to relax, some asshole triggered the fire alarm, and Jack and Mauro evacuated the club together and then had to answer questions when a fire truck rolled in. The wet mess of the sprinklers also washed away what spilled blood had soaked into the carpet upstairs, or at least diluted it into a questionable pool of murk.

When Jack did a cursory tour of the upstairs floor, a pair of deserted Louboutin heels stood tidily arranged on the bar top. Of course, Spadaro wouldn't have been able to carry or drag Andrea's body around in those heels.

Jack took them and threw them in the trash outside on the way to his car.

39

Hours later, Jack could still feel the vibrations of the music in his bones while he steered the car. If this were a normal night, he'd drive home just like that, so he tried to stick as close to his normal routine as possible. It was eerie knowing what else was going on, but he'd lived in two realities for most of his life, as a made man on the one hand, and a legitimate "consultant" on the other. He'd have to navigate those for the rest of his life, though it seemed increasingly likely that he'd add "turncoat consigliere on the run from the Cosa Nostra" to the identities he had to manage.

Though who was he kidding? It hadn't exactly been a "normal" night at The Matador, either.

Once he reached his street, the restlessness sat so deep that there was no way he'd be able to sleep, so he started the engine again and drove. This time of night, the streets were empty except for insomniacs or nightshift workers, or very late revelers. Driving usually helped, so he drove aimlessly around until a sudden impulse turned him toward Memorial Bridge.

He parked the car exactly in the middle, with the same view toward where the river poured itself into the sea, and while he usually avoided the bridge and the whole area for fear of another psychotic break—or whatever it had been—this time he only experienced melancholic peace. On the bridge with the dark water flowing beneath and the wide-open sky above, he leaned on the railing and focused on his breath mingling with the clean air and the smells from the water and ocean blowing in.

Only when the humidity had crept through his clothes and to his skin, did he straighten and reach into his pocket. He turned Andrea's phone over and over in his hands, imagined Spadaro driving bare-footed around town in Andrea's Lamborghini, and likely still enjoying the ride like some girl-faced angel of death. To transport a body in that car, the passenger seat was the only option, and Jack figured that that was the only time in his, well, life, that Andrea would be wearing a seat belt. Jack couldn't help but smile.

He rubbed his face and shook his head. Things were fucked up, Andrea was dead with nobody at the helm of the Lo Cascio, and no one could or would do a damn thing about it. More heads were going to roll, and this whole nightmare scenario he'd fought so hard and so long to prevent simply felt as inevitable and cleansing as a hard late-summer rain. And all of that because Andrea had been a very small man deep down—unkind, petty, and not worth Jack's loyalty.

"Fuck you, Andrea", he murmured and hurled the phone into the river as far as he could manage.

40

As much as he wanted to, Jack didn't call Sal. First, the man would have his hands full waging his war, and neither of them should be distracted now. Second, because of the first reason, this wasn't the moment to ask him to clarify their relationship—whether they even had one. But all it took was closing his eyes to feel the echo of Sal's touches on his skin. How many people knew Sal was both cruel and kind, both controlling and relinquishing of everything? Maybe that was the message—despite the circumstances, Sal had let Jack into his mind, his body—and had shared moments of intimacy outside of sex.

Jack kept a low profile, making sure nobody could spot him from the street while he was sitting in a café. As always, he had the phone close, pondering the right moment to raise the matter of Andrea's disappearance. How to best respond when people began calling him to tell him that somebody was picking off Andrea's capos and soldiers. Spadaro might show up and put a bullet through his head. Or the cops would catch a whiff of the killing happening under the skin of the city and pretend for a little while to give a damn about it.

Without leadership, all the capos were flailing limbs, and all their signals were directed to a brain that no longer responded. Jack focused on plausible deniability. Everybody knew Andrea was erratic. Jack was no longer running a crew. People would try to reach Andrea first if Jack didn't pick up the phone.

He finished his coffee, picked up the phone and dialed Vic Decesare's number.

"Yes?"

"It's Jack. Barsanti. Listen, is there any way I can meet you? I need your advice."

"Business?"

"Yes."

"Not sure how much I can be of help, but feel free to come around. I don't have anything else on my calendar."

"Appreciate it."

"You know the room?"

Yes, he did. He'd already sent flowers and a hamper with everything that Vic liked to that same hospital, along with a hand-written card with measured words of appreciation. "I'll be there in less than an hour. Do you want me to bring anything?"

"A good bottle of wine."

"Consider it done."

After the call, Jack selected a bottle from the specialist dealership down the road. He tried to listen to music to take his mind off everything that had happened, but mostly everything that was about to happen.

The private hospital was the best in the state, and from the outside, it could have been a country club or an exclusive spa.

Jack was on the list of "guests", so they let him pass through, and nobody commented on the bottle of wine he carried.

"Ah, yes, Mr. Barsanti, please follow me," a nurse said.

Last visit, Vic had received him in what looked like a living room, complete with a flatscreen TV, carpets, and antique furniture. Vic had worn what he'd have worn outside on a good day—formal trousers, a shirt and a woolen sweater, top button of his formal shirt open underneath. So seeing him lying in bed in pajamas jarred Jack, especially with a thin plastic tube snaking into his nose.

Vic wasn't a year over sixty-five, but he looked twenty years older. His hair had come back after multiple courses of chemo- and radiotherapy, but it was wispy and colorless, and his dark brown eyes seemed washed out, the white yellowed like antique ivory. Jack could see the lines of his skull clearly under the thinning skin.

Jack stepped up to the bed and set the bottle down next to a bunch of fresh flowers that didn't have a card attached. "I should have come by weeks ago."

"Ah, no. Sit down." Vic gestured toward a chair. "It'll be a nice distraction. How are you doing, son? Who's beaten you up?"

Jack gave an embarrassed laugh he'd practiced enough by now. "Caught my foot getting out of the Jacuzzi. In my defense, I was drunk."

Vic's face lit up with amusement, "You need to come up with a better story." Jack's heart skipped a painful beat.

"That's no way to boast about a war wound. You're always too honest."

"Andrea said I needed a story about a sparring match gone wrong." Because in the reality where he was not a traitor, that was what he'd have said. Not that it mattered anymore that Vic believed him.

"Yes, that sounds a lot better." Vic settled back on his pillow, then clicked some kind of remote control and the head part of the bed rose with an electric hum. "Andrea's been riding you hard?"

So Vic apparently hadn't heard anything yet. "Andrea is … Andrea." Jack shrugged. "He hasn't been so bad lately, so …" He looked around the room. "I don't think you've told us about the situation here."

"No point." Vic looked around with a weak snarl of distaste. "Take a man's guts out, everything follows. Slice by slice. There's more of me in the incinerator than left in the bed. Told them they can't have any more, so they can stop milking my insurance for more money. Fucking vampires."

"Last doc I met was a drug pusher," Jack agreed. "But if you need anything …"

"Eh." The disgust was palpable. "No. Tell me, what do you need?"

"I know we've already talked about it, years ago, but I have some questions about Salvatore Rausa. I met him at the Prizzi wedding and something about him makes me nervous. But I haven't dealt with him much, so I was hoping you have more."

"Shown himself in public, has he?" Vic looked down at his hands which were resting on the covers. "Yeah, I have stories. When the War got bad, Sal Rausa went out and killed his uncle who'd groomed him as his underboss. When the pressure on the Rausa got so bad that they were near breaking, he turned against his own, because Mike Rausa disagreed with him on the direction of the family."

"That's reckless."

"Old Mike wasn't the most effective leader the Rausa have ever had—he was too confident, for one, and thought he was cleverer than he was." Vic made a "what can you do" gesture. "That could have worked to our advantage, but it didn't. Not at first."

"Please explain?"

"With their leadership in the state it was—young boss just taken over, patriarch sleeping with the fishes—I decided it might be worth it to take out Salvatore too. Have them rip each other apart trying to fill the void, so we could focus on the Dommarco."

"It didn't work, though."

"No. The shooter took out the wife. She was driving Rausa's car." Vic seemed to weigh thoughts or memories. "The shooter called before pulling the trigger and told Andrea the wife was driving. Andrea was in charge, and he was agitated, flushed, pacing. We'd been sitting in the office, waiting for the call."

"So Andrea gave the order?"

"Kind of. He shouted, 'I don't care, we kill him next!' and hung up. Then he turned to me all, 'Can you believe it? This bitch is asking me whether I fucking mean it. I do fucking mean it.'" Vic shrugged. "And that was that."

"Wow." Jack swallowed. "How did he have time to call when she was moving?"

"Oh, winding roads. Multiple opportunities for the kill. It's why we'd chosen the spot."

"And I always thought it was an accident."

"Sadly, we never got a shot at Rausa after that, because the War didn't go our way, and by the time we had spare capacities to deal with him, he'd practically vanished."

"Why'd he do that?"

"It's hearsay, but my best guess is, he spent the time weeding out everybody who was loyal to Mike. Some people vanished, so they probably got walked into a room."

Jack remembered a quip from his previous capo that it was only the Cosa Nostra where "a man was walked into a room" wasn't the first line of a Dad joke.

"Rausa's a hard man," Vic continued.

For what it's worth, I think you broke his heart.

"He needs to be." Jack kept his voice level and flat. "Considering he clawed his way to the top. Andrea didn't have to."

"Neither did you. Timing worked in your favor, Jack. When you got out, you carried less baggage than any of the others."

"I'm aware." All of it was moot now, though. His role was no longer set, the shackles had fallen away. There was something liberating in chaos and destruction. "I've played defense so long, shifting to offense will take some getting used to."

"What makes you think it'll be necessary?"

"I approached him at the wedding. Cassaro was there too. Rausa told me to fuck off. He's definitely holding a grudge."

"Might be a good time to revisit the idea of taking him out. Can't imagine you'd even have to talk to the Dommarco about it, though I'd call Cassaro at least. As a courtesy, if nothing else." Vic groaned as he shifted his weight in bed. "I swear, humans are just made of guts and shit. Never get old."

Some humans. Jack gave him a slight smile. "You've given me some stuff to think about." He rose, hesitantly and lingered near the bed. "When we deal with Rausa, there might be some poetic justice if we use the same shooter. Care to share the name?"

Vic smiled with some real humor. "I like your thinking, but he's currently not available. Unlike you, he wasn't exactly a model prisoner, so he should be out in twenty years or so."

Ralphie Galante. He was the only one that fit the description. He'd been a trusted button man for Andrea's father and a noticeable loss when the jury had quite rightly put him away for a long time. Jack hadn't paid a lot of attention to him, except to back him up with lawyers and money. He'd been too busy sweating over the peace treaty with Cassaro.

"That's too bad." Jack checked his phone for the time. "Will they at least let you drink the wine?"

"They didn't keep me from drinking the others." Vic raised his chin in defiance, and Jack assumed some nurses may have decided to indulge a man whose room was crowded with the ghosts of the men he'd killed. "But when you deal with Rausa, do it quickly and decisively. I'm almost glad he'll be your problem now."

"Yeah, agreed." Jack took a few steps back. "If you like that one, I'll have a case delivered for you."

"You're a good man, Jack, thanks."

Appropriate respects paid, he left the room and caught the eye of a doctor making the rounds. "How's he doing?"

"Are you a member of Mr. Decesare's family?"

"Yes, of course. Jack Barsanti. I'm on the guest list."

"You need to understand the care we're providing now is purely palliative."

"I do, thanks. How long does he have left? That might sound harsh, but he has family all over and I'd like to make sure they can all make the appropriate arrangements."

She eyed him but didn't seem unduly alarmed. "I understand Mr. Decesare is making arrangements to be moved to his own home, where a team of nurses will look after him over the next few months."

Even better. "Of course. Gives him unlimited access to his wine cellar. Thanks, doctor." At least that meant that Spadaro wouldn't show up here to terrorize staff, if that was what Sal decided.

What had Spadaro called him? *Last man standing.* Little by little, Jack was feeding his past, his contacts, his former allies to the fire. Vic Decesare still had respect, could still call on people, but the man he'd seen was mostly used up. He could still do damage, but if he did, it was nothing but spite. He wouldn't be able to lead an effective counter-attack, and that was the only thing that mattered.

41

Jack spent the next two weeks pretending everything was normal in anything but normal circumstances. He pretended to care, and at times found himself strangely caring and strangely torn up about the deaths, the panicked phone calls, the attempts by various men to make sense of the avalanche of hurt that Sal Rausa poured out over the Lo Cascio clan.

He entered the Hunting Lodge, a five-star resort less than an hour by car down the coast from Port Francis. Just over two hours away from the airport. He had tickets booked on three different flights via O'Hare, his final destination determined by how long this meeting would take—tomorrow he'd be either in Frankfurt, Amsterdam or Madrid.

The Lodge was mostly regarded as "neutral ground" by the families; the resort was now closed down to normal guests to avoid unwelcome elements creeping in—Cassaro had helped secure it for a "family get together" on short notice.

If any of the staff cared that whatever family gathered here consisted only of men, no women, no children, no elderly family members, they didn't share their suspicions. Jack checked into his room and gave it a cursory look while he undressed. He stepped under the shower to wash off the first part of the day, the last-minute phone calls, and especially the meeting with Petra, whose anguish still reached him.

"What do you mean, we'll just roll over and capitulate? What kind of choice is that?"

"We don't have the strength left to fight. If we negotiate now, we might be able to salvage something."

"Andrea would never allow that."

"I don't mean to be insensitive, Petra, but this is a matter of survival. I'll do my best to make sure you're safe so you'll be there for your children. I owe Andrea to have their interest at heart."

Bringing them up hadn't been fair, and considering her husband had vanished, and Petra clearly half feared and half knew the worst had happened, she'd shown remarkable backbone. She'd tried in her own way to gain an overview and rally what power she had to defend herself. Jack had ostensibly supported her in that, had "tried to find out" where Andrea had vanished to, but both man and car remained gone, and there was no useful coverage from the club. Mauro's best guess had been that Andrea had snuck out with a girl and had been ambushed somewhere on the road.

When Andrea still didn't pick up the phone after twenty-four hours, and capos similarly vanished, everybody realized there was a war on. Some enterprising soldiers had gone out to lead a strike against Sal Rausa, and those soldiers' charred remains were found in a burnt-out car just outside of town early the next morning.

Petra's parting shot still stung.

"What kind of man are you to beg for peace like a bitch?"

In her eyes, he was weak and ineffective, especially when compared to her husband. But he forced himself to accept her derision, nodded with all the calm humility he'd practiced ever since he'd been a Cosa Nostra recruit.

Still in his bathrobe, he grabbed a quick bite from room service in the sitting area, but the beautiful view over a few trees and then the ocean did nothing to relax him. He still had to do this one thing and he'd be free. Then he dressed again and waited.

When the knock came, he was more than ready. It was Enzo, healthy and alive, though the weariness in his eyes betrayed he too had had a rough time.

"Sal's ready to see you now."

"Thanks." They walked through the resort complex, and Enzo chose the longer route so people would be able to get a good view of what was happening. Jack did his best to play himself at his calmest and most dignified. He could have called upon a few surviving soldiers and recruits for some added security, but that wasn't the visual Jack was going for. His presence here, without entourage, telegraphed the power balance very clearly.

They walked into the wood-paneled conference room. Sal sat at the large round table, centered from the door, his unruly hair brushed out of his face. The moment their eyes met, Jack felt the gasp trapped somewhere deep in his chest. None of it had been trickery, or an illusion, it hadn't been due to hysteria or depression or that constant, low-level ache of never belonging. He hadn't thrown himself at the feet of the first man who'd respected him despite knowing his flaws. Whatever had been going on between them, it had been mutual.

Sal wore a tailored suit and was clean-shaven, though Jack decided he preferred him with a bit of stubble.

Enzo moved to the door, clasped his hands there as if he were a security guard at The Matador.

Jack briefly acknowledged the other men—if he wasn't mistaken, all of them Sal's capos. They too, betrayed some of that tension and weariness of the past two weeks, but Sal, he burned as brightly as he always did. Jack wanted to ask whether getting his revenge had helped a little bit with the pain.

"Mr. Rausa. Thanks for seeing me."

Sal folded his hands before him, elbows on the table. "Thanks for coming." A slight grin could be read as sarcasm, but Jack took it as real humor. "I'm looking forward to hearing your proposal, Mr. Barsanti."

Jack walked to the chair directly opposite Sal, but remained standing. He felt the men's eyes on him, but he gave them nothing but studied indifference. In an alternative world, he might have been conflicted, might have been humiliated, might have strategized to salvage as much as possible, but none of that mattered anymore. He was here to wind down the Lo Cascio and end their history in this town, not score the points that were still up for grabs if he played his few remaining cards skillfully.

"I'm here as the consigliere of the Lo Cascio family, Mr. Rausa, and speak on their behalf." Or what headless, demoralized mess was left of them, but Sal knew that. Jack couldn't wait for all of that to finish, and once this was done, he'd retire and count his blessings every day that he'd survived.

"We're offering unconditional peace." After a lot of thinking, he'd whittled his statement down to that sentence and rehearsed it until it sounded neutral and smooth. "The remaining people associated with us sent me to negotiate whatever terms suit you, in return for peace."

Sal smiled. "I'm willing to hear you out."

"Petra Lo Cascio would like to retain interests in certain businesses of her husband, in order to support herself and her family. Other associates are asking to be bought out for a suitable price and leave Port Francis permanently."

The tension in the room dropped, and shifted toward anticipation as the capos considered which piece of the cake they wanted to claim. Sal's focus didn't waver as he seemed to consider the implications. "I doubt Mrs. Lo Cascio will want to hear that from me, but please convey to her that I'll respect her wishes and the safety and security of her and her children. She, too, will be required to leave the city."

"She's willing to do that." Or, in Petra's words, *Damn this whole fucking city to hell.*

"Good. We'll hash out which businesses are of interest to us and what price we're willing to pay to speed up the peace process." Sal lifted an eyebrow. "I trust you brought a list."

"Of course, Mr. Rausa." He handed over a few folded pages. Nothing on there would come as a surprise to Sal, it was all just for show. But however they played this, whatever people might end up thinking, Jack would still forever be the consigliere whose family had been soundly beaten, and who now had the job of clearing away the debris. But the true failure would hopefully be placed on Andrea's shoulders.

Sal stood. "I'll review this. In the meantime, I accept your surrender and that of the Lo Cascio. Hostilities will cease on both sides while we hammer out the details." He offered his hand.

"Agreed." Jack took Sal's hand and shook it. The touch ran like a low, sweet current over his skin. He had to force himself to meet Sal's gaze. They'd barely talked on the phone, just enough to let each other know they were both alive. *We'll talk when this is done*, Sal had said.

"Please have a seat."

Over the next hours, Jack hammered out the details, signed papers that the law firm running the Lo Cascio clan's legit interests would enact, with Petra as one of the main beneficiaries, even though some of those assets changed hands for a song. When all of it was said and done, Sal stepped out to take a call, and Jack stood and walked out too. He didn't return to his room, no reason to—he hadn't brought his suitcase from the car.

This part was a lot harder than he'd feared.

He tightened his hands around the steering wheel of his trusty Porsche, already hating the thought of leaving it behind at the local airport.

Last man standing.

He started the engine.

Port Francis didn't have a place for him. Three generations ago, the Barsanti had stepped off the boat in the hopes of becoming Americans and building a new future in this new world. While they'd succeeded, and he'd made more money than his threadbare, hopeful, hard-working grandparents could even dream of, he didn't have a future here.

The only way to cope with his total defeat was to leave and find a place where nobody knew him.

But he had his life, and the other positive was that, if he should ever meet another man like Sal Rausa—as unlikely as that was—he could now allow himself to feel and slowly explore where that feeling would take him. The thought was sweet and made his heart ache. There might be a place, but more importantly, a someone for him.

He'd almost left the resort grounds, when headlights appeared behind him, and a car was rapidly closing in. If he wasn't mistaken, it was Sal's truck.

Oh no, not happening.

He took the last corner faster than he wanted, but then it was open road, and the turbocharged 2.5-liter flat four generated a purring, smooth 350 horsepower. And after all of his tight control, the fear, the exhaustion, it was exhilarating to finally be able to run, and run fast.

42

"*uck!* I'll call you back." Sal floored the pedal, but his truck didn't exactly offer super car acceleration, speed or handling, and he was not going to wrap himself around a tree trying to catch up to that damned Porsche.

He speed-dialed Jack's phone, but the man had his hands full driving at, fuck, much faster than 130 miles per hour.

At that speed, he didn't *want* Jack to answer the phone.

No response.

Sal slowed down, even though that meant the Porsche was rapidly getting smaller, and speed-dialed Spadaro.

"Yes."

"Jack's just ... fucking vanished." Wrong. He was running, just when everything had looked like it would work out. Where had he gone wrong? Pushed too hard? Humiliated him? He'd fucking *promised* they'd talk, and surely Jack knew by now that he always delivered on his promises. "He's driving. Fast. I need to catch him."

"Where to?"

"He's taken the highway headed northwest." Now, if Jack fled in a straight line, that would take him past Port Francis and straight to ...

"Airport," Spadaro said. "Is he driving his usual car?"

"Yes."

"Nice." A hint of glee in Spadaro's voice. "I'll call when I got him."

Fucking speed demon, but at least Spadaro was on his side. "Great, meet you at the airport."

43

Amsterdam, then. Jack looked at the departure board —the next flight to Chicago O'Hare was already boarding, and he hadn't even checked in, so he wouldn't be able to make the Frankfurt flight. He waited in line for the business class check-in. He'd have plenty of time on the tourist visa to decide where he wanted to live, but right now, a couple years in Europe sounded like just the ticket.

He knew a lawyer in Valletta who could help with acquiring permanent residency in Malta, where one official language was English, and Italian was also widely spoken. Plus, it wasn't Italy and nowhere near his parents or other connections. Excluding fees, that would cost about 150,000 Euros, and if he liked it there, he could always buy Maltese citizenship as a next step. That would open the whole continent to him, giving him plenty of options.

The woman behind the counter smiled and indicated that the gate would open in 30 minutes, and he thanked her and turned away.

Spadaro stood before him, dressed in his biking leathers, helmet dangling from his right arm. "Hi, Dad. I found a seat for us over there." Without taking his eyes off Jack's face for a second, he pointed over to a corner near a luggage shop and a fast-food outlet.

"Do you think it's smart, bringing a weapon into an airport?" Jack asked in Italian.

"Wasn't going to go through security." Spadaro responded in the same language. "Come, let's sit." He took Jack's arm in an unsettling echo of how Jack had offered him support while Spadaro had been wearing a dress and high heels.

Creeped out, Jack allowed Spadaro to lead him over to the empty group of seats. Spadaro sat down next to him, and placed one leg across his knee, taking a lot of space. He could have been nothing more than a manspreading teenager, but his dark eyes remained fixed on Jack, and that made this whole situation a whole lot less casual.

"What do you want? Tying off loose ends?"

"You wouldn't be talking to me now if you were a loose end. No. Sal Rausa wants a few minutes of your time."

Shit. "If I wanted to talk to him, I'd have stayed at the Lodge. In fact, we've talked plenty. Our business is concluded." He forced himself to breathe calmly and evenly, part of him trying to figure out where the gun or knife was. Inside the suit? In the helmet?

"Running from finished business is weird, don't you think?"

"Listen, I need to catch that plane. I'll write you a check for a hundred grand, and you missed me."

For the first time, Spadaro actually smiled an almost normal smile. "Cute."

"Two hundred then." Jack did have the feeling it was futile and, worse, pathetic. But seeing Spadaro not even blink at such a handsome bribe was really fucking disturbing.

"Yeah, sorry, not currently taking any other jobs, but happy to give you my number." Spadaro reached inside his bike jacket and pulled out a card that he slid across to Jack. Jack took it mostly because there was no point in rejecting it.

"I have reasons to leave," Jack tried again. Plan B. A new start. No more responsibilities. Nobody would know him. He could leave this part of his past behind in much in the same way he'd left prison behind for good several years ago.

"We all do," Spadaro said and stood. He focused on something else in the check-in hall, and with a sinking heart, Jack spotted Sal Rausa in an almost full run, behind him Enzo. Sal's face was flushed, but whether it was exertion or rage was impossible to say.

Oh hell. One reason for running was that he hadn't wanted to have this discussion with Sal. This was nothing he could negotiate. All this would do was hurt him more and push out the inevitable.

Sal reached them, breath going hard. "Jack. Fuck."

Spadaro pulled back and shifted his attention to their surroundings, people wrestling with their luggage or digging for their passports or ordering a burger. Jack could barely hear the airport noise over the pulse pounding in his head. The seventy yards to the entrance of the security check area might just as well have been miles. He could raise an alarm and attract attention, but even so these three men could grab him and bundle him into a car before the security guard over there looked up from his phone.

44

Sal honestly didn't know whether he wanted to shake or punch Jack, but seeing him, he was just relieved that he'd caught up to him. Spadaro had spotted Jack the moment he'd entered the check-in area, and then given Sal directions.

And while an airport was not the best place for this, it also wasn't the worst. "What the hell is going on here, Jack?"

"I'm done in Port Francis." He sounded very calm, very reasonable and now straightened in his seat.

Sal sat down next to him, with one seat between them, still catching his breath. "Done with what?" None of this made sense, but if Jack needed to put this into his kind of words, he needed to ask questions and listen to the answers, even if he didn't like it.

"My job. Sal, you got everything you wanted. Every last bit. Everything ..." Jack's voice vibrated with some kind of suppressed emotion that Sal couldn't parse. "Everything and more. You didn't take any losses. Your enemies are dealt with.

You got the money, the power, the businesses. Nobody will ever disrespect you again. It's a fantastic victory. Congratulations."

Yes, and? Why did Jack sound bitter now? "And what's the problem?"

"And I ... didn't."

"Bullshit. You made it possible."

"Possible. Jesus." Jack's eyes narrowed with pain. "And I got nothing. My job ... everything I'm good at, that's all done. You winning always meant I'd lose. Yes, I'm breathing, but that old me, the man I was as part of the Lo Cascio, he might just as well have drowned. And I think I deserve to find out who else I can be."

"Might just as well have drowned."

Fuck. Then who'd the man he'd had sex with been then? Jack didn't even allude to that, though, likely to keep his dignity, but Sal thought he could hear those meanings in his words too.

"Yes, you do," Sal said and meant it.

"Thank you." Jack took his bag, slipped the strap over his shoulder and stood. "Goodbye, Sal." He turned to leave.

"But you can do that here." *With me.* Sal forced himself to remain sitting.

Jack faced him again. "I'll be a traitor. I'll never be anything else."

"And I turned you into that, is that what you're saying?"

Jack's lips tightened. "No. I made my choices. I own them."

Brave fucking consigliere. Jack had always had heart, but his integrity and inner strength kept shining through, and Sal admired him for it. Few men just unblinkingly accepted the consequences of their own actions. At the same time, Jack was definitely being too harsh on himself. "I told you we'd talk about everything. And you didn't even give me a chance for that."

Jack glanced back to the departure board. "I'll miss my flight."

"Talk to me, Jack. After that, I'll let you go. Fuck, I'll even walk you to the fucking gate."

Jack took a deep breath, closed his eyes, then shook his head. "You got everything you wanted."

"I think we both know that isn't true. I didn't get you." Shit, and this was something he'd wanted to say after some languid sex in that huge bed in his suite. Ask Jack whether he could imagine trying for something more. He'd been ready to negotiate the terms of a relationship—and now it seemed that had never been on the table. Sal had never been much of a negotiator, but he realized that had been Jack's whole life. Everything he was. This was little-explored territory for Sal, but he'd be damned it if he walked away without trying.

Jack's face softened and he seemed to waver. "It's not enough. Who would I be if I stayed?"

"Whatever the fuck you want. Retire if you want. If it's not working out, I'll drive you personally to the airport, though a bit more slowly." The attempt at cracking a joke didn't fall completely flat; Jack's lips twitched. "Don't think all of ... all of this happened because I used you. I didn't use you when it came to the personal stuff."

"No, I didn't think you did."

"Then give me a chance." Sal stood when Jack kept looking at him. He wished he knew what was going on in

Jack's head—that was one constant in their relationship. "If it's because of the job, fuck it, you could work as an independent negotiator and act as my go-between with the Dommarco. Or join my people."

"How would that look?"

"Independent then. Reevaluate after a few years. There's plenty of work for a smart man. Fuck, get in with the Prizzi, I'm sure they'd have work for a consultant. Do whatever you want." *Just don't leave.*

Jack was wavering, thinking, and Sal took another step toward him. He wanted to touch him, but they were in public, and he really didn't want to spook Jack now. Not while everything could still turn to shit. Jack could still decide to run, and while Sal had the means to hunt him to the ends of the earth, he'd force himself to let Jack go if he really wanted that. After everything he'd done to Jack, he did owe him that much respect, even if it would hurt like hell.

"For what it's worth," he lowered his voice even more because the last thing he wanted to do was entertain a bunch of travelers while they queued for their burgers, "I'll always respect you. Your choice. If you want my protection, you can have it. If you want anything else ... same. It really is your call this time."

Jack gave him warm smile. "Thank you." It sounded heartfelt, and Sal still expected a "but" and then Jack would walk off and vanish from his life.

But it didn't come. Jack cast another look at the departure board, then plucked his boarding pass from his inside pocket, ripped it up, and threw it in the nearby trash can. He gripped his bag tighter and returned to Sal. "I didn't check out of the Lodge. Should we meet back at my suite? To discuss the ... particulars."

"Of course," Sal agreed and watched Jack go. He didn't quite manage to take a deep, calm breath—he'd do that when he could hold Jack again. Kiss him. Fuck him. Keep him. Of all the things about Jack that intrigued him, of the many ways the man had earned his respect and won his heart, Jack's poise and grace under fire hit him the hardest. But having to go toe to toe with him and being so unsure who'd win in the end still unnerved him. He'd never met anybody else who could turn the tables so completely on him, outwit him with his head under water, even at the cost of his own life. There simply wasn't anybody like Jack Barsanti.

Spadaro stepped to Sal's side. "I don't think I have to chase him down again."

"No, I think he'll listen."

"Good. Battista will be happy about how all of this is going." Spadaro looked around. "No massacres necessary. I haven't done an airport yet. Though it's pretty small."

"Just don't."

"Joking." Spadaro scoffed as if Sal couldn't have possibly thought he was serious. "I'll get going. I'll be around for a few more days. If I don't hear from you, I'll assume all is well. If you need me again, call me."

Sal offered his hand and Spadaro shook it. "Much appreciated."

On the way to the exit, Spadaro put the helmet on and then he was already through the door. Sal gestured to Enzo, who joined him. When he turned to leave, he heard, "Final call for passenger Mr. Jack Barsanti at Gate 8" through the loudspeakers. He exchanged a glance with Enzo, who looked a lot calmer than Sal felt.

"You drive. And before you get sassy with me, there's something else we need to talk about." It was a distraction for himself, but it was also long overdue.

Enzo lifted his eyebrows and gave a small nod. He'd coordinated those parts of the clean-up that Sal hadn't, and taken out a couple capos himself. Those first thirty-six hours had been some of the bloodiest in Port Francis' history, and after his killing spree, Enzo had settled in with a bottle of nice old cognac—not to deal with the blood and murder, but to tamp down on the adrenaline and exhaustion. Spadaro had roamed freely around the city, tying off "loose ends".

"Seems we're growing a lot after this, so we'll need to fill some positions," Sal said softly when they sat in the truck. He noticed how Enzo's shoulders relaxed. "Wait, what were you thinking I was going to say?"

Enzo shook his head and started the engine. "I don't know, something about sex, I guess."

Sal blinked, but decided to stay on his original track. "It's time to fill a certain position. We haven't needed an underboss, but that has changed." He'd also shied away from filling the position because that had been his own launching pad to take over the family. With the low profile he'd kept, it hadn't been necessary to have somebody handle the day-to-day.

Enzo kept his eyes on the road. "You do know I've never played for that."

"But would you take it?" Sal lifted a hand. "No, I mean, will you take it?"

"Well, we can't have some other douchebag doing a shit

job," Enzo growled softly. "And I have a soldier who can take over my crew, and won't fuck it up."

Sal laughed and patted Enzo's thigh. "Congratulations on the promotion."

"Yeah, and fuck you too," Enzo muttered. "Thank you."

"You earned it. And now, since we're nice and alone in the car together, what was that about sex?"

"Jack's a good guy. He'll look after you."

"If we can work this out, yeah. But I don't feel like I'm completely in the clear yet."

"You can be very convincing." Enzo glanced in the mirror and changed lanes. "And you can always count on me in the life and outside of it. But I don't think you need me the same way anymore. That role's been filled by a guy who's better at it than I am. And I'm okay with that, just in case."

"Setting boundaries, are you?"

"Just in that way. It's time for me to move on."

Nothing about Enzo suggested he hadn't thought long and hard about it. Or, really, short and hard. Enzo wasn't the type who ruminated over these things. And he was right, he'd served as Sal's lifeboat too long already. "I respect that. So, you're going back into the dating game?"

"Soon." Enzo shrugged. "A week or so. I'll give it until Saturday."

Until Saturday? How oddly specific. That little piece of information connected with another one in Sal's head. Silvio Spadaro's departure date. "Comparing notes with the Barracuda?"

Enzo jumped a little. "Nothing serious, but he's very good at what he does."

Holy shit. The things that happened under pressure in

life and death situations. He couldn't see those two together, though they'd clearly gelled well when it came to planning and executing a mass killing. "Welcome to the bisexual club. We have the hottest members and plenty of choice, but the heartache is pretty much the same, just saying, sorry."

"I have no fucking clue what he is, but I don't think it matters. Might widen the field. Might not."

"Take it one day at a time," Sal said, echoing what Enzo had told him so often.

"Yep." Enzo smirked. "You think you'll join us for dinner tonight in the restaurant? Boys might want to see your face."

"Won't promise it." Sal patted Enzo's arm. "You cover for me, *sottocapo.*"

45

Jack paced across the cream carpet back in his suite, trying to think through the implications of the new picture, trying so hard to focus, but all he could think of was Sal's stricken face back at the airport.

"I think we both know that isn't true. I didn't get you."

This whole thing was preposterous, impossible, at the very least highly unlikely, not because of Sal, but because of the past, because of who they were or had been, and the idea scared Jack. Always much harder to pick up the pieces than just burn it all to the ground and start anew. He knew very well just how much hard work it was.

But for once, he wouldn't have to do it alone.

A knock on the door, and Jack opened it for Sal, who stepped swiftly inside, but didn't crowd Jack, didn't touch him, though he looked like he wanted to. Instead, Sal Rausa crossed his arms and waited.

"It's madness. You know it is."

"But you knew it wasn't just sex, right?" Sal's voice was

low, as if he made an effort to be non-threatening. Good luck with that. As long as Sal Rausa breathed, he'd be threatening in all kinds of ways.

"I don't *know* anything. I don't exactly have a long history when it comes to sex or relationships." Nothing to measure this against. Sex could mean all kinds of things—just because there was no casual for Jack because he just didn't feel attraction randomly, didn't mean the same standards applied to everybody else. "That is what you're doing, right? Offering me a relationship?"

Sal drew a breath so deep it lifted his shoulders, and then released it. "I'm offering you everything. Independence, protection, dignity, respect, love, a relationship, sex. You don't have to choose, you can have all of it. I'm not going to beg you, Jack, because if this has any chance of working out, I want us to be equals. Regardless of what others may think. And if it doesn't work out, at least we tried. But I need to try."

Jack's heart hurt seeing Sal's eyes so open and vulnerable. Sometimes there was a depth and fragility to him that made Jack ache, but this time was different. There was none of that boundless rage, and without it, Sal seemed more human, more real with all that emotion.

"So we'll … there's …" And he had no real vocabulary for it. He'd never been in a situation where he'd asked somebody to be his partner or his lover, and he assumed it wouldn't get easier even with more practice. "You really believe there's something we can have, something longer?"

"Yes." Just that. No terms, no conditions. "You, and me. I want to know you like I know myself, and I want you to know everything about me. Every last thing."

Jack swallowed hard. "Same."

"It's good to hear it. And say it." Sal offered him a cautious smile and uncrossed his arms. "I want you to stay here with me. I want you in my life, not just in my bed, and I'll do what's necessary."

That exceeded every best-case scenario Jack had ever considered. At most, he'd hoped for an affair, an ongoing thing to explore his own responses, his own emotions. He'd never allowed himself to think further than that, because he couldn't cope with the vulnerability of it. Turncoat consigliere meeting an enemy boss for sex every few days or so? Too demeaning. But Sal offered so much more than Jack would have asked for. "I don't expect you to put a ring on my finger, Sal. I know that's impossible."

Sal's smile widened and he took a step closer. "A ring I can do, I just can't marry you. A ring ... fuck, a ring can be just between two people. I still often wear mine." Sal took Jack's hand and pointedly looked at his fingers, then kissed his knuckles. "Who would even ask why you're wearing one too?"

Jack smiled softly and drew Sal into a firm hug, speechless that those things were even on the table. It seemed he wasn't the only one who had ended up surrendering completely. "I'd wear it," he whispered, because he didn't trust his voice. But he needed even more than this embrace, needed Sal even closer, needed to feel him unguarded, without fear, skin to skin. He reached behind himself and picked up the key card to the suite and pushed it into the pocket of Sal's suit.

"Come back with rope."

"Pushy." Sal grinned. "I like it."

46

Sal slid the card through the lock, and even pushing open the door, he felt the atmosphere inside had changed. It was nothing conscious—most likely it was his imagination because for the first time he had a fair idea what Jack wanted, and the ground under his feet seemed much more solid and reliable. Less of a chance that he'd wade into quicksand or the ground would wash away under his feet.

He hung the "do not disturb" sign on the door handle outside, and closed the door, allowing it an audible click, then he locked it.

He found Jack standing on the balcony, and walked up to stand next to him. "Always the views with you."

Jack turned around and leaned against the railing, displaying his stomach, chest and throat, and looked Sal up and down. "I don't know. This view is maybe even better."

"What are you going for tonight? I cancelled my dinner plans, so I have time."

"I was angling for some more surrendering. To make sure it sticks."

Sal grinned, glad that Jack began to see the playful aspects of it. "Come inside before somebody sees us fucking right here."

Jack seemed to consider the words, then slowly straightened up and walked back into the room. He'd already shed the jacket, now he opened the buttons on his shirt, pulled it out of his trousers and dropped it on the nearest chair without looking. His gaze was turned inward, as he pulled the undershirt free and dropped it on the floor.

Sal took two quick steps and picked it up, but then changed his plan and stayed low. He dropped fully to his knees and reached up to Jack's zipper and belt. Jack ran both hands through his hair and broadened his stance when Sal freed him from his trousers. Giving blowjobs was something Sal loved, and he couldn't wait to get used to Jack's taste and size.

From the trembling in Jack's thighs, his sighs and suppressed moans, he could tell what he liked. He unleashed his bag of tricks, squeezing Jack's balls, adding pressure to the point behind the balls, rubbing and massaging it, while opening his throat to take all of him. Despite the video Jack had watched proving that Sal could more than cope with a little roughness, Jack never pushed, never simply grabbed him and fucked his throat. They'd have to know each other sexually a lot better before Jack felt that confident, but Sal was okay with that too. As long as his partners enjoyed themselves, he was okay with pretty much anything.

Similarly, Jack lacked the experience of other lovers—he

wasn't trying to control this or break it off when he got close. He was mostly focused on the pleasure and on not losing his balance, while Sal moved more harshly, determined to push Jack over the edge. He used one hand to steady Jack, but the other kept working him, adding friction to the suction. Jack came with a choked sound, grabbed the hand that had been steadying him and squeezed it, while Sal slowed down and drew out Jack's orgasm while swallowing the final drops. He pulled back and they were both breathing heavily, Sal to get oxygen, Jack to recover.

"That's something I've wanted to do for a long time."

"I now feel inadequate," Jack said in a low, awed tone.

"I'll let you practice as much as you want." Still on his knees, Sal pulled Jack's trousers and boxers down to his ankles, then helped Jack out of his polished black leather shoes, and then the rest of his clothes. He sat back on his haunches to study his lover's body. From the athletic toned muscles that he'd forged with his unrelenting, almost punishing, gym routine, to the fur on his chest and that beautiful cock, the strong jaw line to his kind, intelligent eyes, Jack Barsanti was goddamned perfection. He still couldn't wrap his head around the idea that Jack had never been touched by anybody, had forbidden himself the pleasure, locked himself away in those most fundamental ways.

"What are you thinking?" Jack asked.

"How lucky I am." A frown formed on Jack's forehead, so he added, "Not because of your history, or any of this. But that I've found you and you trust me."

"If you'd come to the negotiation table back then ..."

Sal laughed. "That would have been a fucking disaster."

"Probably. I wouldn't have been able to let my guard

down. Not like this. Now ... I'm glad I'm alive, and that's new too."

"Good. Because I know I'd lose any race to the airport. I should have slashed your fucking tires."

"You touch my car and I'll end you. And I won't need Spadaro for that."

Sal laughed but sobered quickly and placed a hand against the side of Jack's face, again struck by the soft expression in the man's clear blue eyes. "I didn't think I could have ... this again." This sweet gentle pain of being so close to another soul, of wanting, so badly, to share everything, good days and bad, and life and health, and secrets. To give himself over completely. "And I don't think a part of me will ever be completely over Catia's death, but that's all right too."

"I ..." Jack swallowed, but ploughed on. "Every time you speak of her, it's straight from your soul. I love that. I love how strongly you feel."

Fuck, talk about a killing blow. Sal smiled and blinked his eyes clear. His first impulse was to reach for the ropes, considering Jack was already naked, and he couldn't wait to see the patterns he could draw on the man's skin. He ran a hand down from Jack's collarbones to his solar plexus. "Rope?"

"Yes." Just like that, a calm openness without reservation. If Jack ever did this with anybody else, Sal would definitely brief him beforehand to make sure he was in safe hands, and teach him what to look out for when it came to a rigger, but he also didn't feel like interrupting the building tension between them with a lecture. He was happy to shoulder the burden, and, besides, while he definitely planned to quite literally turn Jack's world upside down with some advanced suspension shibari, for the moment he'd stick to the basics.

"Bedroom."

Jack followed him into the large room. The thick carpet swallowed their steps, but Sal was more intrigued by the four-poster bed. And indeed, considering the posters were solid wood and nicely carved, they gave him options. He opened his toy bag and took out the rope he'd selected for Jack—sky blue, almost electric blue.

Jack looked at the rope and lifted an eyebrow. "For my eyes?"

"Seemed like your color." He loosened the coil of rope and met Jack's gaze. "Any requests?"

"You're way too dressed."

"You're absolutely right."

"What do you normally wear when you do this?"

"Sometimes boots and leather pants. A t-shirt. Sometimes no t-shirt or boots. Sometimes, being barefoot is better when I need some extra grounding. I'm more dressed when it's going to be less sexual."

"Then definitely lose some clothes." Jack grinned.

Normally, Sal liked to set the scene for the other person, which included presentation. One thing Sal had learned was to use fake candles because they flickered so authentically as to be indistinguishable from real flames. When asked, he told his lovers, "*I want to focus on you, not on the other fire hazard.*"

Fragrances were another aspect of it. He would spend some time walking around and sniffing flowers, sheets, and ropes to make sure that everything was just so. At the same time, he'd learned to be subtle. He used leather, wood, tobacco when he was tying up a man, ylang-ylang, rose or musk when he was tying up a woman. Sometimes, play-mates were assigned a specific scent. Sal's had been the deep, warm, sweet and bitter smell of dark chocolate, and the rigger who'd taught him would also rub cocoa butter into his rope marks, further marking him as hers.

Sal took a step backward and undressed. He enjoyed how Jack watched him, attentive and appreciative, gaze flickering between his half-hard cock and his face.

Sal pulled the leather pants from the toy bag and put them on. He turned his body just so that Jack could see that he was getting harder, and adjusted himself before closing the belt.

"Better?" He strode up to Jack, picked up the rope on the way and placed a length of rope around his neck to pull him in for a kiss.

Jack grinned and responded eagerly. One of his hands went to Sal's nipple and gently twisted the bar there, the other cupped him in his pants. "This time I want to feel you inside me," he said in a low voice. "Keep the toys for another night."

The original plan had been to familiarize Jack with having something inside him and take slow steps from there until he was ready to attempt bottoming. They were in no rush, and Sal was determined to make the first time feel as good as possible. "It's not exactly like in porn, you know that, right?"

"I'm duly warned, and I consent to getting fucked." Jack squeezed him. "Even if we need to practice a few more times to get it right."

Well, he'd check if that held up when things actually

started going that way. "All right. You'll still need to talk to me."

"I will."

Sal met Jack's gaze as confirmation, then moved around him and took the rope with him. The contrast against Jack's skin was everything, but so was the shift in Jack's breathing pattern when he began the work. He began slowly, with every touch and slide of the rope a caress that he then fixed in a knot or loop.

It could feel like that—he'd once read somewhere that witches used knots to form and hold spells, and while he didn't particularly believe in witches—or spells—on a different level he got it—the captured tension and energy, weaving a pattern around and into another person like that, could feel magical. He'd barely started the harness when he noticed that very slight sagging at the knees as Jack relaxed into it.

He walked around Jack, immobilizing his upper arms behind his body, making him push out his chest. Then he set to work on the chest, framing the pecs with two and three lengths of rope. He ran his fingers between rope and skin to check tightness, keeping a very close eye on the natural tone and coloring of Jack's skin.

He then stepped around Jack again, and worked on the harness. He noticed Jack's hands opening and closing, until they settled into loose fists. He'd love to add some cuffs to that, but while he could definitely tie Jack down to the extent any small twitch would only tighten the bonds, he was in the mood for something different. He placed knots along Jack's front, running the rope around him until he'd made a perfectly symmetrical pattern that was loose enough to allow him to breathe, but definitely tighter toward the groin.

He ran the rope nowhere near his ass, but created another loop around his thighs. He made sure Jack couldn't reach his own cock in this position, then tied off the ends. Jack was slightly swaying on his feet, and widened his stance automatically. His eyes were hooded and his chin had slightly dropped, and his shoulders only held the tension from the position he was in, and with a caress from Sal, those dropped too. He'd be beautiful in predicament bondage which would test that ability to relax and zone out. Sal closed a hand around Jack's half-hard cock. Jack shivered.

"Enjoying yourself?"

"It's unbelievable. So ... so good."

"And you're amazing." He kept playing with Jack's cock, tugging and jerking, even gave it a small slap, which rocked Jack's whole body, but didn't seem to rip him out of his perfectly blissful state. Another note for later—some cock and ball torture, specifically with shibari that immobilized him, see how far this could be pushed ... But right now, Sal enjoyed simply shifting that full-body awareness from the ropes down to Jack's cock.

He walked around Jack without breaking the touch for more than a second, and leaned into his ear. "I'll fuck you like this. But not quite yet." He took a handful of the ropes at Jack's back, and tightened them, making Jack sway backward, then, because he could feel through the ropes how much Jack was ready to yield to him, he pulled Jack backward toward the side of the bed. "Get on there. Kneel."

Noticeably dazed, Jack obeyed, and Sal kept hold of the harness at all times. He knew how that felt—guidance, strength, control. Once Jack had moved to the middle, he patted the inside of Jack's thigh above the knee. "Open wider."

While Jack obeyed, he took a tube of lube from the toy bag and squeezed some into his hand. He didn't warm it and when he wrapped his lubed hand around Jack's cock, Jack drew a deep, fast breath, and then made a small sound as the ropes made him feel that breath.

"Holy ..."

"Exactly." Sal ran his lubed hand over Jack's cock and worked the tip until Jack was shuddering and glowing with a slight sheen of sweat. He'd pushed his hips forward to chase the sensation as the arousal went from playful to intense. Sal enjoyed pulling him back and down onto his thighs.

Jack caught on quickly and ground back against him. "That's ... God, I can't think. That's like in that video."

"Yeah, I looked at your favorites, but I'm putting my own spin on it."

"I like your version better."

Sal laughed softly. He withdrew his hand and added more lube. Jack's positioning gave him pretty good access to his ass, so he slid his fingers along Jack's naked skin. When he began to circle Jack's hole, the man trembled in the ropes, and lifted up but didn't pull away. He might only believe he was ready, but for the moment Sal took his cues from Jack. One finger went easily, and Jack's breath stuttered. Sal brushed Jack's prostate, making him moan out loud. "You sure you want all of me? You could probably get off with just a couple fingers up your ass."

"Seems like it's you who's scared."

Fuck, sassy rope bottoms. He wouldn't get carried away

with a virgin, but he added another mental note for some things he wanted to try later.

Sal freed his cock, and guided Jack's hand to it. "Does that feel scared to you?"

Jack stroked his length with no more than a feathery touch. "Feels like something I need. Now."

"Careful you don't bite off more than you can chew."

Jack laughed. "Even I know not to chew it. I'm good, Sal. I'll tell you if it's too much." He moaned when Sal pushed two fingers into him and pushed back against the intrusion. All right, so maybe they were at the point where they could risk the next step. Sal reached into his bag to grab a condom.

"I know we ... haven't exactly talked about it, but I don't think we need that." Jack swallowed audibly. "I mean, I ... haven't done this before."

"I have, but my tests are current." Besides, apart from calculated risks with Enzo, he strictly played safe with his various hook-ups; whether he'd known them for a while or not didn't matter.

"Then leave it."

"You don't know what that means."

"I know what it means to me. I want to feel you."

Fuck. He should have raised the issue when Jack wasn't half out of his mind from the restraints. Was Jack in a state to consent to this? Did he really understand? The pros and cons raced through Sal's mind, but he decided to trust Jack in this. The man had been remarkably clear-minded under much worse pressure. He put the condom packet down and instead lubed up his own cock. "Lift up."

Jack did, and again, Sal made sure to grip the harness

firmly. He shifted underneath Jack's ass, then steadied his cock at his hole. "Go slow and down."

And Jack slowly lowered himself, adjusting to where he could feel the pressure, working to get the angle right to allow Sal to enter him. Sal didn't move, didn't push or pull, just held and steadied, trying to control his breath when Jack slowly bore down on him. They both gasped when he breached Jack, and Sal kissed Jack's shoulder while Jack released enough of his weight to slowly, tentatively, impale himself. Sal wished above all else they had a mirror to allow Jack to watch what he was doing.

"Yeah, it's ... intense," Jack breathed.

"Stop if it hurts. Seriously, we can spend a whole lot more time getting you ready."

"Noted." Jack settled more of his weight on Sal's lap and groaned when he rested on Sal's thighs. The heat and tightness were dizzying, but more than that were Jack's breaths that slowly deepened as he got used to the intrusion. Sal placed a hand on Jack's throat and tilted Jack's head further back before he kissed and nibbled the taut skin, feeling Jack's thundering pulse under his lips and around him. He slid his lubed hand past Jack's hip and curled it around his hard cock.

Jack shuddered. "Not ... too much. It's too much."

"Might need to put a cock ring around you next time."

"Might ... might be an idea ..." Jack breathed for a little while, then ground back against him, making them both gasp. In no time at all, he was moving, fingers helping support his weight against Sal's hips, and Sal gave him small, sliding thrusts, while holding the harness to steady Jack and anchor him. Jack took to getting fucked pretty easily and quickly, and

Sal made sure he only got as much as he could take. He took his cues from Jack's movement, meeting him when he moved, but didn't drive or push. Allowing Jack to explore the pleasure while holding him, and letting him work for it, was a complete mindfuck even for Sal and tested his self-control to the limit.

Still, while Jack chased orgasm, he couldn't quite get there—yet. He thrust backward, moaning and almost recklessly hard, and while Sal was close, he held back because this wasn't the time to tip Jack over and fuck him as hard as he could. Not this time, and maybe not for a while.

"Want to come, Jack?"

A swallow. "Yes ... feels like ..."

"Takes more practice." Sal pulled him back against himself all the way. One hand around Jack's throat, another around his cock, he worked the tip with the same harsh movements that Jack used on himself when he jerked off. He increased the pressure against his throat enough to make Jack feel his pulse, but not constrain his breathing.

Jack came gasping, shuddering, his whole body tensed, and it almost pushed Sal over the edge too. Ah, hell, he let his tightly wound control go, and thrust hard a couple of times into Jack's impossibly hot tightness and came too. He had to hold onto the ropes now to steady himself, and was relieved when Jack ground back against him. Sal's orgasm crested and left him as sweaty and shivering as Jack. He stayed inside of him for a while longer, caressing the bound body on top of him, holding him, until he trusted his voice again.

"That okay?" Jack asked, voice rough as if he'd screamed.

"Is that your praise kink?"

"I didn't ... push you too much, did I?"

"Jack." He kissed the sweaty skin right below Jack's ear. "You can push all you want. I just wanted to be the responsible one in the room, that's all. But I don't think I've hurt you."

"No. I think I'd ... like to lie down though. I feel light-headed."

"Yes, of course." He moved away enough to have better access to the ropes. Right after an orgasm, his mind was scrambled enough that loosening the knots represented much more of a challenge than tying them. Though his fingers were sweaty and trembling, he focused on undoing the ropes first, and then helped Jack stretch out. He checked him for rope burn or bruises—his rope marks would fade quickly. Sal paused to appreciate the marks around Jack's chest and especially around his upper arms and caressed them. Jack lay down on his back and took several deep breaths.

"I think I ... get why people are so into ropes. You miss them when they're gone."

"I'd say you're definitely into ropes."

Jack gave a languid smile. "How did you get into it?"

Sal gathered the rope and tied it, then fastened it and dropped it on a chair. "Catia was a fantastic rigger. Turns out, rope in the right hands means you can do whatever you want even with a guy who's bigger and stronger. Up until then, my skills in bed were limited to shit like fuzzy handcuffs." He chuckled.

Jack smiled warmly at him. "After this, I don't think I'd settle for less."

"Definitely get lovers who know their shit. Not worth working with amateurs."

"Not interested. If you'll have me, I'll stick to this."

"You don't know what you're missing out on."

"I'm still not ..." Jack sat up and blinked a few times, clearly trying to focus. "I just want you. The past couple weeks, I had time to think about it, look at other men, ponder ... think what I want out of life. Whether I could get back into the closet, shut myself down again, and I'm not interested in other men. I don't know why. I can see they're attractive, but I don't want to have sex with them."

"Okay." If Jack was only interested in him, that worked for Sal too. He could be happily exclusive.

"It's specifically ... connected to you. I see you and I want to touch you and kiss you. I see some other man, even an attractive one, and there's no spark. Maybe because I think I'm falling in love with you, and it doesn't scare me. It could be that simple."

The second time that night Jack had used the "l" word, if in a circumspect way. Again, it jolted Sal down to the bones, but not unpleasantly. They'd agreed to try a relationship without even saying the word, talked about rings, and Sal had offered everything he had to offer even before that. It now hung between them, and saying it out loud was really only a formality.

In every way that counted, Jack was special, and none of this felt like a hook-up, or an affair, or a friend with benefits. There was a deeper, wider, richer aspect to all of it, much more encompassing. He also appreciated that Jack told him this with his utter honesty that held no demands or neediness. There was something to be said for falling for a guy who was so secure in himself. And Jack also wasn't the type to blurt out "I love you" while overwhelmed by an orgasm. No, if he said it, he meant it.

Sal scooted back onto the bed, grabbed Jack's neck and kissed him. "I love you too, Jack." They hugged tightly, caressing and kissing, a small world unto themselves. For the first time in what felt like forever, Sal let go and drifted in tenderness, soaking up as much of it as possible.

47

Jack sat in the Hunting Lodge's bar, flicking through the links Sal had sent him. Apparently he'd collected images from various sources and had created a "mood board", which seemed to be what architects worked from now rather than detailed specifications.

Jack tended to buy houses as they stood and make changes to them afterward, but Sal had found a plot of land he liked—close enough to reach the center in twenty minutes, but still surrounded by greenery and virgin forest. Jack was sure nobody received new building permissions in that stretch of land, otherwise the city's tech and start-up hipster millionaires would have already turned it into their playground. But Sal had secured a plot somehow. Maybe from an associate, or he'd held it in reserve, or the Prizzi had something to do with it. In any case, the old buildings on it were already being pulled down and new construction began in earnest in spring.

The "mood board" made Jack smile. Sal wasn't the type

to ask his opinion about every little thing, but as he flicked through the images, he had to admit the architects had managed to make the house look like an organic whole, rather than a study in contrasts ripped from a hundred Pinterest boards. The mock-up images included shots of large windows opening out into the forest, and plenty of natural textures, wood grains in multiple colors, marble and sandstone tiles, natural rock walls, granite paving outside. It almost looked like a slightly different take on his own house up in the hills, except it also had the more minimalist and enclosed spaces that Sal seemed to prefer. It would have a basement with a dedicated play area, and Jack wondered what the architects had made of the generous, well-lit and sound-proofed space.

A separate wing, housing a gym and indoor pool, could also be used for entertaining and had enough space for visitors. The other wing of the house was a totally independent living area and so closely matched Jack's preferences for open lines of sight that he felt right at home there even though it didn't exist yet.

A few weeks prior, Sal had told him to meet with Beth so she'd stop worrying about Jack, and he'd kept nagging until Jack had arranged lunch with her in a private restaurant back room. Beth had seemed happy to see them both, and Jack had bit his lips a few times as Sal lied so effortlessly and charmingly to her. She was doing well in her classes to train as an electrician, and after they'd parted, she'd texted him: *"Keeper!!!"* When Jack had shown him the message, Sal had laughed warmly, flattered.

Jack noticed people walk into the bar and pressed the button to switch off the tablet.

Cassaro and Guy Dommarco himself filed into the room, as well as a couple of guys for security reasons. They fell back and remained at the entrance, while Cassaro and the Dommarco boss continued onward. Jack stood and smiled.

"Jack. So good to see you. I was worried." Cassaro sounded genuine enough, though the worry likely included a whole lot more than Jack's survival.

"It's been an interesting time. Let's hope the rest of winter is quieter. Do you want to join me for a drink?"

Cassaro nodded, walked back to Dommarco, said something so low in his ear that Jack didn't catch it, then Dommarco stepped close and shook Jack's hand. "You would have been missed, Barsanti."

"Thank you, sir. I hope you're well?"

Guy Dommarco slid into the booth opposite Jack, and Cassaro came back from the bar a few moments later and sat on a chair. "Now, tell me what I should expect in there."

Jack won a few seconds of time while the server brought drinks and olives and then vanished to the far end of the room to tidy the spotless bar. "Well, I believe Sal Rausa will negotiate about his future business interest in Port Francis, as they pertain to his family and yours. Nature abhors a vacuum, and we all know there have been some significant changes."

Cassaro *hmmm*ed. "What's your position now?"

I'm literally in bed with the enemy, and positions remain interesting. Jack shrugged with a sigh. "Well, after the hostile merger, I've wound down the other business interests of the Lo Cascio. Mr. Rausa has driven a pretty hard bargain, but I also think he realizes that he's unlikely to encounter any meaningful hostilities from that direction."

"What about Vic Decesare?" Cassaro speared an olive.

Sal's face had darkened when Jack had conveyed what he'd learned. After some deep soul-searching, he'd decided to let the natural killer do the work, but not out of a sense of mercy. "No longer a player," Jack said as neutrally as he could. "Cancer's a bastard."

Both men nodded solemnly at that.

The situation with the real killer had been different. The last thing Jack had heard was that he'd committed suicide in prison, helped along by an obliging cell mate whose girlfriend desperately needed help with a loan to keep a roof over her head. With all of that resolved, Sal had then focused on reorganizing his family, as well as those pieces of the Lo Cascio businesses that complemented his interests. They'd spent several days discussing what the Dommarco might offer in return for another peace agreement, and how to sell them the new deal.

Jack turned up his hands on the table briefly and shrugged again. "That's the current state of things. From what I'm catching, Mr. Rausa has no interest in being the only player in town. The actions against Andrea were due to a personal grudge. I didn't know Andrea had his wife murdered, so ..."

"Yeah, I heard a rumor about that. It did seem too conveniently timed." A rumor from Cassaro was gospel truth. "Well, Jack, thanks for giving us the lay of the land. That's helpful."

"Any time. I'm just going to ... you know," he dropped a hand on the tablet next to him and gave another sigh, "count my blessings."

"Indeed", Guy Dommarco said and rose again. "We're

lucky we don't have the city swarming with Feds. Let's keep it that way."

"Exactly."

Cassaro also stood, and Jack followed. "Listen, Jack, we respect you. If you need some new hunting grounds, we could use a good head like yours if you're interested."

"Thank you. I'm here strictly as an independent to help with the negotiations. I'd say Mr. Rausa doesn't quite have my depth of experience when it comes to keeping the peace."

Cassaro's eyes sparked with amusement—he probably remembered that scene at the wedding too. "And after this?"

"Might be in everybody's best interest if I accept Sal Rausa's offer to join him. He's in desperate need of a consigliere. I did consider retirement, but it's not the right time."

"He's taking you in?" Cassaro raised an eyebrow. "How do you feel about that?"

Very good, thank you very much.

"It's a good way to keep the peace. At least Sal Rausa isn't a hothead like Andrea was. Nothing has changed. I still believe peace is better than war, and Port Francis is large enough for all of us."

Cassaro and Dommarco exchanged a glance. That was clearly a surprise to them, and Jack assumed unease warred with relief. Sal would make an effort to sweeten the deal; it wasn't Jack's place to do that, except of course he'd coached Sal on exactly what to say. In the future, they'd probably be glad Jack kept Sal in check. The deeper dynamics were none of their business.

They shook hands and Cassaro, Dommarco and their

security detail left the bar to, no doubt, discuss the new information Jack had given them. Taking his time, Jack finished his coffee.

As he walked back toward Sal's suite, it struck him as strange how much more clear-headed and optimistic he felt about these negotiations. Not only were they acting from a position of strength, but Jack, even though he had no official role as yet beyond "independent", felt much more at ease about his own situation and much better in his skin. For the first time in his memory, that self-loathing and darkness wasn't clawing against his skin from the inside. That alone was a blessing he could barely fathom.

When he slid the key card through the lock to Sal's suite, and entered to the sound of the shower from the generous bathroom, a warmth and calm came over him that made him positively giddy. The real challenge now was to not smile at Sal too fondly, or touch him in public. Much like the exact things they got up to in the bedroom, their love was a secret between them, and one that Jack gladly kept.

Speaking of what they did in the bedroom, they had four generous hours before the negotiations with the Dommarco started, and he'd finally decided that the rope color that complemented Sal's skin best was black.

AUTHOR'S NOTES

If you enjoyed Silvio Spadaro, he appeared first in *Dark Soul*.

I owe a huge amount of gratitude to my alpha readers, Jennifer and Jenny. Both held my hand (or, depending, biffed me gently over the head) when I ended up struggling to make it work and complained to them about that.

Many thanks to my editing crew, Ann, Ali, and Leta, who made the book so much better; the beta crew, Katerina, Tom, Nerine, Elora, Roz, Rhi, Ali, Carole, Valerie, Suzanne, Linda, Elora, Kirsten, Alyssa, and Gaia who all made big contributions, and the sensitivity and sense-check readers, Tim, Fra, and Chiara, who prevented the worst gaffes. All remaining problems and mistakes are mine.

ALSO BY ALEKSANDR VOINOV

Dark Soul

Mean Machine

Witches of London – Lars

Witches of London – Eagle's Shadow

Witches of London – Shadows watching, with Jordan Taylor

Memory of Scorpions (series)

Burn

Skybound

Gold Digger

Return on Investment (Return on Investment #1)

Risk Return (Return on Investment #2)

Nightingale

Deliverance

Incursion

Dark Edge of Honor, with Rhi Etzweiler

The Lion of Kent, with Kate Cotoner

Broken Blades, with L.A. Witt

Unhinge the Universe, with L.A. Witt

Market Garden (series), with L.A. Witt

For a full list, go to www.aleksandrvoinov.com/bookshelf.html

ABOUT THE AUTHOR

EPIC Award winner and Lambda Award finalist Aleksandr Voinov is an expat German living near London, where he works as an editor in financial services. His genres range from science fiction and fantasy to thriller, historical, contemporary, and erotica.

If he isn't writing, he studies world history, mythology, and astrology, or teaches writing or the Tarot. Sometimes he also makes candles. He's a certified Master Hypnotist and NLP Coach, and loves both Buddhism and Ásatrú, though he needs to meditate more often. He is a member of the venerable Society of Authors.

Visit Aleksandr's website at http://www.aleksandrvoinov.com, his blog at http://www.aleksandrvoinov.blogspot.com, follow him on Twitter, where he tweets as @aleksandrvoinov at ungodly hours (UK time), and/or subscribe to his newsletter at: http://eepurl.com/7ijNz.